MIGHTIER THAN THE SWORD

MIGHTIER THAN THE SWORD

Mightier Than the Sword

Civilian Control of the Military and the Revitalization of Democracy

ALICE HUNT FRIEND

STANFORD UNIVERSITY PRESS
Stanford, California

Stanford University Press
Stanford, California

© 2024 by Alice Hunt Friend. All rights reserved.

No part of this book may be reproduced or transmitted in any form or by any means, electronic or mechanical, including photocopying and recording, or in any information storage or retrieval system, without the prior written permission of Stanford University Press.

Printed and bound by CPI Group (UK) Ltd, Croydon, CR0 4YY

Library of Congress Cataloging-in-Publication Data

Names: Friend, Alice Hunt, author.
Title: Mightier than the sword : civilian control of the military and the revitalization of democracy / Alice Hunt Friend.
Description: Stanford, California : Stanford University Press, 2024. | Includes bibliographical references and index.
Identifiers: LCCN 2023034608 (print) | LCCN 2023034609 (ebook) | ISBN 9781503629189 (cloth) | ISBN 9781503638976 (ebook)
Subjects: LCSH: Civil supremacy over the military—United States. | Civil-military relations—United States. | United States—Military policy.
Classification: LCC JK330 .F75 2024 (print) | LCC JK330 (ebook) | DDC 322/.50973—dc23/eng/20230825
LC record available at https://lccn.loc.gov/2023034608
LC ebook record available at https://lccn.loc.gov/2023034609

Cover design: Michel Vrana
Cover photographs: iStock
Typeset by Newgen in Utopia Std 9.75/14.75

CONTENTS

	Preface: Maybe Not These Civilians	vii
	List of Abbreviations	xiii
INTRODUCTION	Why Study Civilians?	1
ONE	Who (and What) is a Civilian?	20
TWO	A Framework for Civilian Control	44
THREE	Civilian Control after the Cold War	69
FOUR	Civilian Control and the War in Afghanistan	102
FIVE	Civilian Control and Capabilities	141
CONCLUSION	The Civilian Ethic	165
	Acknowledgments	181
	Notes	185
	Bibliography	197
	Index	215

PREFACE

Maybe Not These Civilians

IT IS ALWAYS EXCITING TO attend a meeting with the secretary of defense. Spread along a windowed side of the E-ring hallway on the third floor, the Secretary's office suite is wood-paneled and carpeted in a deep blue. One day many years ago, I was sitting in the conference room that looks out onto the Pentagon parade grounds and across the Potomac River at the Washington Monument, trying to appear confident and relaxed. Really, I was buzzing with nerves. I was a midlevel bureaucrat, and I didn't often have the privilege of seeing the man I wrote memos to, the man whose authority I borrowed every day to do my job as a civilian policymaker in the Office of the Under Secretary of Defense for Policy.

The secretary was holding a meeting with the new commander of Africa Command. We had sent him a hefty package of materials to prepare him for any requests the four-star general might make of him, and the general's staff had done the same for their boss. The choreography amounted to a routine accountability mechanism, a standard means for civilian leaders to conduct oversight of the military.

When the secretary strode into the room, we all stood up in a sign of respect for the office he held, the highest ranking one in a department of over two million people. He waved us into our seats, and the commander began his briefing. Not long into the presentation, the secretary interrupted him.

vii

viii   Preface

"Listen," he said to the man sitting in front of him in the pristine coat and shiny black shoes of his service uniform, "I trust you to do the right thing. Don't feel like you have to come ask me for permission."

There was a stunned pause. By law, the commander had to ask the secretary for the authority—or permission—to conduct most meaningful activities. It was the commander's job to justify why the permission he was requesting was consistent with civilian strategic guidance, and it was the secretary's job to grant or withhold such authority carefully. Rather than follow this script, the secretary had deferred judgment—explicitly, and in general—to the military officer sitting in front of him.

I felt my heart sink. I had expected the secretary to issue guidance in that meeting, guidance it would be my job to reinforce with the combatant command in future interactions. Now I wasn't sure what to do. After all, the secretary had told the commander to follow his own judgment. If the secretary waived his own right to exercise control over the officer in front him, what value did a much-lower-level civilian official like me add?

The principle of civilian control of the military in democracies is based on logics of power that most Americans never learn and don't understand. The warning in the Declaration of Independence that the military should never be "rendered independent of and superior to the civil power" seems like an improbable hazard. But without that founding attitude, civilian control becomes a hollow slogan rather than a guiding rule of self-government. In recent decades, Americans' unreflective esteem for the military has fostered an assumption that we can trust it implicitly, including with powers the Founders intentionally gave to citizens outside military institutions. As a result of this shift, the norms and practices that have made the civilian-run US government superior to its military for well over two hundred years have been eroding.

That erosion became obvious after the end of the Cold War. The early days of the Clinton administration were marked by open civil-military disagreement about foreign interventions and social issues, including the wars in the Balkans and LGBTQ Americans' eligibility to serve in the armed forces. The G. W. Bush administration contended with public criticism of Iraq policy marshalled by recently retired officers in the so-called Revolt of the Generals. President Obama had to relieve the commander of operations in Afghanistan because of disparaging remarks his staff made about the vice president and other civilian leaders to a reporter. All three presidents' disputes with their military advisors over the use of force and other military policies were leaked to the press. All three also amassed long lists of retired military officers to endorse their presidential election campaigns, as did their opponents, suggesting that politicians were not qualified to be commander in chief unless the military approved of them.

Then came the presidency of Donald Trump. Trump treated the military like a partisan constituency, used military experience as a qualification for civilian positions, deflected responsibility for operational failures, and intervened in the military justice system to overturn war crimes convictions. By the end of Trump's term, administration officials had used the National Guard in response to protests in Washington, DC, and threatened to use military forces against American citizens elsewhere in the country. After losing his reelection bid in November 2020, Trump fired his secretary of defense and replaced him with a recently retired Army colonel.

To those of us who study civil-military relations, Trump was more of a logical conclusion than an anomaly. We have spent the past thirty years expressing alarm about the de facto power of military voices in national defense policymaking and about the enthusiasm so many citizens show for military leaders in political positions. But even we have been surprised by how little consensus there seems to be about what civilian control of the military means and why it matters.

Partisan polarization has eroded the principle of civilian control even further. It has always been tempting to relax on principles when doing so benefits one's own political party. But in recent years, partisans have tended toward actively rejecting control by civilians they find undesirable. Afghanistan policy is a case in point: depending on the party identity of the president, partisan voices clamored for more or less military influence over decisions and expressed more or less faith in civilian control over war policy. Republicans tended to think President Obama should listen to his military advisors whereas Democrats were fine with him overruling them. Yet many of those same Democrats hoped the military would keep President Trump from a rushed withdrawal. This pattern begs the question: Do

Americans really believe in civilian control in an absolute sense, or just in control by civilians who share our ideological commitments?

The notion that the military's judgment is frequently more objective or more patriotic than civilians' shapes our approaches to recent debates about the job of secretary of defense. In 2017 and 2021 successive presidents, one Republican and one Democrat, nominated recently retired general officers to the post. Because neither nominee had completed the codified seven-year waiting period between service as a military officer and service as secretary, Congress had to pass special legislation to allow each man to serve. The public discussions that ensued revealed that the same country that crafted laws to ensure the civilian identity of senior defense leaders evinced little knowledge of or commitment to the practice of civilian control.

Underlying civilians' worsening reputation is the question of competence. Is the current constellation of civilian leaders expert enough and capable enough to merit the military's obedience? A colleague once encapsulated this dilemma for me. In a loud stage voice they affirmed, "Civilian control of the military!" Then they leaned forward and whispered, "but maybe not these civilians."

This is a book about what I call *civilian controllers*—the civilians in professional and institutional positions with the responsibility for controlling the military and each other. And because civilians' status, functions, and expertise center politics, so does this book. In these pages you will find a definition of "civilian" and a typology for categorizing different kinds of civilians; explorations of the meanings of politics, control, and deference; and in-depth studies of what motivates civilians and their choices to control each other and military activities.

I wrote this book because I worry that Americans have become so used to military subordination to civilian rule that we assume it is a natural condition. I know from both firsthand experience and careful study that it isn't. Instead, civilian control is an engineered outcome—one that requires continuous maintenance. Assuming that civilian control is a given blunts Americans' sense of responsibility and urgency about their own role in making it happen. We have lost our sense of the value civilians bring to bear on military affairs, and our understanding of what it is that civilians do.

Unfortunately, existing scholarship on civil-military relations does not offer a systematic guide to thinking about civilians. If ordinary citizens and practitioners have lost track of what civilians are for, American civil-military relations scholars can only offer so much. Scholars often simplify civilians' role in civil-military relations to bookends, issuing orders and sometime later returning to reward or punish the military for how well it complies with civilian preferences. Much of this simplification is derived from a normative desire to keep the military out of politics, and so to keep politics away from civil-military relations. Such studies leave out not just the quotidian mechanisms of civilian control but also the influence of politics on military policy. They also perpetuate the notion that civilian intrusion into military autonomy is a moral failure. Consequently, there is a substantial gap between normative civil-military relations scholarship and the empirical experience of civilian defense policymakers.

Drawing on new research and informed by my experience serving in civilian roles in the Department of Defense (DoD), this book bridges the gap between civil-military relations theory and real-world practice. As both a scholar of civil-military relations and a defense policy practitioner, I have witnessed some of the senior-most civilian leaders practice the political and administrative art of civilian control of military affairs. Those practices and that art are common knowledge to civilian controllers and their civilian staffs, yet the academy, the American public, and even many military personnel do not understand what civilians do and why.

I also aim to reset the associations readers make between civil-military relations and the word *politics*. Many Americans, including and critically those in uniform, associate politics with hyperpartisanship, corruption, acrimony, and hypocrisy. What this book does is show, over and over, that politics in its pure form is a process that powerful actors use to make decisions, craft rules, allocate resources, and build more power. I focus on the context for political processes, the setting that includes the issues, events, and people that give politics meaning. And I observe that political contexts mean different things to different civilians in different professional-institutional positions. Once the reader can associate politics with the exercise of power, it becomes obvious that the military is a political actor and that the use of military force is a political choice. Politics may produce

xii   Preface

negative outcomes, but it is simply the use of power to make collective decisions. And because humans are a social species, politics is unavoidable.

My hope is that practitioners and academics alike find in these pages a helpful framework for thinking through the civilian aspects of the civil-military relationship. I also aspire to prompt other scholars to expand the effort begun here, conducting more studies to build out the literature on the civilian dimensions of civil-military relations. If this book begins that deeper conversation about the civilian role in military affairs, it will have accomplished its purpose.

LIST OF ABBREVIATIONS

AT&L	acquisition, technology, and logistics
BUR	Bottom-Up Review
CIA	Central Intelligence Agency
CJCS	chairman of the Joint Chiefs of Staff
DARPA	Defense Advanced Research Projects Agency
DoD	Department of Defense
DDR&E	director of defense research and engineering
FYDP	Future Years Defense Plan
HAC-D	House Appropriations Committee–Defense
HASC	House Armed Services Committee
ISR	intelligence, surveillance, and reconnaissance
JPO	Joint Program Office
NDAA	National Defense Authorization Act
NSC	National Security Council
OSD	Office of the Secretary of Defense
RDT&E	research, development, technology, and engineering
SAC-D	Senate Appropriations Committee–Defense
SASC	Senate Armed Services Committee
UAV	uninhabited aerial vehicles

MIGHTIER THAN THE SWORD

MIGHTIER THAN THE SWORD

INTRODUCTION

Why Study Civilians?

THE NEW PRESIDENT WANTED A general to be his secretary of defense. The nomination was unusual. By law, the country's senior-most military officers were not eligible to serve as secretary of defense unless they had been retired from active duty for at least seven years.[1] According to Title 10, the section of the US Code that regulates the armed forces, the leader of DoD had to be "appointed from civilian life." When president-elect Donald Trump named retired Marine Corps general James Mattis secretary of defense, no president had asked Congress to make an exception to that law for six and a half decades.

If the nomination was unusual, the circumstances were unprecedented. Donald Trump had not served in the military himself, nor had he ever held public office. Not only that, but during the presidential campaign he made a number of statements that many foreign policy professionals deemed reckless. Jim Mattis, who served in the Marines for forty-one years, seemed like an "adult" who would steady the neophyte president. Military historian Eliot Cohen, appearing at a hearing before the Senate Armed Services Committee (SASC) on the question of issuing an exception to law so Mattis could be confirmed, said he hoped that "a Secretary Mattis would be a stabilizing and moderating force" in the Trump administration (SASC 2017).

Introduction

In any case, not many people understood why nominating a recently retired military general to run the military was a problem. Civil-military relations scholars stepped into the public square to explain. "In healthy democracies," political scientist Peter Feaver wrote in the *New York Times*, "the command authority is civilian." He added that as a retired four-star general, Mattis would "never become fully civilian" because his values, assumptions, and personal relationships were too steeped in the Marine Corps (Feaver 2016). Meanwhile, the Congressional Research Service explained that the legislators who drafted the provision mandating a break between officership and political service believed it would "preserve the principle of civilian control of the military" (McInnis 2021, 8). Nevertheless, scholars agreed the circumstances warranted making an exception to the rule. Feaver himself endorsed the nomination because of the extraordinary nature of the untested president. So long as the Senate did not make such an exception for any other recently retired general officer for another seventy years, Cohen and others argued, secretaries of defense would continue to exercise sound civilian control over the military.

Four years later, president-elect Joseph Biden nominated retired Army general Lloyd Austin III to run DoD. That Biden picked another general so soon after Mattis's nomination sparked controversy on Capitol Hill. "I supported a one-time waiver in the case of Secretary James Mattis with the belief that the circumstances at the time warranted a rare exception, not the establishment of a new precedent," Senator Susan Collins (R-ME) told reporters (Steinhauer, Schmitt, and Broadwater 2020). Protests on the Hill and in the press were substantial enough that Biden made the rare move of publishing a written defense of Austin's nomination in *The Atlantic* magazine: "Why I Chose Lloyd Austin as Secretary of Defense." In the piece, Biden argued that although Austin's primary experience was as a military leader, that same role had tested his diplomatic skills. Moreover, Austin had "served as a statesman" when he led the withdrawal operations from Iraq, proving he was "a true and tested soldier and leader" (Biden 2020).

The problem with Biden's argument was that it didn't acknowledge that being drawn from civilian life is normally a prerequisite for the role. Ignoring this fundamental gap in Austin's professional experience blunted the argument that his personal qualities and time as a military leader were sufficient.[2] Although Biden demonstrated his personal confidence in Austin, he did not grapple with the central questions before lawmakers: Had a career in the military become the best preparation for running the DoD?[3] Were Mattis and Austin proving that the requirement for the secretary of defense to have a primarily civilian identity was no longer necessary? In the end, the Senate confirmed both men, but confusion lingered about the value of civilians in the civil-military context.

Americans weren't always so fuzzy about the unique value of a civilian background for managing military affairs. The history of Americans' approach to civilians roles in national defense reveals that generations of government leaders thought civilian control over military affairs was essential to self-rule. Yet the emphasis on civilian dominance of military policy has atrophied over time. Why?

Historical Trends for Civilians in Civil–Military Relations

Wariness of military power was one of the ideas that helped found the United States. In the prerevolutionary era, seventeenth-century English pamphleteers persuaded American colonists that large, permanent militaries posed a danger to society. One influential pamphlet authored by British parliamentarian John Trenchard warned that "unhappy Nations have lost that precious Jewel *Liberty*" because "their Necessities or Indiscretion have permitted a standing Army to be kept among them" (Trenchard 1697, 4).[4] In other words, there was a correlation between a permanent army and government oppression. Under King George III, the colonists began to see this correlation for themselves. "The keeping of a standing army in several of these colonies," the Continental Congress declared in 1774, "without the consent of the legislature of that colony in which such army is kept, is against the law."[5] The Declaration of Independence protested the king "affected to render the Military independent of and superior to the Civil power." The king's policies, according to military historian Richard Kohn, "made hatred of the standing army axiomatic in American politics" (Kohn 1991, 82).

Importantly, Americans did not blame the military itself for their oppression. It was the king who was threatening their liberty. The army

4 Introduction

was a mere instrument; the despot in possession of the army was the real problem (Bailyn 2017). "The time may come, when we may have to contend with the *designs of the crown, and of a mighty kingdom . . . backed by a* STANDING *army*," read another colonial pamphlet (Dickinson 1768, 45).

This keen recognition of the source of danger was essential to the eventual structure of the American federal government. Because it was really overly powerful rulers that put freedom at risk, the American founders worried mainly about controlling civilians who commanded the military. If every politician or functionary could act like George III or Oliver Cromwell, then no civilian could ever be allowed to amass too much power, let alone the personalist loyalty of a full-time army (Bailyn 2017). "It is of great importance in a republic," wrote James Madison in *Federalist* no. 51, "not only to guard the society against the oppression of its rulers; but to guard one part of the society against the injustice of the other part."[6] Early Americans were not just worried about guarding the guardians, but also about guarding the guardians' guards. Civilian control of *civilians* was the paramount necessity. And those civilians could not have too large a military force at their disposal.

Centralized control over the military thus became a problem for the nascent American democracy. To constrain power-hungry civilians, the Founders divided control over military affairs into different civilian roles. Under Article I of the Constitution, Congress has the authority to "raise and support armies" and "provide for a Navy," regulate the military forces it creates, collect taxes and allocate funds for national defense activities, declare war, define violations of international law, and "call forth the militia" and set standards for its training and equipping. Congress itself, being divided into two chambers, also cannot wield power as a unified group. Meanwhile, Article II makes the president "commander-in-chief" of the Army and Navy and of the militia when Congress activates it for national service. The division of labor was deliberate: one civilian body prepares for defense in peacetime and another leads in wartime, yet neither achieves its goals for long without the other. Without Congress, the president has no military with which to use force; without the president, Congress cannot actually launch whatever war it declares—at least not effectively. Civilian control of civilians would prevent a tyrant from total power over the military in the United States, but civilians would remain in overall control of the military instrument.[7]

The division of peacetime and wartime labor worked more or less as the Founders intended for a century and a half. In war, the size of the army ballooned rapidly as an emergency measure, and then shrank back to a small standing force in peacetime. Civilian control of civilians was most imperiled during these wartime episodes—most notably during the Civil War, when President Abraham Lincoln invoked controversial if effective military measures. Generally, however, the US maintained its constitutional system through major wars and kept to its "axiomatic" bias against large standing armies.

But in the years after World War II the United States changed its mind about a large, permanent military force. That period began a slow fading of the distinction between peacetime and wartime, and with it a steady shift in primary responsibility over controlling the military to the executive branch. To many influential Americans, the speed and destructiveness of modern warfare had obliterated the notion that it was safe to dismantle military capacity (Herring 1941). Long-range flight, missiles, and nuclear weapons collapsed the time envisioned in the Constitution for observation and political deliberation before military action. There had to be a permanent vigilance, a belief that drove an urgent need for structures able to ready forces, call upon industrial resources, and generally organize policy with speed and intelligence. The lessons of the war were also fresh in terms of military organization. Competition between the War (Army) and Navy departments had generated grave inefficiencies. Despite the modern sense that America's triumph in WWII was inevitable, it felt much more like a near-miss at the time, and policymakers pushed for military unification into a single department to avoid further hair raising.

Regardless, Americans were as adamant as ever about the importance of civilian control over the military, but the introduction of a standing army shifted the balance of their anxiety away from the sense that civilians themselves needed to be controlled. For the first time, Americans had a military that truly had the capacity to upend democratic governance on its own (Hogan 1998). Americans in the 1940s worried about making civilians powerful enough to constrain this unprecedented military organization. For this reason, Presidents Truman and Eisenhower both insisted on centralized civilian control over the nascent DoD. When Congress passed the National Security Act of 1947—the law that unified the military services into a single department, among other changes— civilian preeminence over the entire institution was an explicit priority. In his letter to Congress supporting the law, Truman best summarized the era's faith in centralized civilian control. Acknowledging the concern "that the concentration of so much military power would lead to militarism," he assured Congress, "there is no basis for such fear as long as the traditional policy of the United States is followed that a civilian, subject to the President, the Congress and the will of the people, be placed at the head of this Department" (Cole et al. 1978, 13). As assistant secretary of war for air (and later secretary of defense), Robert Lovett asserted at one of the House hearings on military unification, it was "not just the theatre that needs unity of command, but the country as a whole needs it—at the top."[8] The effect of the debate was to minimize concerns about excess in a single civilian's control over the military and to maximize anxiety about military subordination to civilians.

But crafting the secretary's role to give the position full authority over military activities proved challenging. A series of amendments to the original 1947 law progressively amplified and centralized the secretary's power over the military departments. In 1949 Congress expanded the secretary's bureaucratic capacity by laying the foundation for a civilian staff, providing for a deputy secretary and three assistant secretaries, including a comptroller to oversee service budgeting (Stuart 2008). The 1949 amendment also clarified the all-encompassing nature of the secretary's jurisdiction, stipulating that the secretary exercises "direction, authority, and control over the Department of Defense" (Cole et al. 1978). This latter phrase, the House Armed Services Committee (HASC) Chair Carl Vinson explained, was "the heart of this legislation."

> Direction means the act of governing, management, superintend[ing]. Authority means legal power; a right to command; the right and power of a public officer to require obedience to his order lawfully issued in the scope of his public duties. Control means power or authority to manage, to direct, superintend, regulate, direct[sic], govern, administer, or oversee. So under

Why Study Civilians? 7

> this law the Secretary of Defense is to have clearcut [*sic*] authority to run
> the Department of Defense. (Cole et al. 1978, 145–46)

Even this was not satisfying to President Dwight Eisenhower—himself a retired Army general who understood the difficulty of controlling military affairs. In 1958, Eisenhower wrote to Congress asking them to remove statutory authority for military operational command from "any official other than the Secretary of Defense" (Cole et al. 1978, 180). Eisenhower also informed Congress of his plans to create unified command structures, strengthen the secretary's power over research and development, give the chairman of the Joint Chiefs of Staff (CJCS) and the secretary more control over military three- and four-star flag officer appointments, and give the secretary more budgetary "flexibility" (Cole et al. 1978, 177). In the final DoD reform of the period in 1958, the service secretaries were told to "cooperate fully with personnel of the Office of the Secretary of Defense" to ensure the secretary of defense's authority would be carried out.[9] That law also expanded the Office of the Secretary of Defense (OSD) once again, to include a new director of defense research and engineering (DDR&E) and assistant secretaries for legislative affairs and public affairs—all three moves designed to shift power from the services to OSD. By 1959, the secretary of defense had ten assistant secretaries, a general counsel, and the DDR&E.

To align itself with the new organizations in the executive branch, Congress also redesigned its own committee structure, combining the committees that had overseen the War and Navy departments into unified armed services committees. But in their determination to strengthen immediate civilian control over the newly sprawling defense enterprise, national leadership duplicated many congressional responsibilities in OSD, shifting the initiative for defense budgeting and much of the regulation of the armed forces from Congress to the DoD itself. Some members of Congress at the time expressed alarm about the rebalance of power. Senators Mike Mansfield and Paul Douglas worried that the law "clear[ed] the way for a major transfer of constitutional legislative powers and duties to the Executive Branch" (Stuart 2008, 226). Even Carl Vinson fought the 1958 reorganization because he feared it would cede too much authority

8   Introduction

to the president. In the HASC's report on the law, he protested that "the organization of our national defense system must . . . at all costs, be the creature of our form of government—with the responsibility for national defense placed equally upon the President, as commander in chief, and the Congress."[10] But it was too late. In the span of just under twenty years, Congress ceded much of its predominance over military policy and budgeting to the DoD. Civilian control over civilians hadn't been eliminated, but it had been handicapped.

Instead, much as Eisenhower had worried, the appropriate balance between civilian and military influence over decision making became a major point of contention. Once the DoD was established, the center of gravity for civilian control of the military increasingly fell between the secretary and the uniformed leaders of the military services—the Joint Chiefs of Staff. Civilians at DoD and the White House wrestled with how to include military leaders in the policymaking process without being overwhelmed by service parochialism. "The problem of the proper set-up of the Joint Chiefs of Staff," Secretary of Defense Robert Lovett had written to President Truman in 1952, "involves the striking of a proper balance between civilian and military control." Although civilian control of the military was "fundamental to our form of government," he continued, "civilian judgment must be based on adequate military advice given by professional military men in an atmosphere as free as possible from service rivalries and service maneuvering."[11]

At the time of the 1947 law and its amendments, lawmakers prevented unified military advice because they feared that the United States would duplicate the German "general staff" model, which they viewed as the engine of German militarism that sparked World War II. But the failed war in Vietnam made many in Congress conclude that the Joint Chiefs of Staff needed a stronger voice in the policymaking process. In 1980, the disastrous failed attempt to rescue American hostages in Iran and subsequent military operations in Grenada and Panama also spurred new thinking about military organization and the role of military advice in policymaking.

To reform the military advisory system, the Ronald Reagan administration's Blue Ribbon Commission on Defense Management recommended that the CJCS become "the principal uniformed military advisor to the

President, the National Security Council, and the Secretary of Defense" (Cole et al. 1978). The Goldwater Nichols Department of Defense Reorganization Act of 1986 implemented the recommendation, putting the CJCS in charge of spearheading strategic, contingency, and logistical planning, and developing joint doctrine and training for the services.

In contrast to the reforms of the 1950s, civilians—the secretary and OSD—received no new powers. It was not that the law's proponents felt civilian control of the military at DoD was unimportant. It was simply that they did not think it needed reinforcing. As SASC staff wrote in their summary of the history of American civil-military relations, "the military has never posed a serious threat to civilian control in the United States." Consequently, "fears that the U.S. military might threaten American political democracy are misplaced."[12] This declaration of victory for civilian control marked a turning point in practitioners' perspective on civilians in American civil-military relations: In contrast to the post-WWII generation, government officials in the last decade of the Cold War weren't concerned about reinforcing civilian preeminence. They had faith that civilians were suitably ensconced at the top of the military hierarchy (Locher 2002, 439).

More recently, Congress has moved to reduce the civilian voice at DoD. In 2015, Senator John McCain, chairman of the Senate Armed Services Committee, launched a review of DoD's structures and practices and found that failures in the wars in Iraq and Afghanistan and bureaucratic waste could be attributed to top-heavy DoD headquarters. Skeptical of the size of OSD and the service secretary staffs, McCain asked rhetorically, "Is the quality of civilian oversight and control of the military better?"[13] The results of the study shaped the 2017 National Defense Authorization Act (NDAA), which required the secretary of defense to "streamline the organizational structure and processes of the Office of the Secretary of Defense" no later than eighteen months from the enactment of the bill and downsized the number of civilian Senior Executive Service members by 25 percent.[14]

Yet the same law expanded the role of the CJCS by making it "responsible for" the "strategic direction of the armed forces" including "developing strategic frameworks and preparing strategic plans, as required, to guide the use and employment of military force and related activities across all geographic regions and military functions and domains."[15] According to

10   Introduction

the SASC summary of the bill, the changes were intended "to improve military advice to civilian leaders" and "strengthen the Chairman's ability to assist the Secretary with the global integration of military operations."[16] But it ceded initiative to the chairman, the "global integrator" role echoing the global force management authority of the secretary of defense. Although the law stipulated that the chairman had to act consistently with the national defense strategy that the secretary wrote, and the secretary was free to revoke those delegated authorities at any time, the law obscured the distinction between the secretary's strategic functions and the chairman's.

Over American history, as the military grew and Congress ceded influence over budgeting, force structure, and war policy to DoD, civilians' distinct professional and institutional contributions to military policymaking were subsumed in a more collaborative civil-military model. The permanent wartime of the Cold War, reinforced by the "forever war" on terrorism, atrophied best practices for civilian control over the military and elevated the status of military expertise relative to political expertise. Given the ground civilians have lost legally and bureaucratically, doubts about the unique value of a civilian background for positions of control over the military—such as the secretary of defense—are easy to understand. This book aims to revive that lost sense of civilians' value to military policymaking.

Civilians in Scholarly and Contemporary Context

In the United States, civilians have distinct status, functions, and expertise that revolve around the exercise of political control. It is through political processes that national values are articulated, national priorities set, and national resources apportioned. Civilians' ability to integrate military policy into national politics makes democratic control of the armed forces possible. Civilians decide how large or small the force should be, manage the division of labor among the military services, and decide whether and how those forces will be used. Civilians author national defense strategies, make decisions about global military basing, approve contingency plans, and buy weapons. They provide for military justice frameworks, nominate and confirm general and flag officers, and provide guidance on readiness, recruitment, retention, and promotion for military personnel.

Yet civilians are underappreciated, understudied, and underestimated. Neither practitioners nor the public pay much attention to the roles civilians play in military affairs, and scholars have built little systematic knowledge about who civilians are or how they fulfill their responsibilities. Political scientists tend to treat civilian elites' supply of money, strategy, and oversight as givens (Betts 1991; Feaver 2003). Historical treatments contain rich descriptions of civilian wartime and defense policy leadership, but are often limited to an individual, a role, or an era rather than providing systematic patterns and findings (e.g., Halberstam 2001; McPherson 2008; Moten 2014).

In contrast to our limited knowledge about civilians, we have a detailed sense of what it means to be "military." A rich library of military studies examines military professionalism, military institutions, military coups, military influence over policymaking, and the militarization of foreign policy (e.g., Huntington 1957; Janowitz 1960; Abrahamsson 1972; Dubik 2017; Lupton 2017). Civilians are not absent from these analyses—even those studies that are not explicitly couched in the civil-military relations subfield often examine the relationship between militaries and regimes. But these studies tend to simplify the roles civilians play and minimize civilians' influence on military affairs. For example, the military innovation literature often argues that civilians are irrelevant to advances in military technologies or doctrine (Rosen 1991; Avant 1994). Ideas about military professionalism often focus on the "unique expertise" the armed forces provide in the policymaking context (Dempsey 2012, 4). Because there is no commensurate concept of civilian expertise there is little sense of what value civilians bring to military affairs.

There are practical reasons that academics and practitioners alike neglect studying civilians as intensively as they study the military. Scholars see the military as a tractable unit of analysis. Civilians are not institutionally organized or culturally homogenous, making them harder to aggregate into meaningful categories. "The military ethic," wrote political scientist Samuel P. Huntington, "is concrete, permanent, and universal. The term 'civilian' on the other hand, merely refers to what is nonmilitary.

No dichotomy exists between the 'military mind' and the 'civilian mind' because there is no single 'civilian mind'" (Huntington 1957, 89). There is the military, and there is everyone else. This perspective has allowed analysts to lower civilians' profiles so that even civil-military relations scholars often treat civilians like supporting characters: there to react to military initiatives or restrain military impulses, but not to shape the military's actions.

But if civilian control is a prerequisite for democratic order, we need to know as much about civilian superiority as we know about military obedience. To build such knowledge, we must specify which civilian actions precede and complement military subordination, and why civilians choose to take such actions in the first place.

The fixation on the military and the definition of military professionalism as apolitical has also obscured the effects of politics on civilian control of the military. Samuel Huntington's edict that civilians ought to isolate the military from domestic political disputes and that politicians ought not to meddle in operational matters generally has inhibited much of the subfield from incorporating civil-military studies into relevant political contexts (Huntington 1957; Brooks 2020). More recent scholarship has tried to call attention to this discrepancy. Drawing on Prussian military theorist Carl von Clausewitz, Eliot Cohen argues that war is a political activity and so politicians' interventions in military strategies are consistent with the logic of war itself (Cohen 2002a). And Risa Brooks shows that equating the military profession with an apolitical identity blinds the military and those around it to the political drivers of military actions (Brooks 2020). Because civilians engage in politics to manage military affairs, methods of civilian control that emphasize insulating the military from politics just marginalize civilians from civil-military analysis more.

Scholars and practitioners alike need a revived concept of "civilian" in civil-military relations, not just to understand the role civilians play in American military policymaking, but to reinvigorate and perhaps even redeem it.

Main Argument and Plan of the Book

This book argues that being a civilian in government confers status, functions, and expertise distinct from the professional military. These three dimensions of the concept of "civilian" build on each other and indicate the activities civilians undertake in the civil-military context. First, civilians have the status of authoritative leadership in governance. The civil-military relationship is hierarchical, and civilians have the superior status in that hierarchy. Second, civilians' functions flow from their superior status. Their essential function is to ensure that national political decisions drive military policy and to administer government implementation of those policies. Civilians serve these functions in two major ways. The first is familiar to even casual students of civil-military relations: Civilians control the military. But the second is both a condition of American democracy and a complicating factor for the first: Civilians also control civilians. Civilian control of the military is the key mechanism that ensures the armed forces implement politically validated policies. Civilian control of civilians, expressed here mainly in the division of civilian labor between the legislative and executive branches, is the key mechanism for reconciling military policies with politics.[17]

Finally, to serve their essential political and control-exercising functions, civilians develop and use political expertise. Expertise in politics combines procedural and interpersonal skill. Procedurally, civilians understand how to win elections and legislative votes, and how to run policy-making processes and conduct effective oversight. Procedural success in a political context in turn relies on communication skills, especially persuasion and coalition and consensus building. Civilians also understand how to influence human social behavior to drive the outcomes they want. Using their political expertise, civilians perceive and build sufficient democratic support for the size, shape, capabilities, and uses of the military instrument.

With this comprehensive description of what defines civilians and their role in civil-military relations, the book then builds a framework for understanding why, when, and how civilians exercise control. It takes a different approach from much of the civil-military relations literature, which often explains civilian control choices with how civilians anticipate the military will respond. But tying civilian choice so closely to the prospects for military compliance does not adequately account for the other reasons civilians choose to control or defer. In my efforts to focus on what

14   Introduction

makes civilians tick, I leave the effectiveness of control to other scholars and instead focus on the sources of civilian choices and actions prior to the military's response.[18]

The book identifies two main sources of civilian control choices: civilians' professional-institutional types and political context. Civilians, as Huntington noted, are not a monolithic group. But civilians involved in controlling the use of the military are distributed in professional categories and across institutional positions. Although all civilian controllers engage in politics, some are professional politicians while others are professional administrators. Additionally, some civilian controllers are situated in the legislative branch while others are in the executive branch. The combination of a civilian's profession and institutional position structures their beliefs and incentives regarding military policy in systematic ways.

At the same time, civilians' functions make politics the most important factor in their decision making. I use the term *politics* to mean the interactions among powerful actors to make governing decisions. Political context describes the distribution of power among actors, the issues they are considering, and what they value. All other commonly cited factors in civilian control—the structure of the international environment, military threats and their severity, the degree of military professionalism—are less important to civilian controllers than political context. Why? Because political success is the key to both the viability of military policies *and* to politicians' electoral survival, and to all civilians' reputations and advancement. Legislative and executive politicians who wish to keep their jobs or, later in their careers, secure their legacies will make choices about military policy consistent with those aims. Meanwhile, legislative and executive administrators will exercise control over the military in ways that protect and enhance their reputations. If civilians misread the political context (and sometimes they do) the consequences can lead to military failure and curtail their careers.

Reading the political context is not an easy feat because civilians interact with politics on many levels at once: international (or strategic) politics, national (or domestic) politics, and bureaucratic (or interagency or institutional) politics. There are also interest group politics, network politics, and personal politics. These different levels and kinds of politics can

Why Study Civilians?   15

present contradictory incentives. The memoirs of presidents, secretaries of defense, and chairs of the armed services committees are cacophonies of issues and countervailing pressures. On a single page of his memoir, President Bill Clinton recounts selecting Ruth Bader Ginsberg for the Supreme Court, getting the fiscal year 1994 budget through the Senate and setting up a "war room" to secure its full congressional approval, and ordering missile strikes on Iraq to punish them for plotting to assassinate former president George H. W. Bush (Clinton 2004, 525). Clinton was concerned about senators' views on all of these matters because support for one could translate into a roadblock to another. Similarly, one chapter of former secretary of defense Donald Rumsfeld's memoir covers civil-military cooperation at the Pentagon, hiring a deputy secretary, the "transformation agenda" for military capabilities, and the global defense posture review (Rumsfeld 2011). Each of these items had a different, but overlapping, array of military stakeholders whom Rumsfeld would need to implement decisions or cooperate with civilian officials. Both examples show that civilian leaders work with the same counterparts on a variety of issues, their interactions involving multiple simultaneous negotiations and requests.

How do politicians and administrators make sense of the morass of political contextual factors and come to control decisions? By answering two basic questions: whether proposed ideas align with public opinion, and whether other politicians will oppose or support them. Administrators ask themselves whether ideas align with what their politician bosses want, and whether the bureaucracies they lead will embrace or reject them. The answers to these questions tell them whether it is in their interests to exercise control and whether doing so will be politically possible. They also tell civilians whether to exercise strong or weak control or to defer control to others.

Although much of the preceding is about structural pressures, I also argue there is a civilian ethic in the civil-military relations context. Authority and responsibility are aspects of each other, and the civilian profession in the context of democratic military policymaking involves obligations to institutions and fellow citizens. More precisely, the civilian ethic is to make rules and allocate resources in ways that accomplish two goals: to create and preserve a military capable of fighting wars effectively

16 Introduction

and to prevent any use of the military that oppresses the population or changes the nature of government.[19] As with many normative standards, the civilian ethic in civil-military relations is not an iron law of nature but a vulnerable social expectation, and the book explores moments of tension between political exigency and the principled aspects of civilian control.

I present the argument in two parts. In the first part, I develop the concept of "civilian" and establish a framework for analyzing civilian control decisions. This chapter lays out the motivations for the book and explores the historical context for Americans' conceptual, legal, and structural approaches to civilian roles and responsibilities. It shows that Americans' historical expectations of civilians are for them to control the military and to control each other's use of the military, but that both expectations have faded over time. Chapter 1 develops a concept of "civilian" and a civilian typology that together equip analysts with a foundation for civilian behavior. Chapter 2 then offers a framework for understanding civilian control choices. I argue control may compel or constrain action, and then focus on the kinds of mechanisms civilians use to control other civilians and the military, examining why civilians sometimes relinquish control altogether and defer to others. There are many mechanisms to control the military, but the primary three are guidance, budgeting, and force management. Chapter 2 ends by showing how civilians refer to their motivations to evaluate the political contexts in which they make their control choices. Importantly, the military itself forms a key part of those political contexts.

The second part of the book applies the analytic framework to cases of civilian control choice and specifically examines the control mechanisms of guidance, budgeting, and force management. I put the argument through several robustness checks by examining the association between political context and civilian control choices under a variety of conditions. In each chapter I compare the control choices of politicians and administrators and compare congressional and executive branch control over the military and other civilians. In Chapter 3 I use the immediate post–Cold War period from 1989 to 1995 to show how political context affected civilians' use of all three major control mechanisms. I use the change in presidential administrations to control for party affiliation and for different individuals in civilian control roles, while the international and domestic political contexts—including civil wars in Somalia and Bosnia—serve as constants over the case period. At the same time, the administration change demonstrates whether the SASC chair, who did not turn over in this period, shifts in his reliance on political context when the parties in the White House change.

The uniqueness of the historic moment of the Cold War's end, however, is not a sufficient test of the framework on its own. I run a second check in Chapter 4 by examining the ways that three presidents, three SASC chairs, and four secretaries of defense controlled the military and each other over the course of the war in Afghanistan from 2001 to 2017. Because of the war's length and complexity, I focus on control choices regarding force management—specifically troop levels. Chapter 5 examines the connection between political context and civilian control choices regarding military capabilities. I focus on the development and uses of uninhabited aerial vehicles (UAVs) from the 1980s through 2016. Again, I use changes in presidential administrations and congresses to control for party differences and explore how civilian types affect decisions.

Together, the cases demonstrate that the interaction of civilians' professional-institutional type and the political context explains civilian control choices. It is politics, not threats, that shape civilian choices. The cases show that civilians consistently consider politics as part of their choice calculations—even the secretaries of defense who are dismissive of politics demonstrate responsiveness to political incentives. But politics do not have a direct effect on civilian control, because an individual civilian interprets political contexts through the lens of their professional-institutional type.

This book contributes primarily to the literature on civil-military relations and addresses the long-term imbalance in the scholarship that favors examinations of the military over civilians. It also adds to public policy studies, providing an explanation for military policies that synthesizes the roles of ideas, institutions, and interests (e.g., Kingdon 1995 and John 2012) at the domestic and individual levels of analysis. For evidence, I draw on primary and secondary sources. To get inside the heads of politicians and administrators, I rely on interviews and memoirs. Because former

18   Introduction

government officials are not always reliable narrators, I validate their memories by cross-referencing them with other first-person accounts, government documents, speeches, contemporary reporting, and histories.

The book's expansive topic calls for careful scoping to keep focus on what is essential. Unlike many other studies of American civil-military relations, the chapters that follow do not dwell on the profession of arms, officership, or military subordination.

The focus is on civilian roles and responsibilities in the civil-military relationship, particularly civilians in positions of control over the military. But even narrowing just to the civilians directly involved in military policy-making and oversight in the United States is an encyclopedic undertaking. In the Pentagon alone, there are more than a hundred political appointees below the secretary, including the secretaries of the military departments, the undersecretaries, assistant secretaries, and deputy assistant secretaries. Thousands of civilian staffers work in the Pentagon, and hundreds of thousands of civilians work across the entire DoD. Congress, the National Security Council (NSC), the Department of State, and the intelligence community crowd the stage more. Moreover, in some sense every civilian in a democracy has a share in controlling the military. This book therefore concentrates on those who exercise more control than most, trading breadth for depth. The case studies concentrate on the president, the chairs of the congressional armed services committees in the Senate and the House of Representatives, and the secretary of defense. These four civilian roles grapple with the full range of military policy choices and wield the legal authorities to exercise civilian control under the Constitution and Title 10 of the US Code. Moreover, civil servants and other civilian bureaucrats generally act based on the legal authorities vested in the president, armed services committee chairs, and the secretary, making those four the ultimate fulcrums for civilian control. However, where the exercise of control cannot be captured without reference to lower-level civilians, I include their choices as well—an approach most evident in the chapter on UAVs.

Focusing on the often-neglected civilian side of civil-military relations clarifies what it means to be a civilian and deepens our understanding of why, when, and how civilians exercise their control functions in the American context. The founders of the United States intended a government where neither the military nor civilians could use violence without a democratic process of coalition building, and where no single civilian amassed enough power to coerce the domestic population. The democratic design of the American government therefore made politics essential to the civil-military relationship. Although military officers may develop political skills, civilians have comparative advantage in terms of wielding national-level authority derived from representative institutions. Civilians are ultimately accountable for the use of force and for the priority the United States gives to developing and sustaining military capabilities. To be a civilian in the civil-military relationship is to have profound responsibilities. Every citizen, whether in uniform or not, should have a sense of what those responsibilities are and be able to evaluate whether civilian controllers are exercising them well.

ONE

Who (and What) is a Civilian?

AS WITH OTHER SOCIAL IDENTITIES and categories, civilians share some key features while also exhibiting important variation. This variation is partly responsible for scholars accepting Huntington's argument that little unites civilians beyond their exclusion from being in the military (Huntington 1957). Yet some of the variations among civilians are systematic, linked to their professional positioning in the structure of the US government. This combination of stable social distinctions and variable professional positions renders a typology of civilians that not only describes those who control the military but also contributes to the explanation of what motivates how they exercise that control.

In general, a student can more easily learn what a civilian is not, rather than what a civilian is. If those studying civil-military relations begin with the laws of war, they learn that civilians are noncombatants.[1] If they move on to the organization of those who do fight, they learn militaries take rigid, hierarchical forms with precisely defined functions: platoons, squadrons, brigades, branches, services, and so on. Civilian organizations, in contrast, are structurally diverse, and participation in them is more flexible. Being a military officer connotes a profession with a sense of corporateness, a body of knowledge and expertise, and a culture or cultures that guide individual and institutional actions (Huntington 1957; Janowitz 1960; Finer

1962; Builder 1989). But no one has defined a civilian professional identity.[2] Scholars and practitioners need a concept that specifies the meaning of civilian in the civil-military context across time and governments, along with descriptions of the unique structural positions and traditional-legal responsibilities civilians occupy in any particular system.

This chapter develops a concept of "civilian" in the context of democracy generally and the United States specifically.[3] The chapter explores the stable elements of the civilian role in a democracy, identifies types of civilians in the American government, and specifies the key civilian positions in that system. The goal of this chapter is to develop a concrete, specific understanding of what and who civilians are. With this knowledge in hand, we will later be able to analyze how and why civilians behave in the ways they do in the civil-military context.

Civilian: Concept and Typology

Beyond the general "not-military" categorization, scholars tend to use the term *civilian* to refer to two broad social groups. The first group comprises the general public: voters, citizens, and members of civil society. The second group consists of nonmilitary employees of the national government. Of these civilians, a subset are those with the authority to shape and use the military. These are the civilians in which I am interested because they occupy positions of civilian control in the government civil-military relationship.

CONCEPT: STATUS, FUNCTIONS, EXPERTISE

I define the concept of civilian along three dimensions: status, functions, and expertise. Each dimension reflects lasting characteristics of civilians in the civil-military context. Together they depict civilians' position and value in government relative to both the military and the broader society. These dimensions can relate to the military, but they also exist on their own. After all, in the American context civilians create the military and use it as an instrument of national policy. If civilians come first and are doing the creating and controlling, then they exist independently of what

22   Chapter One

is being controlled. Hence, civilians would have status, functions, and expertise even if the military were unnecessary.

Existing scholarship already acknowledges the first dimension of the concept. Civilians control the military because of their superior *status* relative to the military. That status does not only exist in the civil-military relationship, however, but in governing generally. Civilians are in charge of government. In the United States, the source of civilian status is power delegated to civilians by an ultimate authority. Reflecting a devotion to representation and participatory government, the Declaration of Independence identified "the consent of the governed" as the source of that authority. Citizens, through the mechanisms of elections and other representational processes, choose civilian leaders to protect and advance public interests in government. Representative government lays the foundation for ideas about civilian control of the military because it gives those vulnerable to military coercion nominal control over it.[4]

Public sources of power mean public sources of legitimacy. Legitimacy is the idea that one's authority is justified because it is consistent not just with formal rules and institutions (such as elections) but also, as sociologist Morris Zelditch Jr. puts it, "with the norms, values, beliefs, practices, and procedures accepted by a group" (2001, 33). Legitimacy indicates widespread agreement that a person, office, rule, or institution has rightful power. To be a civilian is to have the status of legitimately occupying positions to control the mechanisms of government (Weber 1964; Peter 2017). Moreover, authority must not just be legitimately won; it must also be legitimately exercised (Lipset 1959). If it is not, democratic systems have further mechanisms—elections, divided government, and rule of law—to monitor and punish those who govern.

This means that civilians' status makes them, above all, creatures of politics. Politics is the interactions among powerful actors to make governing decisions. In political processes, these powerful actors set agendas and select decision-making procedures (Riker 1986). Politics therefore determines whose interests are reflected in decisions about government activities and resources. Social scientists maintain two general approaches to the idea of politics. The first emphasizes the acquisition and use of power (Tucker 1985). The second incorporates power into ideas about legitimate governance. Subordinating power to commonly held values is the main goal of democratic systems. Rather than power being seized coercively, in a democracy citizens confer power—and revoke it. To achieve high office and stay there, civilians must earn public endorsement and ongoing approval through political processes. Civilians' ability to participate in all aspects of politics—not simply voting—along with the legitimate governing authority they wield are what define civilians, not their lack of military characteristics.

Civilians' *functions* follow from their status. Civilians use their status to organize and regulate society and government, including the military.[5] Their position in politics involves them in "the activity of giving direction to the community of citizens in the management of their common affairs" (Tucker 1985, 3). The very word *civilian* has been used over time to mean a class of people who create and maintain social order. The root word "civil" comes from the Latin *civilis*, "relating to a society, pertaining to public life, relating to the civic order."[6] To order social life by controlling the organization and actions of government—including the military—is civilians' essential function. But because government covers a broad range of issues, the span of civilian control is far, far wider than just military affairs.

The diversity of social interests and preferences and the scarcity of public resources to satisfy those interests means that ordering social life requires identifying and prioritizing interests, diagnosing situations and problems, and articulating solutions (Tucker 1985; Phillips 2009). Because groups do not automatically come to consensus on goals and do not easily agree on the means to achieve them, society needs to overcome collective action problems (Olson 1971; Lopez 2020). This is the essential work of politics. Civilians prioritize and devise solutions to social problems, elicit group participation in solutions, and discipline decision-making and implementation processes to maintain group commitments and ensure desired outcomes (Shepsle 2010; Ahlquist and Levi 2011; Beerbohm 2015). Civilian leaders break the deadlock that often results from competition among preferences.

Civilians do not just impose order; they sustain it. Sustaining social order means getting group members to contribute to that order on a routine basis. To incentivize these persistent commitments, civilians use political accountability mechanisms (Shepsle 2010, 467). Accountability entails verifying consistency between promises and results, corresponding rewards or punishments, and learning lessons and making updates to governing approaches as appropriate. Accountability mechanisms can be legal, administrative, and political. They can also be vertical—whereby superiors hold subordinates accountable or vice versa—or horizontal—whereby peers hold each other to account (Kuehn and Levy 2021). Civilian control of other civilians can be both horizontal and vertical modes of accountability, whereas civilian control of the military is only vertical.

The presence of accountability mechanisms also indicates moral evaluation. Early Americans tended to associate order with justice, believing leaders' purpose was to maintain public peace and to act as advocates and guardians for those "Unjustly Molested and Injured" (Estabrook 1718). Consistent with concepts of legitimacy, the order civilians imposed and regulated aimed to be "humane and moral." Those in civil power were expected to suppress "Prophane-ness, Licentiousness, Intemperance, Uncleanness, Pride, Prodigality, Covetousness, Mur[d]er, Cursing, Swearing, and the like" (Fisk 1731, 35). Although modern society tends to associate corruption and egotism with the word *politics*, the purpose of politics is to identify and protect what a community values, and to adjudicate among those values in cases where they cannot coexist (Medvic 2018). Civilians' function is not mere order, but moral order: to generate peaceful social order by making, implementing, and enforcing ethical rules and laws. The civilian function in the context of military policymaking—the key arena in the civil-military relationship—is to determine when and how to use the military to produce and protect that social order.

But occupying a position of control is about obligation as much as power. There is thus an ethic to being a civilian controller. That ethic comprises two principal responsibilities. The first is the responsibility to use the military as a resource that belongs to society, works on its behalf, and does not harm it. Civilians have an obligation to strike the balance between maintaining a military capable of defending the society but disincentivized from menacing it (Feaver 1996). The second rule is that civilians are responsible for preventing the military from becoming a partisan actor or a tool used to empower domestic political factions. The military's nonpartisan professional ethic plays a major role in domestic political stability—acting as a complement, in fact, to the efforts civilians make to prevent each other from becoming despotic—and civilians are stewards of military nonpartisanship by reinforcing it. The civilian ethic is to act as society's trustee, using the military responsibly and ensuring that other civilians do the same.

As function follow status, so *expertise* follows function. Civilians' responsibility for generating and maintaining order compels them to develop expertise in two principal areas: politics and administration. Civilian expertise in politics is essential in the civil-military context. Political decisions must be made about military affairs, too. Use of force decisions, budgetary allocations, war termination—all are produced by political processes. Politics is also how politicians are elected to office, and how they gain decision authority, including authority over the military. Politics is how the public registers its preferences for the use of the military and how politicians persuade the public to endorse military operations. Politics provides the comprehensive context for the military's existence and missions.

Navigating political contexts requires expertise in political processes. In a democracy, politics is conducted through persuasion and negotiation rather than force. As then SASC chair Sam Nunn once explained to a reporter, working in Congress is not just about a policy itself, but "knowing how to relate it to the timing and knowing how to relate it to other people's thoughts and ideas and knowing how to express it and knowing how many people and who you need to bounce it around with to get their input before you ever do it" (Rasky 1990). This process of political socialization happens at both the domestic and international levels. Domestically, civilians represent coalitions of interests that must be adjudicated at the national level to determine how finite resources will be distributed. Internationally, civilians are responsible for diplomacy and negotiations, for seeking order among foreign powers that protects domestic security. Perhaps the most valuable skill is the ability to form coalitions to make and enforce decisions. Frances Townsend, an advisor to President George W. Bush on national and homeland security, once explained:

> I remember walking around [the White House], thinking, *Oh, my goodness, how do you get all of these incredibly bright, talented people to put aside personal preferences? . . . The answer was that they don't really put*

26   Chapter One

aside personal preferences nor substantive knowledge, but they do look for policy allies. It was like watching magnets either attract or repel each other. In the policy world, at that level, as issues are prepared for decision, it became clear to me that they work diligently to identify *Who is my policy ally?* And *Who is my policy opponent?* They were very smart and all had a natural ability—They had not gotten there without having that skill and the ability to do that really well. (Miller Center 2010, 66–67; emphasis in original)

Civilians implement political outcomes through administration of government, which actualizes political decisions and generates order on a day-to-day basis (McCubbins, Noll, and Weingast 1987). Administration requires knowledge of law and policy, as well as the processes that produce laws and policies. Overseeing government requires expertise in organizing interest groups, parties, committees, agencies, and offices; gathering information; implementing laws and regulations; spending allocated resources and auditing financial activities; developing rules and procedures for organizational decision making, prioritization, and workflow; and evaluating the outcomes of government activities.

In the civil-military context, civilian administrators run legislative and executive operations in ways that directly affect the uses of the military. Administrators develop budgets for the military departments, oversee major acquisitions, and audit service finances. Administrators also issue guidance to the military in the form of strategies, frameworks for military plans, deployment orders, and manage personnel policy and approve senior leadership changes. The DoD—which includes the Office of the Secretary of Defense, all three military departments, and numerous other organizations—is the largest government bureaucracy by far. Managing it consumes the full-time efforts of more than sixty Senate-confirmed senior civilians.[7]

Crucially, administration means not only working with and within bureaucracies, it also often involves getting bureaucracies to change—to adapt to new circumstances or adopt new technologies. Whereas running an organization's existing processes to achieve long-held goals efficiently requires one set of management techniques, driving change through bureaucratic resistance takes other skills. The workforce must embrace new

Who (and What) is a Civilian?   27

priorities, which takes a mix of persuasion and incentives, like aligning funding and personal rewards with new goals. Efforts need to be sequenced. And leaders need a network of other powerful figures to contribute their time, efforts, and credibility to new ways of working. A secretary needs those sixty-odd senior officials to reinforce her vision.

In sum, civilians have the legitimate status of controlling the government, including the military, and they maintain that legitimate status by developing the political and administrative expertise to organize, prioritize, coordinate, and hold others accountable.

CIVILIANS AND THE MILITARY: DISTINCTIONS AND OVERLAPS

So far, I have mentioned the military sparingly, because most of what defines a civilian is independent of military considerations. But there are important areas of overlap between what civilian and military leaders do. Despite their distinct roles and attributes, civilian and military activities at senior levels are not all mutually exclusive. This section explores which activities are unique to civilian roles in military policy and which activities are more about emphasis than exclusion.

Civil-military relations often revolve around debates about the correct balance between military autonomy and civilian intervention. Military officers sometimes criticize civilians for micromanagement, and civilians sometimes rebuke the military for intervening in political decision making. But in practice civilian and military activities frequently overlap.[8] Senators, secretaries of defense, and four-star generals all work on strategy, policy, and budgeting. As the history of civilian roles in civil-military relations from the previous chapter showed, the overlap is most pronounced inside the DoD, where civilian and military leaders collaborate extensively. The deputy secretary of defense cochairs the Deputy's Management Action Group (a major decision-making body) with the vice chairman of the Joint Chiefs of Staff, and the secretaries of the military departments and the uniformed service chiefs appear together at congressional budget hearings to justify resourcing and answer questions about strategy, as do the secretary of defense and the chairman of the Joint Chiefs of Staff. In preparing for such hearings, these leaders' civilian and military staffs must coordinate which official should tackle likely questions about the use of force, military objectives, and capability needs. This exercise makes plain that senior military officials and senior civilians collaborate. The question is, to what extent do their roles overlap?

Recent debates focus on expertise, especially the proper role of military advice and how much deference civilians should show to it (Cartwright 2015; Brooks 2020; Karlin 2022). These debates rest on the premise that civilians can never know as much about the military as the military knows about itself. Although civilians in control positions often have deep military expertise, their knowledge can still seem shallow compared to military personnel. On the extreme end, there is even a sense that military expertise is exclusive to people in the military. This view holds that military expertise gained from military service is "unique" and therefore indisputable. This frames military expertise as both in competition with and superior to other forms of expertise (Golby and Karlin 2018; Brooks and Grewal 2022). If a situation involves or may involve the use of force, so the logic goes, expert advice from military personnel should dominate discussion.

But the use of force is a policy decision, where military technical expertise is secondary to civilian political expertise. The military's technical acumen in current operations and tactics, although almost always more up-to-date and more granular than any civilian's, is also less relevant to questions of political priorities, costs, and benefits. Military advice can also be highly biased by service or command interests, or simply by the narrowness of their areas of responsibility. A civilian's use of military expertise is also different from how professional military officers see the uses of their advice. Although both civilians and the military want to know the probabilities of military actions' failure and success and the likely costs in lives, equipment, and funds, civilians need that information to calculate the political consequences of military action. Fundamentally, civilians and the military have comparative advantages in expertise. It is not that civilians know nothing about military matters and the military is ignorant of politics. It is the combination of civilian political expertise and technical military knowledge that renders informed policy decisions. Civilians have expertise in the political meaning of the use of force.

The division of labor between politicians and administrators can obscure the line between the technical and political utility of military expertise, and thus confuse participants as to which type of expertise should drive decisions. Military advisors tend to view military feasibility as the major determinant of decisions about strategy and the use of force. If an operation is unlikely to succeed, or if resourcing may hamper swift success, a military officer will likely advise against such a policy. But a civilian will consider public opinion, congressional pressures, and international legitimacy, among many other political considerations, all of which can constrain freedom of action. A stark example of confusion over civilian and military functions is the Johnson White House's famous proclivity for selecting bombing targets in Vietnam. The service secretaries and uniformed service chiefs bicker routinely over their ambiguously delineated responsibilities. And the CJCS's "global integrator" role sparked debate over whether such a function, with its strategic and political implications, was inherently civilian. Yet the basic civilian function of establishing order, prioritizing resources and efforts, and fitting military policy into national politics remains firmly in civilian hands. In fact, the reason the global integrator debate arose is because it impinges on the secretary's comprehensive authority, direction, and control over the department's resources, as well as his role in representing DoD to other civilians outside the department. Regardless, when it comes to civilian functions, the fact that civilians rely on a collaborative relationship with senior military leaders does not mean civilians have ceased to perform their unique tasks.

Where there is no dispute over the boundaries between civilians and the military is in their relative status. Military subordination to civilians, who control military actions, is an accepted norm among scholars and practitioners alike. Scholars of American civil-military relations have often affirmed that a military coup is a low-probability event. However, civilians' status is under pressure as the public, the military, and even politicians question the justification for automatic civilian superiority. The logical connection between status, functions, and expertise also makes status the linchpin in a meaningful concept of "civilian" in the civil-military context. Without it, the distinction between the military and the government itself will dissolve.

Civilian Types: Politicians, Administrators, Executives, Legislators

A key challenge to defining the concept of civilian is the claim that variations among civilians can be attributed to personality traits. For example, former secretary of defense Robert Gates and former president Barack Obama's different approaches to military policy could be products of their different dispositions. But a closer examination reveals that the two men's professional backgrounds and institutional positions played significant roles in shaping their choices.

Writing in 2014 about his four and a half years at the Pentagon, Bob Gates expressed discomfort with the prominence of politics in military policymaking under the Obama presidency. Obama was "determined from day one to win reelection" he wrote. "Domestic political considerations therefore would be a factor, though I believe never a decisive one, in virtually every major national security problem we tackled" (Gates 2014, 584). That politics were not the "decisive" factor in Obama's decision making was a saving grace in Gates's estimation. A few pages later, he praised both George W. Bush and Obama for making decisions they "believed to be in the best interest of the country regardless of the domestic political consequences" (Gates 2014, 588). To Gates, politics and national interests were incompatible.

In the first volume of his own memoir, Obama evaluated Gates's performance as secretary of defense using a very different perspective on the relationship between politics and military policy. "Gates understood as well as anybody congressional pressure, public opinion, and budgetary constraints," the former president wrote. "But for him, these were obstacles to navigate around, not legitimate factors that should inform our decisions." Obama concluded, "what he dismissed as politics was democracy as it was supposed to work" (Obama 2020, 436). To Obama, politics revealed and prioritized national interests, guiding military policy in logical and ethical ways. Interests and politics were interrelated: one a set of preferences and the other a means for evaluating and choosing among them.

This disagreement between a president and his secretary of defense about the influence of politics on military policymaking reveals how different civilian experiences generate different perspectives and how different civilian positions confer different incentives. Obama and Gates were both civilians, but they had different professional and personal experiences and therefore different values and expertise. A career Central Intelligence Agency (CIA) analyst, Gates spent decades in the halls of Washington's foreign policy bureaucracies cultivating expertise in the substance and procedures of policymaking. He eventually affiliated himself with the Republican Party, agreeing to become secretary of defense under the presidency of Republican George W. Bush. Barack Obama had been a lawyer, activist, and state and federal senator. He pursued the craft of politics, developing the communications, agenda-setting, and negotiation skills to work with civil society, with government bureaucracies, and within the Democratic Party. Obama and Gates also occupied different institutional roles that produced different demands. The president, a politician concerned with reelection, concentrates on the preferences of the politically powerful, including the public and other politicians who represent them. The secretary of defense, an administrator, focuses on policy implementation and organizational management. That the two men were also from different political parties made their institutional divide even wider.

Although all civilians in the civil-military relationship have status, functions, and expertise, there is a typology of civilians divided into professional and institutional categories: civilians are either politicians or administrators on the one hand, and either executives or legislators on the other.[9] A typology provides description and generates intuition about why certain civilians behave in the ways they do.[10] Being an elected official is different from being an appointed official because the duties of office and the pathways to power are different. Being a civilian on Capitol Hill is different from being a civilian at the DoD because the institutional rules and professional pressures are not the same. By identifying the specific types of civilians, we can understand the fundamental incentives, resources, and constraints on their governance choices and thereby explain why they exercise control over each other and the military in the ways they do.

POLITICIANS AND ADMINISTRATORS

There are two main professional types of civilian controllers: politicians and administrators. Presidents; chairs of SASC, HASC, and the subcommittees

32   Chapter One

for defense on the appropriations committees (SAC-D and HAC-D); and other senators and representatives are the key politicians in the American civil-military relationship. The secretary, deputy secretary, undersecretaries, and assistant secretaries of defense; the national security advisor; and the staff directors of the armed services and appropriations committees are all administrators. The key distinction between politicians and administrators is their immediate path to power: politicians are elected by the public, while administrators are selected by politicians.

Many well-documented consequences flow from politicians' electoral imperatives (Bueno de Mesquita et al. 2003). The requirement to petition others for votes and funds to achieve power encourages politicians to make choices that cause their constituents to vote for them and financial backers to give them money for campaigns. In most democracies, the United States included, a civilian must be a member of a political party to develop the social and financial resources necessary to run for office successfully. Parties, like constituents, apply pressure on politicians to adopt their preferences. The electoral imperative thus imposes both incentives and constraints—politicians do what will get them votes and money, and do not do what will lose them votes and money.

The key reference point for an office-holding politician is reelection—for which they seek attention, approval, and endorsement (Mayhew 1974). Politicians therefore prioritize issues that will affect their electoral survival. Politicians' incentives and constraints are not all deterministically binding, however. In addition to high-profile topics on which constituents hold strong views, there are also topics on which voters and funders are indifferent. When voters and funders are indifferent or inattentive, politicians have fewer constraints but also more variance in motivation. Voter indifference may allow politicians to follow their personal beliefs and preferences or may allow a politician to pay an issue very little attention. Where military policy is concerned, the more procedural, abstract, classified, or future-oriented an issue is, the less likely it will be to have widespread voter interest, while technical issues will attract the attention of constituents whose livelihoods depend on them. The nuances of security assistance policy or the process for approving operational plans are just two examples of issues that few voters watch closely. Communities and politicians from California, Colorado, Arizona, and elsewhere care about government investments in missile defense, whereas the voters of Maine and Mississippi keep an eye on shipbuilding. Yet these issues do not sway presidential elections and do not have general influence on congressional races. Politicians have specific, parochial incentives regarding military policy.

Politicians may attempt to change voters' minds through persuasion and by manipulating incentive structures. Successful politicians know how to win a critical mass of support through persuasion, how to forge sufficient consensus, and how to operate within party organizations. They also know what do in office to remain in office. They are therefore reputationally motivated, although their reputations are vulnerable to unfavorable interpretation. Those who fail at electoral politics and the reputational and issue-based politics that underwrite them are simply replaced by more capable politicians.

In contrast, administrators are not elected by voters but appointed to organizational leadership roles by politicians. Administrators manage government departments, agencies, and congressional committees on politicians' behalf. Administrators also have constituents, but their stakeholders do not cast formal, equal votes, and administrators do not campaign and therefore do not need donors. Instead, their stakeholders are their personal network of current and former colleagues, including superiors and subordinates, across a range of public and private organizations, expert groups, and the media. Although some have national profiles, they care primarily about Washington politics. They do not worry about appealing to a wide range of voters and funders to get and keep their jobs (especially given the relatively minor role that military policy plays in American electoral politics); they worry about impressing gatekeepers in the political class.

Administrators get nominated for their positions through a far less transparent process than elections, often against unknown competitors, based on personal relationships as much as on merit and reputation. William Perry had worked in and around the Pentagon and the defense industry for decades and became President Bill Clinton's nominee for deputy secretary of defense because of his reputation as an expert in defense technologies and his ties to key members of Congress, including SASC chair Sam Nunn. He later became secretary of defense in part because of his relationship with Vice President Al Gore. Administrators also require confirmation by politicians in the Senate—a probable but not guaranteed outcome. President George H. W. Bush's first nominee for secretary of defense, John Tower, was not confirmed, and it is more and more frequent for senators to place holds on nominees to extract (often unrelated) concessions from the president.[11] Another indicator of administrators' dependence on politicians is that their tenures are tied to electoral cycles. When the president or SASC chair leaves office, so do their administrators.[12]

Administrators' expertise combines politics with military affairs and organizational management—many secretaries of defense have had backgrounds in managing business enterprises. But this combination of duties and conflicting political demands makes administration of the DoD nearly impossible. In a speech at the University of Michigan titled "Managing the Defense Department: Why It Can't Be Done," former secretary of defense Harold Brown explained, "the pull of the need to fight a war, will always limit the peacetime efficiency of the defense establishment. . . . The pull of conflicting domestic interests represents democratic government" (Brown 1981). Even without the countervailing pressures, administrators have substantive portfolios that are so capacious that no single person could ever maintain comprehensive knowledge about all their areas of responsibility. In his memoir of his time as secretary of defense, Robert Gates wrote, "Nothing can prepare you for being secretary of defense. . . . The size of the place and its budget dwarf everything else in government" (Gates 2014, 82). Moreover, classification issues often prevent all but a few administrators from enterprise-wide knowledge in any case. Even the few who are authorized to access everything cannot learn about all of it. "I'm not going to live long enough to be briefed on everything," one senior DoD administrator told the *Washington Post* (Priest and Arkin 2010). Limits on civilian capacity, including classification restrictions, contribute to information asymmetries among civilians and between civilians and the military that I will discuss more in the next chapter.

EXECUTIVES AND LEGISLATORS

Politicians and administrators are embedded in institutional settings. Institutions provide structure, rules, and procedures to guide action, conferring additional constraints and resources on civilians. In democracies, these settings are typically divided into executive and legislative arms of government. In the United States, the Constitution adopts the executive-legislative division of labor to facilitate civilian control of civilians. While each branch is further subdivided into specialized organizations, the overall functions of passing laws and budgets on the legislative side and executing military policies and operations on the executive side provide the second major dimension of civilian types. This institutional dimension of the civilian typology reflects what Huntington called the overlap in "hierarchical" and "conciliar" structures of the American system (1961, 123).[13]

Hierarchy marks the executive branch, with the president at the top of a pyramid built of advisors in the White House and department and agency administrators. The key civilian control roles other than the commander-in-chief are the national security advisor, who runs the NSC staff and process; the secretary of defense and the deputy secretary of defense; the undersecretaries of defense; and the service secretaries. Clear superior-subordinate relationships among civilian positions, including explicit orders of precedence, assist in settling disputes—there is almost always a higher office that can decide on an issue, an authority to which subordinate elements may appeal for decision.

Beyond the roles and prerogatives given to them by the Constitution, executives wield authorities provided for in law. These authorities add detail to their status and functions, and demand specific types of expertise. For example, under Title 10 of the United States Code, the undersecretary of defense for policy reviews military plans on behalf of the secretary, giving that role superiority over military planning and requiring the incumbent to apply expertise in issues like planning assumptions, coordinating lines of operation, and force deployment phasing.[14] Executive politicians and administrators tend to have clear job descriptions with associated authorities and responsibilities.

The legislative branch contains both hierarchical and flat organizational elements. The principle of one member of Congress, one vote, ultimately decides most issues rather than higher authorities. In other words, the ultimate arbiter is a process rather than a person. But the institution is also composed of hierarchical elements: an upper and lower chamber; ranks in terms of seniority and in roles like speaker of the House and Senate majority leader; and the division-of-labor structure of committees that give some members more access to information and control over agendas than others (Johnson 2006). This mixed form of organization makes coordination and decision making a complex task, and an effective legislator is familiar with both procedural rules and gatekeepers. An individual politician's or administrator's accomplishments thus depend on whether her party is in the majority or minority, how senior she is, and her ability to navigate the byzantine committee and chamber rules.

The muddle of civilian ranks matches the ambiguity over roles. Politicians outrank administrators in each branch, yet the secretary of defense has more power over military affairs than most members of Congress. Compare the secretary and the SASC chair, however, and the balance of power becomes far more complicated. The former controls the entire DoD, but so does the latter—not to mention that the chair confirms the secretary for office, as well as all the secretary's immediate subordinates. Likewise, when it comes to operational control over the military, the president has power the SASC chair does not. But the president depends on the SASC chair for the underlying authorities and capabilities he needs to initiate and sustain successful military action. As the previous chapter revealed, the Founders put this design in place to enable civilians to control each other's use of the military. But as later generations of Americans have discovered, such constraints sacrifice coherence.

Comparatively, the legislative branch is heavy on politicians and light on administrators, while the executive branch has just two politicians (the president and vice president) wildly outnumbered by administrators. Subordinate elements of executive and legislative institutions further specify civilian positions—a civilian might work at the DoD or on the NSC staff, or on a senator's personal staff or for a committee. Political parties supply additional institutional affiliations, and politicians and administrators on the Hill have the distinction of being in the majority or the minority. Each civilian in government therefore answers to multiple, sometimes competing, institutional demands. Senior military and civilian leaders in the DoD may oppose a military intervention, but the secretary is still asked to support the administration's intervention policy. A legislative vote may help a party advance its national agenda but harm a representative's reputation with his constituents. Onetime HASC chair, Democrat Ike Skelton, represented the people of Missouri's 4th District for thirty-four years but lost reelection in 2010 because his Republican-leaning constituents believed he voted too frequently with his party (Lieb 2010).

Although these professional and institutional types can be sticky, they are not fixed. A member of Congress may become an administrator in the executive branch—in fact, seven secretaries of defense were former senators or representatives. A former DoD administrator may be elected to Congress, as in the case of Senator John Warner of Virginia; so could a former civilian staffer, like Representative Elissa Slotkin of Michigan. That civilian types reflect professions and institutional roles people step into and out of suggests that being a civilian is just a job. In the narrow sense we are interested in here—civilian controllers and what shapes their choices—being a civilian in the civil-military relationship is defined as a job, a job with status, functions, and expertise.

But there is another aspect of being a civilian that is, in a sense, a job requirement: being a civilian means having a civilian identity. The elements of an identity may be professional, but they are also, and above all, social. As Title 10 puts it, administrators in civilian control positions at DoD must be "drawn from civilian life." Civilians accumulate relationships, experiences, values, and perspectives that also inform their life choices, not just their policy choices. People choose to become politicians or administrators—or military officers—in line with their values and the kind of work they want to do. They build experiences over time that reinforce and refine their beliefs. The debates over the eligibility of retired Generals Mattis and Austin to be secretary of defense turned on the assumption that becoming a civilian is about more than leaving one job for another. The debate over the provision in federal employment law known as the "veterans' preference" is another focal point, as some analysts

Chapter One

	LEGISLATIVE	EXECUTIVE
POLITICIANS	• Senators • Representatives • **Chair SASC** • **Chair HASC** • Chair HAC-D • Chair SAC-D	• **President**
ADMINISTRATORS	• Staff directors of HASC, SASC, HAC, SAC	• National Security Advisor • **Secretary of Defense** • Service secretaries • Other Senate-confirmed officials

FIGURE 1. Civilian Typology

wonder whether the provision overrepresents military experience in the demographics of civil servants at DoD (Burke and Eaglen 2020). Again, the assumption is that "military" and "civilian" are durable identities. *Civilian* is not only a governing status but a more general social identity as well.

Presidents, Chairs, Secretaries

This book focuses on the three most prominent civilian controllers: the president, the SASC chair, and the secretary of defense. These three positions have the most expansive civilian responsibilities over military policymaking. To be sure, the HASC chair, the chairs of the defense appropriations subcommittees, the national security advisor, and the many other administrators at the DoD, the National Nuclear Security Administration, and arguably the Intelligence Community are also important civilian controllers.[15] But the president, SASC chair, and secretary represent the span of civilian control activities and reflect the degree to which being a civilian is a profession, an institutional designation, and an identity. The real people who exercise control over military policy demonstrate patterns of civilian professional and institutional experience that generally led them to these roles. In many ways, these patterns exemplify the status and expertise outlined above, but there are shortfalls, too, especially in the representational aspects of civilian status.

The average civilian controller enters office with high levels of education and specialized experience, belying the stereotype of politicians and government leaders as charlatans who buy or charm their way to the top. Senior civilians are almost uniformly college graduates, and many have advanced degrees, most commonly in the law. Those in elected office have years of service at the state or local level along with extensive experience in political campaigns. The most common professional backgrounds after the law and politics are business, academia, and prior government appointments. Most civilians in leading control positions also have at least two years of military service—56 percent of HASC chairs, 66 percent of Army secretaries, 76 percent of secretaries of defense, and 85 percent of SASC chairs have served in the military.[16] Those few who have not served in the military often have other professional experience at DoD or in research institutions focused on military affairs. Generally, they have been elected to representative office or selected to senior governing positions by other civilians multiple times prior to assuming their positions of military control. Being a civilian, much like being a military officer, is an earned identity.

Nowhere is this clearer than in the civilian commander-in-chief, the president. In general, the post-WWII presidents got into politics soon after finishing school and made their careers as elected officials. All but one, Barack Obama, has been a White man. All but two, Dwight Eisenhower and Donald Trump, held congressional office or governorships before becoming president. All but one, Harry Truman, received a college education, but only six had advanced degrees, five of which were in law. Every president from 1947 to 1993 served in the military. Wartime service includes WWII but not Vietnam, even though four were age eligible for the latter. Of the five men who have been president since 1993, only one has served in the military, in the Air National Guard.

In the seventy-five years since the position of secretary of defense was created, twenty-seven men have served in the role.[17] Selection of the secretary has tended to target the ranks of previous government officials, suggesting presidents are inclined toward experts and technocrats. The path to secretary of defense involves an advanced degree at least half the time, often master's degrees of some kind but in six cases a law degree, and for six others a PhD (in economics, physics, math, and Russian history). Military service is also the norm, although the trend there has shifted over the years. Whereas most of the early secretaries served in WWII, their service averaged fewer than three years. Only nine secretaries never served in uniform. The last three men to serve as secretary of defense had more than ten years of active-duty military service each, and two each clocked over forty years in uniform. Aside from those two recent exceptions with military careers, secretaries tend to have professional backgrounds in the law, academia, and business. Although SecDefs usually identify with the president's party, this is not always true—Presidents Bill Clinton and Barack Obama both selected Republicans to serve in their Democratic administrations—and even the copartisans frequently are often marginal participants in political campaigns.

The road to chair of the SASC or HASC is long and depends heavily on party favoritism. A senator or representative only becomes chair of an armed services committee by first serving on the committee, usually for many years (Taylor 2019). Strict seniority requirements for promotion to chair were dropped in the 1970s, but putting in the time still matters "heavily" in the competitive caucus selection process.[18] SASC chair Senator Jack Reed joined the committee in 1998 and was a member for twenty-three years before ascending to the top spot.[19] Each chamber of Congress has its own rules for assigning committee chairs, but in all cases the party in the majority fills the chairs. Each party caucus sets the rules for how a senator or representative becomes a chair, and typically sorts out committee assignments shortly after a new Congress takes office (CRS 2021). Chairs are then formally assigned through chamber measures.[20] Once a member has become chair, they may stay for an unlimited number of terms, meaning that the tenure of chairs varies by reelection, majority status, and personal circumstances. Senator Carl Levin was SASC chair for ten years; Senator John McCain was chair for just three and a half years, forced to step down early because of the cancer that took his life. Since the committees were formed out of the disparate Navy and Army oversight committees in the late 1940s, fourteen men have chaired SASC and sixteen men have chaired HASC.

A noticeable feature of these actual civilians who have served in positions of civilian control is that they are not a representative sample of the American population. With just a few exceptions, the people who have become civilian controllers have been overwhelmingly White and male. Readers will see in the chapters that follow that not a single armed services committee chair, secretary of defense, or president has been a woman. The reasons for the narrowness of the civilian cadre have to do with the pipelines to power. For one thing, the pools from which these leaders are selected are already more homogeneous than the general population.[21] Entry into the groups that vie for political and administrative roles in government is not equitable today and has been even less so in the past. Careers in politics have financial and social barriers to entry; structural biases have historically suppressed minority participation in senior government positions, and many groups are only now beginning to catch up, unevenly. Because civilian controllers are selected from the already-narrowed pool of elites, and because they self-select based on their own political and personal interests, those in civilian control jobs tend to represent elites drawn from the portion of the population with direct interests in military affairs. That proportion is not small, but neither is it representative of the general US population.[22]

The relative homogeneity of civilians in positions of control over the military undermines the democratic nature of that control. There is a stark contrast between the broad range of backgrounds and beliefs present in civil society and the narrow range of demographic backgrounds civilian controllers directly represent. There has been some progress toward greater representation in recent years, especially with more women and people of color in DoD administrator positions. But civilian control remains far from representative.

This problem is compounded by the fact that, except for election to the presidency, the ultimate processes through which civilians gain control positions are not democratic. The public doesn't choose congressional committee members or their chairs, nor do voters select cabinet officials or presidential advisors. Instead, narrower institutions select civilian

42   Chapter One

controllers (Bueno de Mesquita et al. 2003). As one special assistant to the secretary of defense for White House liaison—the person responsible for orchestrating the political appointment process in the DoD—put it, being selected for political appointments is "the ultimate insider's game."[23]

Despite these shortfalls in the representational element of status, civilians still represent public interests better than the military because civilian roles are explicitly responsive to those public interests. Even if they are more trustees than true representatives, civilians nonetheless are more accountable to the public than the military.

Conclusion

Being a civilian in government means filling certain roles—officials act in civilian capacities. They have status, functions, and expertise that are independent from the military's but also define their positions and shape their choices in the civil-military context. Being a civilian is also an identity. A person is a civilian by experience, associations, values, beliefs, and biases. An individual can change roles quickly, shedding one set of duties and taking on another. But the same person cannot shed identity so swiftly. Her experiences, values, and loyalties stay with her, and her perspectives change only as she accumulates more and different experiences. That there are both civilian roles and civilian identities makes the meaning of "civilian" complex and variable within certain parameters. The SASC chair's duties and background are not the same as the national security advisor's. Yet both are civilians, because they share a status, ordering and control functions, and expertise in matching political interests to military policies.

Within this conceptual definition is a heterogenous group with different combinations of motivations and responsibilities. Order can be imposed on diverse civilians by categorizing them according to their type and institutional role. The civilians most implicated in control functions are generally politicians and administrators who are distributed across the executive and legislative branches. A civilian's type provides insights into their core motivations—what they care about and what they believe—as well as their experience, expertise, and identity. Additionally, each civilian institutional role has a unique set of resources, constraints, and relationships to the military as a policy tool and as a political actor.

Situating any given civilian in her professional and institutional contexts reveals information about her power, her incentive structures, her networks, and her likely path to her particular role. In sum, civilians have comparative advantages in political and administrative expertise. They come in types that combine professional careers as politicians or administrators with executive or legislative institutional positions. The status, functions, and expertise that define all civilians along with the type expressed by any individual civilian role provides the basis for the framework to analyze civilian control choices presented in the next chapter.

TWO

A Framework for Civilian Control

DEMOCRACIES EXPECT CIVILIANS TO CONTROL the military, and the founders of the United States designed the government so that civilians would control each other. But people do not always live up to expectations. What makes civilians choose to control each other and the military, and how do they attempt to do so? To answer that question, analysts need to know what control is, the mechanisms civilians use to exercise it, and why civilians sometimes defer control to others.

Building on the concept of *civilian* developed in Chapter 1, this chapter argues that whether and how a civilian decides to exercise control over other civilians or the military depends on the interaction between her professional-institutional type and the political context. Political context is composed of issues and people, and appears at different levels of analysis, from the interpersonal to the international. A civilian observes the political context and interprets its meaning for her control choices using the motivations and resources conferred by her professional-institutional type. Resources include the information and institutional capacity at her disposal. Combining motivations and resources with political context explains where a civilian's choices land on the continuum from control to deference.

This chapter proceeds in three parts. First it explores the idea of control, elaborating its mechanistic aspects and its inherently political character. Then I discuss the idea of political context and how it interacts with professional-institutional civilian types to produce control choices. I then demonstrate the framework by applying it to the case of the military intervention in Libya and conclude with a reminder of the extensive empirical tests in the chapters that follow.

What Is Control?

I define *civilian control* as a series of efforts to cause desired behaviors or outcomes. Civilian control efforts happen through political processes that devise, articulate, and enforce those desired outcomes. Civilians exercise control over each other through such political processes. Civilians exercise control over the military through three primary mechanisms: guidance, budgeting, and force management.

Much of the civil-military relations subfield literature views control as a state or outcome. When the military habitually does what civilians want, scholars consider civilians in control. This state is brought about by international and domestic "conditions," often threats (Desch 1999), but also by aspects of democratic regimes like civilian institutions and a strong civil society (Kuehn et al. 2017). Another way of looking at control is to assess civilian dominance of policymaking, whether civilians have "uncontested decision-making power" (Croissant et al. 2010, 26).

These approaches confuse the exercise of control with civilians' status. It is not sufficient for civilians to be thought of as legitimately holding power; they must do something with that power. As Lindsay Cohn puts it, exercising control means choosing "the mechanism by which the expression of a direction or prohibition has effective influence on the target" (Cohn 2011, 384). For civilian control to obtain, civilians must communicate instructions and do something to make the military comply. In other words, control consists of choices followed by a set of actions; control is not merely a state, status, or outcome. In contrast to scholars who ask if civilians *are in* control, I ask whether and how civilians *are controlling* each other and the military.

If we want to understand civilian control, we need to understand what those civilian actions are, what civilians do to exercise control. Yet few studies, particularly those with case studies of the United States, do more than confirm that civilian control appears to be happening. There are studies that provide important exceptions, the most prominent of which is Peter Feaver's book *Armed Servants* (2003). Feaver accounts for civilian control with a model of civilian efforts to hold the military accountable for policy decisions. Civilians choose whether to monitor military compliance with their preferences and whether to punish the military if it "shirks." Although this approach captures more civilian control activity than most studies, Feaver is still only covering part of what civilians do to exercise control. In his model, control happens after policies are already in place, without much exploration of where those policies come from, how civilians choose to convey them, or if they specified how they want them implemented. This framing of control captures the policing aspect of control but much less of the policymaking.

Some scholars dig into the exercise of civilian control by focusing on methods of governance (Cottey, Edmunds, and Forster 2002). Such studies move beyond treating institutions as conditions by examining what civilians do with and within those institutions. They ask if civilians are conducting defense planning or providing strategic guidance. Such studies consider whether civilians are unable to exercise control for reasons of few or poor institutional mechanisms, poor education, a lack of capacity, or excessive delegation to the military (Pion-Berlin, Acacio, and Ivey 2019; Beliakova 2021). Civilians can also "harness and shape" military culture to generate obedience to orders (Cohn 2011). Feaver himself examines how civilians exercise control over the military by devising policy and issuing decisions in his article on the surge of forces to Iraq (2011). In short, civilians have many mechanisms of control at their disposal.

I follow the scholars who focus on governance and group mechanisms for civilian control of the military in three categories: guidance, budgeting, and force management. *Guidance* comes in written form and in verbal instructions. It may be a law, strategy, directive, or order. Guidance specifies and codifies what civilians want others to do, and frequently contains instructions intended to constrain and compel. The War Powers Act of 1973, the annual NDAA, National Security Decision Memoranda (or Presidential

Decision Directive, etc.), executive orders, the National Defense Strategy, the Defense Planning Guidance, and presidential and secretary of defense operational orders are all examples of guidance. But unlike orders, which are generally issued under exigent circumstances and intended to shape near-term action, most policy guidance applies for at least two and often four or more years. Laws last until a new Congress amends or abolishes them, and a directive issued by the president may last until it is overturned by a subsequent president. A National Defense Strategy (previously called the Quadrennial Defense Review) has a four-year shelf life, as does the Defense Planning Guidance.

Budgeting describes setting programs and spending levels, and comprises an ecosystem of activities that determine which efforts merit resources, at which level, and over which period. Budgets are a tremendously influential mechanism of control over both civilians and the military, because of the myriad stakeholders in the funding they disburse, including military organizations, businesses, and constituents who work in or benefit from the defense industry. Budgets confer power and structure incentives. Using budgets, civilians can compel military activities, research and development, and acquisitions, and constrain the military and civilians from pursuing activities by denying programs resources. In 1986 a *New York Times* profile of one DoD administrator provided a colorful illustration of the contentious nature of civilian control over civilians using budgetary levers. Anthony Battista, a HASC staff member, expressed skepticism that DoD administrators imposed any discipline on military spending. "I don't see anyone over there saying, 'No, you can't have it, I'm killing it,'" the *Times* quoted Battista. "I don't know why they didn't offer HIM the job," Undersecretary of Defense for Research and Engineer Donald Hicks shot back (Keller 1986).

Control via budgeting, however, is not a lever that is easy to pull: it requires deep procedural and substantive expertise and persistence over multiple budget cycles to lock in investments. Defense budgets typically authorize two years of funding (recall from Chapter 1 that this is a mechanism for civilian control of civilians as well as the military), and DoD plans budgets for five years at a time but revises those plans each budget cycle.[1]

48   Chapter Two

To get the military to make big changes through the budget, civilians have to exercise control consistently over time.

Guidance and budgeting often go together. In the executive branch, the OSD and the Office of Management and Budget coordinate to link budgets to defense and national security strategies, at least nominally. For example, as later chapters will explore, the 1993 Bottom-Up Review (BUR) strategy accompanied a budget submission and a Future Years Defense Plan (FYDP). Sometimes, to the chagrin of strategists, budgets drive guidance. "Show me my budget and I'll show you the strategy" is a well-worn Washington aphorism. This was largely the case in the development of the BUR, which was revised to fulfill candidate Clinton's campaign pledges. On the legislative side, the annual NDAA provides guidance and budgeting simultaneously—although the separate appropriations process allocates the actual funds. For example, the NDAA might authorize military construction projects in a combatant command's area of operations and the spending limit to go with them, but the appropriations bill might only allocate half the amount authorized. This can occur because the armed services committees develop the NDAA whereas the appropriations committees write the checks, and the two groups do not always see eye-to-eye.

Control via *force management* tends to involve shorter timelines than guidance and budgeting, both in terms of the process that produces control actions and the length of time over which the control is exercised. The term *force management* has a technical definition at DoD, but I borrow it here to indicate a range of control activities from making decisions about the use of force in contingencies to the routine processes of authorizing nonconflict (or "presence") missions around the world.[2] Control over force management decisions has an indirect effect on control over civilians because it can prevent the president from using the military the way he wants. The control over the military is direct, giving civilians a precise lever to direct military assets where civilians want to use them. Much like budgeting, force management can be a highly technical activity demanding expertise to conduct effectively.

In the United States many of the mechanisms for civilian control are institutionalized in law, organizations, and standard processes. Many of them are cyclical and automatic. Although civilians must make some effort, routines and legal requirements often help spur them to perform their control responsibilities. They also reduce resistance among those who are controlled, or at least redirect resistance into attempts to influence the use of the mechanisms themselves. The military planning process is a good example. By statute, the secretary of defense, with the assistance of the undersecretary for policy, must review combatant commanders' operational plans on a regular basis. Because it is a statutory part of his job, bureaucratic practices in OSD—including the existence of an entire deputy assistant secretary for plans—somewhat automate that mechanism of civilian control for the secretary. So long as OSD enforces this requirement, the Combatant Commands and the Joint Staff will focus their energy on persuading civilians to accept their plans. The military may want to resist civilian preferences, but the formal nature of the relevant control activities force that resistance into the open.

Both competitors for control and the targets of control may choose to contest control efforts. Competitors would rather be in control themselves and may attempt to undermine the efforts of their rivals. Meanwhile, if both competitors and targets are unable to prevent principals from using control mechanisms, they may seek to change the mechanisms themselves—by changing legal requirements for strategic reviews, for example. But control mechanisms vary in their malleability, and therefore vary in how contested they may be. Their susceptibility to change descends from nearly unalterable at the level of government structure to highly flexible at the level of department and agency procedures. Because departments and agencies themselves usually establish their own procedures, these can be changed internally without resort to complex and time-consuming legislative action. The process of selecting senior officers for nomination for promotion, for example, is at the discretion of the secretary of defense in consultation with the service chiefs (Hoehn, Robbert, and Harrell 2011). Changing the Constitution to restructure the government, however—to a parliamentary system perhaps— would require national collective action that is difficult to envision. Thus, control mechanisms that DoD can alter on its own are often contested; the overarching structure of government checks and balances are not.

But even unalterable mechanisms are only meaningful if they are used. Civilians do not always choose to exercise control; sometimes they defer or default to each other or to the military. In cases of deference, civilians are aware of their opportunity to exercise control and either choose not to try or give up trying and cede influence to others (Beliakova 2021; Friend and Weiner 2022). One explanation for Congress's abdication of its war declaration authority to the president is that most members of Congress do not want to be held politically accountable for failed military operations, and so pass the responsibility on to the president (Fisher 2013). The president or the secretary of defense might believe that military advice is incontrovertible, and so defer to the military's recommendations for action. They may also believe that there is political advantage in military agreement, and they may be willing to cede control to obtain it (Kanter 1983; Friend and Weiner 2022).

Sometimes, control over military policy is too difficult to exercise either in an absolute sense or in the context of the governing activities competing for time and attention. Principal-agent theory is full of evidence of principals who, despite their best efforts to control their agents, eventually default to agents' ways of doing business. And civilians are frequently burdened with far more issues than they could possibly manage, sometimes making them ignorant of opportunities—or in extreme cases, their fundamental obligation—to exercise control. A member of Congress who is not aware that forces have been deployed to West Africa is failing to exercise control over military affairs. Although some deference can result from simple disinterest, it does not always indicate that a civilian has stopped caring about the issue that raised the question of control in the first place. Deference could even be a strategy if a civilian's interests in an issue will be protected by the military or other civilians.

Civilians' ability to lean into or avoid exercising control indicates that control is best measured on a continuum from weak to strong (Cohn 2011). Civilians don't merely choose whether to control, but how firmly to do so. In fact, as the above discussion points out, civilians often bind themselves or each other to mechanisms of control such as annual budgets and guidance documents. In such cases, a modicum of control is baked into the process, and civilians choose how precisely to use those tools, how much military and other civilian input to allow into the process, and how rigorously to enforce the directions they issue.

To capture degrees of control, I identify its progressive types. They essentially move from generality to specificity, in two basic categories: actors can *constrain* each other *from* taking certain actions, and they can *compel* each other *to* take certain actions. Constraining is the more limited activity: it involves denying an actor what she needs to act, typically by withholding permission or resources. Constraint is familiar to students of civil-military relations. Often when scholars and practitioners use the term "civilian control," they mean that civilians (or, often, military leaders themselves) have constrained the military or prevented the military from taking over roles in government reserved for civilians—the military does not coup, or it does not exercise "undue influence."[3] Similarly, civilian control of civilians is designed to constrain authoritarian or unilateral executive coercion. This may be easier said than done. A famous example of civilian control of the military via constraint is the Cuban missile crisis, when the Kennedy administration monitored the Navy's blockade of Cuba very closely to prevent actions that might provoke a Russian escalation. Compelling an action is even more difficult because it requires a more complex arrangement of instructions and incentives, including an unambiguous description of the desired action, the resources to accomplish it, and compliance incentives.[4] But most difficult of all are what political scientist Sam Finer called "strategies of control" (Finer 1962), activities that constrain and compel at the same time. Long guidance documents tend to mix these forms of control (Friend and Karlin 2020). Rules of engagement are another clear example of mixed control.

Because civilians are also responsible for controlling each other's efforts to control the military, guidance, budgeting, and force management are also arenas of civilian competition. The mechanism of civilian control over other civilians is political competition, typically conducted through political processes as well as some complementary administrative processes.

The policy formulation process represents the first and critical stage in the exercise of control. Policy determines the actions desired, and the mechanisms of control described above are civilians' means for achieving them. To formulate policies, civilians must come to a consensus among themselves about their preferences. The methods for doing so are the stuff of political expertise: agenda setting, bargaining, compromise, and commitments. Such consensus building is necessary in cases of civilian control of the military as well as civilian control of civilians. Most citizens of democracy understand intuitively that the checks and balances of divided government are inherently political, making civilian control of civilians a naturally political activity. But it is less common for people to think of civilian control of the military as a political process. Yet the premises and the exercise of control are both political acts. Forging consensus approaches to complex military problems—or opposing an approach—is a political process. Powerful actors vie for influence over what the government does with its resources. And whether a preference or policy prevails may depend as much on who supports it as on its substantive merit. Furthermore, if forging policies is a political process, the mechanisms to exercise control are political as well. To the extent that politics is just competition for dominance and resources among powerful actors, if there is contestation over control mechanisms, then their selection and use are also shaped by politics.

Civilian control of both the military and other civilians are thus inherently political activities. They involve bargaining and strategic maneuvering among those with resources and power. They also involve values, weighing what is important to a society, how to confront ethical questions, and even when to compromise morals. In his memoir, former secretary of defense Donald Rumsfeld quoted Winston Churchill: "If Hitler invaded hell, I would make at least a favorable reference to the devil in the House of Commons" (Rumsfeld 2011, 372).

In the political science literature, the politics of civilian control actions often take an analytical back seat to the military's response to civilian preferences. Yet civilians not only have to devise military policy that other civilians will help them enforce—or at least not hinder—they must also come to a policy they are reasonably confident the military will implement (Brooks 2008; Cohn 2011). Both scholars and practitioners acknowledge that civilian control of policy itself is often a function of the relative influence of civilian and military preferences (Avant 1998; Desch 1999; Travis 2019; Friend 2020a). This means that the military is involved in the political process of consensus building around both policy and the means to enforce military compliance with it.

The same sort of politics continues to factor into civilian control after policies have been formulated. Even control mechanisms that are somewhat automatic do not just "work." They require three elements to be effective: sufficient civilian unity (Friend 2020a), expertise in the technical aspects of the mechanism itself, and the acquiescence of the target of control (Cohn 2011). How much unity among civilians is "sufficient" varies depending on the issue, its complexity, and the length of time the policy must be implemented. But in general, those civilians critical to enforcing and/or implementing control must agree to do so. Expertise in control mechanisms means understanding institutional standard operating procedures. For example, the budget reconciliation process in the House of Representatives is a means for appropriators to constrain authorizers' budgeting. At DoD, the Program Objective Memoranda cycle is a key forum for civilians to provide guidance and compel or constrain military service budgets. In both cases, civilians need to understand the timelines, procedures, veto players, and administrative requirements to use the process to compel or constrain the military and/or other civilians. Finally, for control to work, civilians need to know whether the target is capable of doing what is asked, whether they will resist, what resources they have to enable their resistance, and what incentives may induce their compliance. Principal-agent theorists address this stage of the politics of control extensively: the military works or shirks, and civilians choose how to monitor and, if necessary, punish shirking (Feaver 2003). This framework extends ideas about monitoring and punishment to civilian control of civilians.

In sum, civilian control is a political process that comprises formulating, expressing, and enforcing compliance with policies. Because it is so institutionalized, a great deal of civilian control is not a question of *whether* it is exercised but how, how much, and how well. Control may constrain, compel, or both. And because it is costly in terms of time, effort, and political capital, civilians sometimes simply default or defer to others— Congress may allow the executive branch to decide whether to use force, or executives may defer to military judgment to craft policies. But in much of the day-to-day mechanisms of control, civilians at least impose some constraints on each other and the military. The question is: What makes civilians proactively attempt to exercise control or choose to defer to others?

Civilian Control Choices: A Framework

To make up her mind about how and how much to control military affairs, a civilian uses the motivations conferred by her type to interpret the meaning of the political context. In this section I explore the dimensions of political context, civilian motivations, and institutional resources. I then show how these factors relate to the civilian types introduced in the previous chapter and present the framework for analyzing civilian control choices.

POLITICAL CONTEXT

Civilians' core function in military affairs is to engage in political processes to identify interests and to design military policies that protect and advance those interests. As explored above, control itself is an inherently political process, meaning that the broader political context informs how civilians exercise it. Politics is the process of negotiation that powerful people and groups engage in to make collective decisions, coordinate action, and distribute resources. *Political context* describes the distribution of power and the preferences of powerful actors.

Two main factors comprise the political context: issues and people. *Issues* can be events or ideas, and civilians evaluate them in terms of meaning and salience. *Meaning* supplies an issue's importance and consequences. *Salience* has to do with how much attention people are paying to an issue. Issues may become salient for a variety of reasons, but often by becoming more immediate and/or urgent. For example, Russia's nuclear weapons have threatened the United States for decades, but that threat became more immediate with the onset in 2022 of the war in Ukraine (Sanger and Broad 2022).

People make up civilians' professional networks and political constituents. Each civilian will have a slightly different array of actors who can apply meaningful pressure on them, or whose opinions matter to them. People have influence over a civilian's survival and over her ability to exercise control. Civilians don't value everyone's opinion, but there are people whose opinions they must take seriously if they hope to survive politically. For example, a president will care about the entire voting population, whereas a senator may care only about the voters in her own state. A president will also care much more about the views of foreign leaders than a representative of a district in Wyoming if that district does not rely on trade with foreign countries. In situations involving military affairs, military actors are key people in the political context, but their pressure may affect different civilians differently. Members of the military can influence a civilian's survival—for example, by contesting the wisdom of policy decisions—and almost always participate in the networks that implement civilian control.

Because only some people matter to any given civilian, different civilians facing the same issue at the same time may deal with it in different political contexts. In many cases, one civilian can feel countervailing pressures from different people who matter to her survival and beliefs. A politician's constituents may want a no-fly zone, but her national party may wish to support the president's policy opposing a no-fly zone. Or the president could be sympathetic to using the US military to defend humanitarian aid corridors, while the secretary of defense's military advisors may urge him to resist the policy. Conversely, a civilian may feel something is important, but other actors he needs to help him exercise control over the military disagree. Even for the secretary of defense and the chairs of the SASC and HASC, whose roles are designed to make all issues touching on the military salient to the incumbents, not all issues are equally urgent nor equally important to their networks and constituents.

Civilians evaluate the political context at the international and domestic levels, where different groups of people coalesce around the same issue. At the international level, foreign leaders, international organizations, foreign publics, and the domestic politics of key allies and partners make up the politics civilians care about. At the international level, civilians rarely consider issues from a purely bilateral perspective. Instead, they consider how third parties will perceive actions. For example, during the Russo-Ukrainian war, Washington considered how China would interpret NATO actions affecting Russia. Sometimes issues at the international and domestic levels interact and reinforce one another, and sometimes they are contradictory (Putnam 1988). And there are more than just two levels of politics: below the domestic level there are partisan,

56 Chapter Two

interest group, bureaucratic, and interpersonal politics. Issues can play across many levels of politics at once, making the political context layered and complex.

The reader might ask if there is a difference between the strategic context and the international political context. To the extent that politics is defined by power and the processes of getting and wielding it, there is no difference between a country's strategic environment and the international political context. Strategy, after all, is about the interactions of goal-seeking, interdependent players (Schelling 1960). Practitioners often use the terms *strategic environment* when they mean the security dimensions of international relations and *politics* to refer to domestic interest group machinations. But political processes are strategic, and the strategic context at the international level is nothing but the integration of politics and military capabilities. While international politics might be more overtly coercive than domestic politics, the threat of enforcement exists in both. Another way to look at it is if we accept that war is politics by other means, then the strategic context is just another label for the international political situation. And because civilians' key function is to engage in politics, then the most important factor in fulfilling their function is to understand the political context—international and domestic—facing them at the time when their leadership is necessary.

Political contexts are dynamic. A single issue may vary in importance over time. For example, the military missions to Somalia in 1993 and to Niger in 2017 were completely off public and political radars alike until American forces died in combat. Then the mission they were on became highly salient to the public and to voters in congressional districts where the fallen soldiers were from, making the event much more important to politicians' survival and administrators' reputations. The war in Afghanistan had become little more than background static to many civilian leaders, but the unfolding tragedy of the withdrawal over the summer of 2021 made it much more salient. A wise civilian might also perceive that an issue that is not salient today will become so later. This can inspire them to avoid it or act contrary to the crowd, as Barack Obama did with his public opposition to the Iraq War in 2002 and 2003 before his election to the Senate in 2004.

Political contexts are strategic and vary across issues, time, and international borders, and civilians constantly adjust accordingly. How and why civilians make the adjustments that they do—how and why they make certain military policy and control choices—is a function of what type of civilian they are.

Choosing Control: Civilian Types and the Interpretation of Political Context

Although issues can be associated with some degree of consensus, whether, how, and how much they matter to national security and military affairs is subject to interpretation (Kier 1997). An issue can matter in different ways to different people, causing them to disagree over the appropriate policy response. The Russo-Ukrainian war is a case in point. The nuclear dimension of the crisis activated the reputations of administrators working on nuclear policy and nonproliferation. Meanwhile, politicians with Ukrainian-American constituents focused on the human suffering triggered by the invasion (Hohmann 2022).[5] Some in the public focused on humanitarian aspects of the issue advocated for a no-fly zone over Ukraine (Lieberman 2022) while others focused on the military risks of that proposal—including the risk of direct confrontation with Russia (Pietrucha and Benitez 2022). The correlation between constituent interests and politicians' focus on the humanitarian aspects of the war is a quick illustration of how a civilian's type interacts with political context. Below I sketch out the motivations and information that civilians draw on when interpreting political contexts and the major questions they ask themselves to calculate control choices.

MOTIVATIONS

Civilians' types both indicate what motivates them—because they are drawn to certain professions—and structure their incentives once they occupy institutional positions. Once there, they also tend to want to hold onto power and gain more. I refer generally to civilians' motivations as *survival*. The concept of political survival is a familiar one to scholars of

politics, and, as explored earlier, often concentrates on the desire to be reelected (Mayhew 1974; Bueno de Mesquita et al. 2003). But those civilians
who do not stand for election also want to protect their reputations as a
means to keep and expand power (Schlesinger 1966). Even once a politician
or administrator has decided they may soon retire, they want their legacy
to be well situated. This desire to maintain power and prestige exercises
extremely strong influence over civilians, including in the civil-military
context (Avant 1994). To ensure their survival, civilians monitor the opinions of their key constituents—for politicians, voters' and other politicians'
opinions are most important, and for administrators, political bosses and
bureaucracies' preferences matter most.

But professional-institutional survival isn't the only thing civilians
care about. Not every civilian wants power for power's sake alone (Peter
2017). Most also have core beliefs that motivate their desire to hold public
office in the first place and shape the ways they approach their positions.[6]
A civilian might care strongly about nuclear weapons, or military readiness, or military families. These beliefs are generally stable, and some
are so strong, or are so threatened in some circumstances, that civilians
might risk their political survival to defend them.[7] More often, however,
civilians will choose to survive in office—often with the faith that remaining in office will allow them to defend their beliefs under more favorable
conditions.

Because motivations are so close to civilians' values and personal fortunes, they precede instances of choice and persist beyond them. But motivations are not invariant—as described, a dearly held belief may outweigh
survival and vice versa. Sometimes a situation does not activate a belief or,
conversely, does not threaten survival. Civilians calculate the total value
of their motivations dynamically, and this ongoing calculation informs
whether they exercise control or deference.

RESOURCES

A civilian cannot accomplish her goals without the means to do so. Resources affect civilian control decisions in two ways. At the most basic
level, civilians need funding and political capital to exercise control.

The distribution of resources also factors into civilians' evaluations of the political context because it affects the power of other players.

Two types of resources matter in the context of control and deference: information and institutional capacity (Friend 2020a). Information enables civilian control by helping civilians understand the political context and the military. Civilians seek two kinds of information: information on the political context itself and information about military capacity and capabilities. Politicians and administrators will seek different kinds of political and military information, however. Whereas politicians focus on electoral and grand legislative politics, administrators will want information on the legislative and bureaucratic politics specific to their budgets and organization. And while politicians will want to understand high-level summaries of military activities and their predicted outcomes (e.g., casualty estimates), administrators will seek detailed information about financial and opportunity costs, how capabilities will be used, impacts on military organizations, timelines, and so on.

Civilians turn to a variety of sources for information about politics and the military. To understand the political context of any given military policy decision, a politician may turn to opinion polls, the news media, other politicians, advisors, even friends and family. Such sources can inform politicians about political context at all levels. For example, a politician from an allied country may supply insight about alliance politics, just as a member of Congress may give a president information about likely committee votes. Some politicians gather information from direct engagement with constituents at speeches, rallies, townhall meetings, and the like. Administrators will also scrutinize the news, but less for general public sentiment and more for details about activities in other agencies and on the Hill, and as a way to monitor their own organizations. As secretary of defense, Dick Cheney called general officers into his office for disciplinary conversations more the once because of something reported about them in the press (Cheney 2011; Powell 1995).

Information germane to control over military affairs often comes from military sources, but civilians also draw on academic, commercial, and other perspectives. Civilians may also develop their own expertise through education and professional experience. A professional network

60   Chapter Two

extends personal knowledge, providing intelligence about people and political maneuvers across the government. Others' substantive expertise is also an important information source and is housed in government-run and independent research institutions, like the Government Accountability Office, the RAND Corporation, and the Council on Foreign Relations.

But most of the substantive and procedural expertise used by government officials grows in the defense and military bureaucracies. Because information can influence decisions, bureaucracies guard it, meaning civilians often have partial and different information from each other and from the military (Moynihan 1998). Such information asymmetries mean that those in the know have leverage over those in the dark. Often where the military is concerned, classification, or secrecy, can prevent civilian access to information and therefore understanding. A civilian's network and political skills are vital for gathering information the bureaucracy does not want to reveal.

CALCULATING CONTROL

To analyze the sources of civilian control and deference decisions, we need a sense of how civilians measure and assess these factors in combination. I focus on the individual level of analysis, examining what motivates a president's, secretary of defense's, or SASC chair's choices. Ultimately, however, military policy often is not made by "a single decision maker with coherent preferences" (Bawn 1995, 70) but by coalitions across institutions. Civilians rarely make control choices at unique decision points but instead refine and calibrate them over time according to their interpretations of the evolving political context and their negotiations with each other and with the military itself. In the case studies, I show these collective, iterative decision processes.

Political context will also look different to different types of civilians. Politicians will consider the probable electoral effects of an issue, and then the electoral effects if they exercise control or defer. Administrators will gauge what an issue will mean for their bureaucracy, their influence, and their eligibility for future roles. Politicians worry about public politics, and administrators focus more on the politics of Washington, DC. Regardless, even when motivations and political context together suggest that exercising control is desirable, that doesn't mean civilians have the resources to exercise that control effectively.

A consideration often invoked by military strategists is the degree of risk that certain courses of action invite or mitigate. Risk is a measure of potential losses, and decisions about risk hinge on how willing the society is to tolerate those losses. "Blood and treasure" is a term referencing a country's dear expenditures and is associated with political evaluations of a military policy's success or failure. A particularly American measure of risk tolerance is the degree of casualty aversion, and tolerance for casualties is highly affected by how political leaders frame military operations (Feaver and Gelpi 2004; Gelpi, Feaver, and Reifler 2009). Other scholars have examined the relationship between financial costs and public support for the use of force, noting that the political mobilization of wealth in ways that offset the costs for the public drives up war willingness (Caverley 2014). In his book illustrating that waging war requires political leadership, Eliot Cohen notes that in cases spanning democratic regimes from the mid-nineteenth to the mid-twentieth centuries, "the balance of risk required a political decision" (Cohen 2002a, 10). One of the main differences between civilian and military leaders is this responsibility for evaluating overall risks and deciding how much risk to life and national wealth to assume.

Civilians' assessments will almost certainly be biased, and occasionally flat wrong—they may not have up-to-date pictures of their resources, or they may misjudge their abilities to activate their networks to help. They can miscalculate and be wrong about the political forces acting on them. Regardless, they go through a process of weighing their motivations and resources (derived from their types) against their political contexts to estimate the desirability and feasibility of control.

What does this process look like? Individual civilians begin with their motivations and resources, and then encounter political contexts. They evaluate the meaning of the political context through their motivational lenses, each type asking two key questions. Politicians ask what the voting public thinks of the issue at hand—deploying or withdrawing troops from a war, for example—and what other politicians think of a proposal. Administrators ask what their sponsors—the politicians—think, and then evaluate

62   Chapter Two

the preferences of the bureaucrats they lead. For each type of civilian, their main focus is the consent of their relevant stakeholders and gatekeepers.

From there, civilians develop preferred degrees and methods of control. Sometimes a crisis prompts the choice to control or not and sometimes it is prompted by one of the aforementioned routine, cyclical processes. Under both routine and crisis conditions, civilians will develop a preference either to control or defer, and if control, they will choose whether they would like to constrain, compel, or mix the two. In the case of routine control, the choice is not whether to defer or control, but how strongly to exercise control—again, whether to constrain, compel, or both.

Motivations will focus civilian attention on what the political context means for their survival and beliefs. Generally, concerns about survival will matter to civilians more than beliefs. But civilians with strong beliefs may act on principle at the risk of their survival. Meanwhile, information works on civilian choice in two ways. First, civilians draw on information to understand the "facts" of the political context. The more information they have, the more expertise they can apply to an issue. Second, civilians use their institutional capacity to exercise control over the military or other civilians.

To filter the political context through their motivations and resources, civilians might ask a series of questions based on their type and role. A SASC chair may ask who is calling attention to an issue, and who is championing or opposing a competing initiative. The national security advisor might ask herself if she has allies who are willing to join her effort. She might also ask if exercising the type of control she wants with the mechanisms she is considering will alienate the military or other civilians. As a secretary of defense evaluates the political context, he may consider how it affects other things he cares about. He will estimate the potential for his action to grow or shrink his reputation. Will he make new enemies? Will he appear inexpert or disloyal?

Although the above sketch reflects the overall process civilians follow to make control choices, civilians are idiosyncratic about how they weigh their decisions. Some civilians prefer to engage a wide range of stakeholders, whereas others consult just a few advisors. Some are transparent about their reasoning, and some are secretive. Some may emphasize their motivations more than their resources or vice versa. Some may fixate on one aspect of the political context, such as a political enemy or a single poll. The factors highlighted here are analytical categories to aid probabilistic reasoning, not absolute determinants. They tell the researcher and practitioner alike where to look to understand why civilians choose to exercise a particular kind of control through their available mechanisms, or why they choose to defer.

However in general, and in sum, politicians will choose to exercise control over other civilians and the military when doing so is, at a minimum, not harmful to their electoral prospects and are most likely to do so when control could be beneficial to their electoral fortunes. They evaluate the probability of risk or benefit to their reelection by checking the people and issues at hand—the political context. Finally, they will exercise control if they have the resources necessary to do so. If the benefit they will derive from exercising control combined with their informational and institutional resources is large, they will attempt to compel the military or other civilians to use force in specific ways. If the combination of benefit and resources is not great, they will either attempt to constrain or defer to the military and to their peers.

Administrators follow a similar calculus, with the important distinction of eschewing electoral issues and constituents and instead evaluating the impact control choices may have on their reputation with other civilian elites and with their bureaucracies. For civilian administrators at DoD, this can mean greater incentives to defer to the military itself, since the military forms part of their political context. But at the same time, their own subordination to politicians means that they must ultimately follow politicians' lead. And if a secretary of defense cannot persuade a president to make a particular control choice, that secretary must implement the choice the president does make.

Applying the Framework: The Example of Intervention in Libya

The 2011 NATO intervention in Libya illustrates the civilian control framework in practice. It shows how civilian controllers evaluated the political context through the lenses of their professional-institutional types

64   Chapter Two

to attempt different kinds and degrees of control over each other and the military.[8]

In February 2011 protests erupted in the eastern Libyan city of Benghazi against the government of President Muammar Qaddafi. The protests inspired a wider uprising, spurring repressive violence from the Qaddafi regime. By late February, high-level officials in the Qaddafi government began to resign and flee abroad, and foreign embassies evacuated official personnel and private citizens. The violence attracted the attention of international media, the United Nations and NATO. The North Atlantic Council, NATO's political decision-making body, met to discuss aid to the rebels. As the fighting on the ground grew more organized and more violent, international institutions increased their rhetorical and formal commitments to aiding the insurgents. In mid-March the Arab League called for a no-fly zone over Libya administered by a multilateral coalition.

Civilian controllers in the United States faced a series of decisions: Should they use military force to stop the violence in Libya or not? How could they influence the views of other civilians to forge a policy consensus? And how should they use military force, and how could they compel the military to do what they wanted?

Making their individual evaluations of the political context and then engaging in political processes to arrive at a policy formed the first set of civilian control activities. The differing perspectives of the president, secretary of defense, and chair (and ranking member) of SASC were immediately evident. On February 23, President Obama released a statement affirming the universal human rights of Libyans and warning that the Qaddafi regime would be held accountable for violence against civilians. In contrast, on February 24, Secretary of Defense Robert Gates gave a speech at the US Military Academy at West Point calling for American restraint, and on March 2, gave testimony on the Hill warning that implementing a no-fly zone over Libya would be an act of war. On March 3, Obama called for Qaddafi to step down. On March 4, Senators John McCain and Joe Lieberman of the SASC signed a joint statement calling for consideration of a no-fly zone and recognition of the anti-Qaddafi Libyan Transitional National Council. For his part, SASC chair Carl Levin publicly and privately supported Obama's approach as it unfolded.

As the crisis in Libya began, Obama's own network of political stakeholders were similarly divided. Public opinion polls showed most Americans did not support intervention, but many of his advisors and many members of Congress called for action. In domestic politics, President Obama was adjusting to the Democrats' loss of the majority in the House of Representatives and narrowing majority margin in the Senate in the midterm elections just three months earlier. In his memoir, Obama quotes his chief of staff at the time, Bill Daley, saying, "I don't think we got clobbered in the mid-terms because voters don't think you're doing enough in the Middle East" (Obama 2020, 656). His own reelection seemed to be at risk, and he worried about engaging in an intervention that voters did not support. But his personal beliefs counterbalanced these concerns. He had hired journalist and human rights activist Samantha Power at the NSC in part because he shared her principled approach to humanitarian intervention. She, UN Ambassador Susan Rice, and eventually Secretary of State Hillary Clinton, along with some members of Congress on the foreign affairs and armed services committees, formed a bloc in favor of military action. Vice President Joe Biden, Secretary of Defense Gates, Chairman of the Joint Chiefs of Staff Michael Mullen, Daley, National Security Advisor Tom Donilon, and Deputy National Security Advisor Denis McDonough were all skeptical of the use of American or other NATO allies' military force. "My brain was churning with calculations," Obama wrote (Obama 2020, 658). Demonstrating the electoral sensitivities of an executive politician, but also his personal beliefs, Obama went on,

> I knew . . . outside of Washington, there wasn't a lot of support for what America was being asked to do, and that the minute anything about a U.S. military operation in Libya went south, my political problems would only worsen.
>
> I also knew that unless we took the lead, the European plan would likely go nowhere. Gaddafi's troops would lay siege to Benghazi. At best, a protracted conflict would ensue, perhaps even a full-blown civil war. At worst, tens of thousands or more would be starved, tortured, or shot in the head. . . . I was perhaps the one person in the world who could keep that from happening.

For his part, Gates was nearing the end of his service as secretary of defense and admits in his memoir that his patience was thin. He was not worried about keeping his job, but he was worried about the health of DoD, and in his recollections, he repeatedly emphasizes his belief that the use of force should be a last resort and that proposed humanitarian actions in Libya did not meet that criterion. As he explains,

> I believed that what was happening in Libya was not a vital national interest of the United States. I opposed the United States attacking a third Muslim country within a decade to bring about regime change, no matter how odious the regime. I worried about how overstretched and tired our military was, and the possibility of a protracted conflict in Libya. I reminded my colleagues that when you start a war, you never know how it will go. (Gates 2014, 511)

Gates was thinking like an executive administrator. He worried about the health of his organization and the likely outcomes of an intervention policy in terms of its effects on military readiness but not in terms of its electoral consequences. The politics Gates worried about were international—hence the comment about invading Muslim countries—and interbranch, as he was defending the DoD budget before Congress around the same time and still trying to preserve resources for operations in Iraq and Afghanistan.[9]

In public pronouncements, SASC Chair Levin supported Obama's policy as it evolved into an intervention in Libya. This was likely motivated by party unity, a key part of the political context for Levin. Levin had a track record of acting to constrain the executive's use of the military in targeted ways. He opposed the surge of troops in Iraq and supported congressional actions to constrain President Bush's use of force after 9/11 (to be detailed in Chapter 5). Yet in the Libya case, copartisanship with the president appeared to be a deciding factor. In one call with reporters, he also insisted that Congress would vote in favor of giving war powers to the president for the intervention (Bresnahan 2011). Levin was not up for reelection again until 2014, but the president would face voters in 2012, and Democratic unity going into a presidential election year was important.[10]

In the end, Obama chose a compromise between his electoral survival and his personal beliefs. The US would use its military "capabilities" in limited ways "for which we were uniquely suited" (Obama 2020, 659) but would swiftly hand the military mission off to NATO allies because Obama calculated that multilateralism was more popular at home and abroad (Hastings 2011). Obama compelled this specific use of the military over the objections of many politicians and even his own secretary of defense, but with the support of key civilian elites and humanitarians. He issued this guidance through Gates and the NSC, which led a process to guide military planning and coordinate with NATO via the State Department and DoD.

Gates followed the president's decision once it was made, executing civilian control through the procedures of operational orders and the allocation of funds via reprogramming budget accounts.[11] Up to the point of decision, however, he remained aligned with Chairman Mullen and hewed to defending DoD's institutional interests. Senator Levin also supported the president's policy, making the case in multiple venues for its wisdom and touting the "international coalition" backing the military intervention (Tau 2011).

As this brief sketch shows, Obama, Gates, and Levin filtered the political context through their professional-institutional types, and charted control courses in ways that would benefit their professional survival and strength. Both Levin and Gates wound up deferring to Obama in the end, Levin because he calculated it was beneficial to the survival of his political party and Gates because Obama wielded greater formal institutional resources in the form of superior authority. For Gates, deference to the president meant exercising control over the military in ways he would not have chosen to otherwise. For Obama, the complexity of the international, national, and even bureaucratic political contexts illustrated the multivariate nature of the determinants of civilian control choices. The framework does not necessarily predict what choices civilians will make, but it can help analysts perceive, retrospectively, why they made them or, prospectively, narrow the range of possible choices to the most likely.

Conclusion

Civilian control is a complex set of activities that combines policymaking processes with guidance, budgeting, and force management mechanisms

68   Chapter Two

to compel or constrain other civilians and the military. The sources of civilian control choices pertain to politics and what the political context—the issues and the people involved—means for civilians and what they care about as defined by their professional-institutional types. For politicians, the electoral imperative makes them focus on the electoral salience of military issues and the likely electoral consequences of control choices. Presidents' constituents are the entire voting population of the country as well as politicians in Congress, international counterparts, and other powerful actors. SASC chairs primarily concern themselves with their voting constituents, the members of their committee, other members of Congress, powerful members of their political party, and financial backers. For administrators, concerns about their own reputations and the management of their bureaucracies make them focus on the interbranch, interagency, and bureaucratic salience of issues and the budgetary and readiness consequences of control choices. Secretaries of defense worry most about their standing with the president and their relationships with members of Congress, especially the SASC chair, and with the senior military. As civilian controllers evaluate the political context, they consider the issue at hand and the views and preferences of their primary stakeholders.

The remainder of this book illustrates how politicians and administrators—particularly SASC chairs, presidents, and secretaries of defense—evaluate the political context to make choices about how and how much to control the military and each other, and whether and when they defer to others. The cases cover the span of time between the end of the Cold War through the Donald Trump administration and demonstrate why and how civilian controllers used guidance, budgeting, and force management to integrate national political priorities and military policy.

THREE

Civilian Control after the Cold War

"THE COLD WAR IS BEHIND us," declared the BUR, the first major defense strategy of Bill Clinton's presidency. The question the BUR then asked was, "How do we structure the armed forces of the United States for the future?" Over the first few years after the Soviet Union collapsed, the United States reconsidered its fundamental approaches to the military and used the armed forces frequently for so-called operations other than war. The period provided a laboratory of civilian control, demonstrating how different civilians in different professional and institutional positions interpreted the political context and controlled military affairs through the mechanisms of guidance, budgeting, and force management.

The case reveals the interaction between civilian control of civilians and civilian control of the military, as well as the range of control choices, from compelling to constraining to deference. SASC and HASC chairs used the mechanism of (strategic) guidance to either constrain or defer entirely to the president, but exercised more compelling control over the executive branch and the military through the defense budget. Meanwhile, Congress tended to reserve exercising control via force management decisions to times of crisis, mostly prominently in Somalia. Presidents, meanwhile, could do little to compel Congress, instead attempting to constrain it or deferring to the SASC and HASC chairs outright. The presidents varied in

70   Chapter Three

their use of strategy and directives as a compelling control mechanism, sometimes imposing guidance on the Pentagon and sometimes leaving their civilian secretaries of defense and the CJCS to propose military missions and joint objectives, and instead exercising constraining control through revisions of Pentagon ideas or deferring outright. Such negotiations between presidents and secretaries were also expressed via defense budgeting. Presidents constrained the whole Pentagon, civilian and military, with defense budget cuts, even as secretaries often deferred to military actors over the remaining funding and authorities. These differences between civilian types in the strength of control they exercised via different policy mechanisms drove tension between executive guidance to the military and executive-legislative defense budgeting.

The relative power of civilian and military actors at any given time affected how civilians perceived their political contexts. If a powerful civilian or military actor—or a coalition of them—opposed a policy option, civilians often deferred control rather than taking the political risk of losing a policy fight. Each civilian type also sought the others' support and assistance to influence military affairs. Coalitions among members of Congress or between presidents and SASC and HASC chairs were particularly effective, demonstrating that civilian unity within and across branches of government could compel military activities. Meanwhile, secretaries of defense and presidents especially needed cooperative relationships with, and public support from, the CJCS.[1] These two civilians along with their counterparts in the legislative branch often borrowed the chairman's own evaluation of international and domestic political contexts to judge the feasibility of policy alternatives. Sometimes, civilian controllers drew so heavily on the CJCS that they allowed him to replace their own judgment, deferring control over strategic guidance to the nation's top military officer.

Finally, the case illustrates that politicians and administrators have different relationships with politics, and therefore use political context differently to inform their control choices. Presidents' and armed services chairs' professional survival depended on politics directly. Administrators, in contrast, banked on their reputations and personal relationships with a cross-section of politicians (especially those who sponsored them for appointments), other administrators, the military itself, and key outside opinion leaders. They didn't care about electoral accountability on their own accounts, but on behalf of the politicians they worked for. Politics signaled to politicians what they should care about. Administrators, much as President Obama observed of Secretary Gates, saw politics as features of the environment to be navigated. For politicians, politics often drove deference to each other or to the military. For administrators, politics often caused disunity among civilians in ways that confounded their own efforts to exercise their control responsibilities.

This chapter is broken into two parts: An exploration of the political contexts provides background conditions informing civilian choices, and an examination of each of the essential civilian controllers during the period explores how each man (and they were all men) exercised control and sometimes deferred to others. I examine how these civilians exercised control through the guidance mechanisms of the Base Force and BUR at the Pentagon; the budgeting mechanisms of the FYDPs submitted in 1991 and 1994; and the contrasting force management challenges of the missions in Somalia from 1992 to 1994 and Bosnia from 1992 to 1995. For each of these periods in the case, I show who controlled whom, how, and why.

The Political Context

With the fall of the Berlin Wall in November 1989 and the rise of the reform-minded Mikhail Gorbachev to the presidency of the Soviet Union in 1990, the dissolution of the Warsaw Pact the same year, and the final collapse of the Soviet Union in August and September 1991, the four-decade threat of a Soviet invasion of the European continent dissolved before the West's eyes. The financial costs of the American victory in the Persian Gulf War in 1991 notwithstanding, heady talk of a "peace dividend" filled the halls of Congress and presidential campaign trails. In fact, the Gulf War only added to the sense of optimism and possibility, because the American military had demonstrated its unrivaled capabilities in an operation swiftly and professionally executed in little over three months. American foreign policy elites had a sense of sitting astride the world victorious, the sole remaining superpower.

72   Chapter Three

The feeling would be short lived. Domestic politics in the United States filled the vacuum of political attention left by the crumbling USSR. A stagnating economy preoccupied citizens and politicians alike. The Graham-Hart-Rudman legislation loomed, threatening automatic spending cuts if Congress and the White House did not achieve target levels of deficit reduction. General economic anxiety was justified as the US slumped into recession by 1991 (Walsh 1993). The 1992 Los Angeles Uprising revealed a social crisis over race, class, and justice to go with the economic strains. Together these issues contrasted the long era of international stewardship and were emblematic of long-deferred needs at home.

Sensing the country's mood, Congress and both presidential administrations moved to reduce spending on defense as part of the overall effort to shrink the deficit. The politics of the defense budget thus focused on the total budget for the year, or "topline" level of authorized spending. Focus on DoD spending accompanied the notion of transition into a "new world order," raising questions about how big a military the US really needed for a world of small regional conflicts rather than the major conventional and nuclear threats posed by the now-defunct Soviet Union. Growing consensus about reducing the topline and changing force structure meant that among themselves, civilians did not debate whether to cut, but what and by how much.

The Bush administration committed to a 25 percent cut in the "end strength" or total number of military personnel along with other spending reductions. As for a strategic reorientation, the Pentagon proposed the "Base Force," a structure that emphasized regional deterrence rather than preparation for global war. During the 1992 presidential election, candidate Clinton claimed he would take an additional $100 billion out of the defense budget between 1994 and 1997. The BUR, the comprehensive strategy review that Clinton's first secretary of defense Les Aspin ordered, provided sweeping guidance to the military about its missions, capabilities, and force structure.

Despite the initial strategic optimism coming out of Washington, the new post–Cold War world presented mostly disorder in the 1990s, and civilians encountered opportunities to exercise control over military affairs not just through abstract guidance but also force management and deployment questions to manage real crises. Although the 1990–1991 Persian Gulf War was the first major American military engagement of the post–Cold War era, the two crises that both Bush and Clinton addressed were in Bosnia and Somalia. In 1990, Yugoslavia began to separate into independent republics, and Bosnia became a war zone between Serbian forces and Bosnian Muslims. The European Community and then the United Nations both levied an arms embargo on the former Yugoslavia in 1991 to try to quell the fighting. But Serbian forces were brutal in their tactics, and it became clear by 1992 that they were committing a genocide against the Muslim population. In October 1992 the UN Security Council voted to establish a no-fly zone over Bosnia-Herzegovina, with NATO participation.

Meanwhile in Somalia, a civil war and catastrophic famine had killed tens of thousands of people. In July 1992 the UN Security Council endorsed a humanitarian food delivery mission, and in August the Senate passed a resolution by voice vote encouraging the president to send American forces to secure the supply lines. President Bush deployed 26,000 troops that December. When Clinton walked into the Oval Office in January 1993, the mission appeared to be succeeding and in February and May the Senate and House passed additional resolutions approving the use of force. Over the course of the year the American force proceeded through a drawdown and transitioned the lead for the mission to the UN. At the same time, however, the UN itself shifted toward hunting for the primary warlord in Mogadishu, Mohammed Aideed. Over the summer, Somalis became more bellicose, ambushing and killing Pakistani peacekeepers and seven American soldiers. On October 3 and 4, a contingent of US Army Rangers launched a raid on Aideed at the UN's request. But Somali forces shot down one of the Black Hawk helicopters on the mission, and in the crash and ensuing battle, eighteen Americans and by some estimates over a thousand Somalis were killed. Clinton and Aspin, along with Secretary of State Warren Christopher and other lower-ranking Defense officials, faced fierce questions from Congress and the media. On October 7, 1993, in a televised address from the Oval Office, Clinton announced that America would provide short-term reinforcements to complete the mission and would then withdraw completely by March 31, 1994.

74   Chapter Three

In Bosnia, the Serbs steadily took over more and more territory until the summer of 1995 when their attacks on civilians in Srebrenica and Sarajevo prompted stronger Western—particularly US—intervention in a campaign of air strikes against Serbian targets. By then, the 1994 midterm elections had swept away the Democrats' majority in Congress and brought on new chairs of the defense committees. In November 1995 the parties met in Dayton, Ohio, to agree to a peace settlement, which was followed by a UN peacekeeping operation.

The Civilians

From 1989 to 1995, there were nine key civilian controllers: SASC Chairs Sam Nunn and Strom Thurmond; HASC Chairs Les Aspin, Ron Dellums, and Floyd Spence; Presidents George H. W. Bush and Bill Clinton; and Secretaries of Defense Richard Cheney, Les Aspin (who moved over from the chairmanship of the HASC), and Bill Perry. Bush, Cheney, and Aspin had experience as both politicians and administrators. The others were career politicians except for Perry, the lone career administrator. Five (Nunn, Aspin, Dellums, Clinton, and Perry) were Democrats and four (Thurmond, Spence, Bush, and Cheney) were Republicans.

This section reviews each civilian controller role by type. It first discusses the legislative politicians, the SASC and the HASC chairs. It then covers the executive politicians, the presidents. Finally, it examines the executive administrators, the secretaries of defense.

THE CHAIRS

Senator Sam Nunn had been the SASC chair since 1987, the year after Congress passed the most sweeping DoD reform bill since the department's creation forty years prior. He was first elected to the Senate from Georgia in 1972 and had served on the SASC starting his first year in office. Nunn came from a political family, the grand-nephew of Representative Carl Vinson, the influential WWII-era HASC chair, and spent a stint in the Coast Guard before becoming a lawyer and then getting into politics himself. By 1990 he was an experienced budget hand and had sparred with the Nixon, Ford,

Carter, and Reagan administrations. He had a reputation for being a true defense expert, and a track record as an adroit and often bold political operator, if ideologically moderate to conservative (Blumenthal 1991). His bipartisan bona fides were reflected in both Bush and Clinton considering him for secretary of defense. Bush's offer came right after the presidential election, and Nunn considered it for a few days (Jones 2020). Clinton asked him more than once. Regardless, as Nunn told *Meet the Press* host Tim Russert, he felt he could serve the country best right where he was in the Senate.

The first evidence that Nunn used political context like a politician was his persistent interest in his constituents' views. As many members of Congress do, Nunn asked his staff to provide the "top ten" list of topics raised in constituent correspondence each week. His staff then divided these into subtopics, so that the topic of "defense" might include letters about "procurement" or "gay rights." In one illustrative week in 1987, defense, foreign policy, and foreign relations comprised just over 21 percent of the letters constituents wrote to Nunn (O'Reilly 2022).[2] That defense and foreign policy topics made up just over a fifth of the things that interested his voters meant that military policy was a matter of political survival to Nunn. He was also aware that as a moderate Democrat from a Southern state, he was on a rapidly melting iceberg, and often worked to use his defense expertise as a bridge to appeal to moderate voters not just at home but nationally (Jones 2020). He considered running for president in 1988, but told an interviewer some twenty years later that he decided against it: "I was more conservative than most of the active elements of the Democratic Party," he said. "And therefore, getting the nomination would've been my biggest problem" (Nunn 2013).

His views on the end of the Cold War were informed by his interest in nuclear security and the health of the armed forces, and by his natural caution. Like everyone, he agreed that the collapse of the Soviet Union presented opportunities for both military savings and change. But, especially in 1989 and 1990, he saw the situation as unfolding in still-unpredictable directions and judged that the US military posture should not be changed hastily. Although he understood the general view in Congress that a "peace dividend" was reasonable, he cautioned against "severe disruptions to our

76   Chapter Three

military personnel programs and operations" and as a result urged his colleagues to focus on items that would generate savings in the future (Dewar 1990). In 1990, Nunn gave a series of four speeches on the Senate floor to lay out his prudent vision for slow American transition from superpower confrontation to a globe with numerous nonexistential threats. Above all, Nunn wanted to ensure a proportional relationship between the international political environment, the defense strategy, and the defense budget.

In the domestic political environment of 1990, that was much easier said than done. The Republican Bush administration faced a Congress with Democrats in the majority, and the pressure for a peace dividend did not result in consensus views about how to achieve it. Although Democrats generally wanted to reorient money that normally went to DoD toward domestic programs, specific base closures and weapons systems cuts could have direct effects on jobs in their home districts. The result was countervailing pressures from individual members. There was also the matter of navigating the broader debates over federal deficit reductions—a situation with increased urgency because of the conditions set by the 1985 Gramm-Rudman law, which could trigger huge cuts in international and domestic spending if revenue minimums were not met to shrink the deficit. The defense budget was often treated more like an auction item in the domestic politics of the fiscal situation than a means to control the military (Snider 1993). Nunn placed policy ideas on the defense agenda, but he did not have the permissive political context to compel particular policies directly or through the budget.

Across Capitol Hill, Representative Les Aspin, Democrat of Wisconsin, was steeped in these caucus politics. Aspin had served in the Army for two years as a systems analyst in the Pentagon after earning a PhD in economics from MIT. He took off the uniform and two years later was elected to the House of Representatives. His tenure as chair had been mercurial. He had ascended to the top of the HASC by gathering enough junior colleagues together to reject the seniority system and catapult him to the chairmanship far ahead of schedule. Just a few years later he almost lost the job because of his tendency to reject compromise when he disagreed with other members' substantive analysis, neglecting the political aspects of legislative negotiations. He learned from this experience to cultivate his committee members personally and meet his own need for political survival by catering more to his colleagues' need for theirs. For example, Representative Gene Taylor, Democrat of Mississippi, credited Aspin with saving a shipbuilding yard in his district, and three thousand jobs with it (Woodward 1993).

Aspin's power on the HASC gave him the opportunity to attempt a trick of civilian control: He tried to control the military and military policy for the twenty-first century by controlling executive civilian guidance decisions. He was aware that the end of the Cold War and the pressure on the administration from his Democratic colleagues (he was one of sixteen members who were proposing deeper defense cuts than the administration's plan) were providing him an opportunity to exercise control over the military by shaping the defense strategy and force structure (Gunzinger 1996). Using the Persian Gulf War and the interventions in Panama and Somalia as analytical frameworks, he developed a series of force structures that met the demands of "two major regional contingencies" at once. He used the HASC staff to prepare an alternative plan to cut force structure, programs, and overall costs beyond what the Bush team proposed in January 1990 for FY 1991. The cuts left the force with 9 active-duty Army divisions, 18 air wings, and 340 ships, a reduction of 3 divisions, 8 wings, and 110 ships compared to the actual numbers in 1993 (*Washington Post* 1993). Aspin also commissioned a Congressional Budget Office report to question the administration's budget math (Snider 1993). In making his arguments, Aspin referred to not just the domestic political demand for less spending but also the American people's support for the use of force itself: "Our citizens understandably will be reluctant to pay for defense unless there is a clear linkage between the forces and the threats those forces are designed to deal with" (Aspin 1992).

The contrast between the chairs of the SASC and the HASC during this period shows how legislative politicians try for different degrees of control over executive branch civilians and the military itself. Nunn's objective was not to legislate a specific defense strategy but to press the Bush administration to present a coherent plan that adapted to the moment. He was less wedded to any specific strategic vision than he was committed to spurring the White House and the Pentagon into greater initiative. Partisanship

78   Chapter Three

made little difference to his pursuit of that fundamental goal, although he was more willing to go easy on Clinton in public. Aspin wanted to seize and maintain control over events and defense choices, partly for reasons of ego and partly for Democratic dominance of policy (Woodward 1993). Nunn chose to control via constraints; Aspin wanted to compel specific actions.

Nunn's exercise of constraining control continued across the Bush-Clinton presidential transition. During Bill Clinton's presidential candidacy and then his administration, Nunn often gave him public political support but pushed back on his budget and force management proposals at the same time. Clinton's first FYDP provided a case in point. Although Nunn supported the cuts Clinton proposed, cuts deeper than the Bush administration's, he publicly "questioned several fiscal assumptions on which the reductions and potential cost savings were based" (Jones 2020, 250). Nunn also expressed consistent skepticism about the Somalia mission. On *Meet the Press* he said that he wanted the mission "narrowed"—constrained—and he helped the appropriations chair, Senator Robert C. Byrd (D-WV), include language in the annual defense authorization requiring the administration to present Congress with its plans for the Somalia mission. (By the time President Bush had committed forces to Somalia, Les Aspin had already become the president-elect's choice for secretary of defense and so, in that time before confirmation, kept mum.)

Replacing Aspin once he became secretary of defense was Representative Ron Dellums of California, the first and so far only Black American to chair the HASC. Dellums was from Oakland, CA, once an enlisted Marine and then a Vietnam War protestor with a reputation for both fairness and far-left views, including a bias against military intervention and high defense spending (Gross 1993). Dellums wasted no time on the latter, pressing now Secretary Aspin during his first hearing to enact more cuts to the budget than he had inherited from the Cheney proposal (Schmitt 1993b). Dellums, however, was on one side of a split party and of Congress itself, with moderates and conservatives fretting that the proposed cuts were already too drastic. This included the ranking member of the HASC, Representative Floyd Spence of South Carolina (Gellman 1993). The polarization meant that Dellums had little room to maneuver with his own colleagues.

Partisan divisions defined Dellums's two years as chair and limited his ability to exercise control over the military. Like most Democrats, he was initially patient with the administration's handling of the mission to Somalia. But over the summer of 1993 the UN shifted the mission from aid delivery to man-hunting. When US forces began taking casualties, members of Congress began asking questions about what the administration's Somalia policy had become. "Who gives us the right to determine who deserves to emerge in power in Somalia?" Dellums asked during floor debate over a nonbinding resolution requiring the administration to ask for congressional authorization for the mission (Krauss 1993). The debate came just days before eighteen Army Rangers died in a failed raid on Aideed, the Somali warlord the UN had singled out as driving the ongoing violence.

For his part, Nunn exercised effective constraining control over the president as well as his fellow members of Congress during the Somalia debacle, brokering the agreement between the White House and the Hill that forced the American withdrawal with an amendment to the appropriations bill that cut off funding for the mission on March 31—a compromise with members who wanted forces out by the end of January (CQ Almanac 1993). Nunn also looked skeptically at intervention in Bosnia, declaring publicly that Congress wanted the administration to provide a timeline for the end of any US mission in the Balkans. Nunn's ability to forge civilian unity on the Hill and represent the general congressional view was strengthened when Republicans on the Senate Foreign Relations Committee echoed Nunn's views to Secretary of State Warren Christopher in an open hearing (Sciolino 1994). The incident demonstrated how unity across civilians could strengthen control efforts.

Where Bosnia was concerned, the 1994 midterm elections meant that after two years of equivocating, the Clinton administration was now contending with a Republican-controlled legislative branch. Dellums and Nunn were out as chairs of the HASC and SASC, and Floyd Spence and Strom Thurmond were in. Meanwhile, Senate Majority Leader Bob Dole was exploring a run for president against Clinton in 1996 and used Bosnia policy to try to impose electoral costs on Clinton, saying that the administration's "policy on Bosnia needs to be checked hourly" (Sciolino 1995).

80   Chapter Three

But the Republicans weren't quite as unified as their campaign victories made them seem, at least not on military affairs. In contrast to the effective Hill control over the executive branch's Somalia policy, the lack of unity on Bosnia and the budgetary mechanism limited the GOP-led congress's ability to exercise control over the military and the president. The new HASC chair Floyd Spence wanted to increase the defense budget by $120 billion over the FYDP, but his colleagues on the Budget Committee demurred (Schmitt 1995). The Senate side of the Hill was more muted in its divisions, and the SASC itself, though technically no longer under the formal control of Sam Nunn, still followed his leadership. When Strom Thurmond took over, he was ninety-three years old and reputedly slowing down. He trusted Nunn and relied on him, as Nunn's biographer wrote, "as his right arm in running the committee" (Jones 2020, 263). This dynamic drove continuity for the SASC but undermined meaningful GOP control of military policy on the Hill.

Thurmond was first elected to the Senate from South Carolina in 1954. Although their party differences suggested they ascribed to very different ideologies (not to mention that Thurmond was a long-time segregationist and Nunn was not), their Southern constituencies shared similarities as did their largely moderate approaches to defense. Like most Republicans, Thurmond was skeptical of military interventions on behalf of the United Nations, and Nunn was only somewhat more open to them. In the House, Spence and Dellums were quite distinct, and faced challenges unifying the large committee. The overall effect was that the Clinton administration had less protection from congressional interference than it had previously, but the Hill struggled to compel defense strategy, budgeting, and use of force choices, meaning that despite individual legislative politicians' efforts, Congress's control of executive civilians and the military became generally weak.

The Presidents

The presidents felt the variation in congressional control efforts and experienced their own challenges exercising control over secretaries of defense and the military. George Herbert Walker Bush spent a career in

Washington and much of it in foreign policy positions. He was a decorated WWII Navy pilot and had been the US ambassador to China, the US representative to the United Nations, and the head of the CIA. He had also done a stint in the House of Representatives and been Ronald Reagan's vice president. He wrote in the memoir he coauthored with Brent Scowcroft, his national security advisor, that his government experiences had given him his "own guiding principles and values." Among these were an orientation toward details "so I could make informed decisions without micromanaging" alongside a willingness to delegate to his experts and cabinet secretaries (Bush and Scowcroft 2011, 52). As president he was an executive politician, but he had a background as an administrator and often approached governing the executive branch from that perspective.

His overall view of the political-strategic situation in Eastern Europe was cautious, and he placed a premium on building international consensus around the US response (Chollet and Goldgeier 2008). The implication for military policy was continuity, at least initially. In one of his first NSC issuances, "National Security Review 12," (NSR 12) Bush signed his name to a declaration that "it would be reckless to dismantle our military strength . . . and foolish to assume that all dangers have disappeared" (Bush 1989). The studies directed by NSR 12 were led and largely staffed by senior civilians at the NSC and foreign policy agencies and were premised on the sense that America was running out of money and that threats would soon be regional rather than global (Snider 1993, 19). As time wore on, however, and Moscow relaxed its control over Soviet satellites and planned its own force reductions, it became harder for Bush to argue to Congress that the world was not changing profoundly.

Bush decided he wanted to make defense cuts that were reciprocal to the Soviets' own reductions, a decision that involved confronting the Joint Chiefs. In 1989, prodded to find money in the federal budget by his economic team, Bush proposed a 25 percent cut in end strength, and CJCS Admiral Jonathan Crowe counterproposed a 10 percent cut (Larson, Orletzky, and Leuschner 2001; Bush and Scowcroft 2011). This tug-of-war dynamic was not unusual, but it also revealed the importance of the military's political support to Bush. Crowe's proposal "did not seem to me to be much of a reduction," Bush later wrote, "but I was reluctant to ignore

82   Chapter Three

the unanimous advice of the Joint Chiefs. Generally speaking, I wanted proposals that the executive made on the use of force or arms control to have their unequivocal support if at all possible" (Bush and Scowcroft 2011, 145). Crowe's term as chairman was soon up, however, and at Secretary of Defense Dick Cheney's strong urging, Bush nominated General Colin Powell to replace the admiral. By the time Powell took office in October 1989, it was just a month before the Berlin Wall came down. In the wake of that historic change, Powell more easily accepted the sense of Congress and the administration that larger defense cuts were coming (Powell 1995).

Bush also illustrated the possibility that civilians do not always interpret the political context in ways that benefit their own political survival—but they still use that context to shape their control decisions. In this case, Bush focused on what the political context suggested for force management choices (Chollet and Goldgeier 2008). He especially viewed changes to US force presence in Europe through Gorbachev's eyes. About the US and the Soviets pacing each other in terms of force reductions, Bush wrote that he thought his administration "could support freedom and democracy, but we had to do so in a way that would not make us appear to be gloating over Gorbachev's political problems with Party hard-liners as he moved away from the iron-fisted policies of his predecessors" (Bush and Scowcroft 2011, 212). He added, "We had stepped carefully in Poland and Hungary and had avoided aggravating the Soviets, whose military presence still loomed there. It was a good start. But I understood that the pressure on Gorbachev from hard-liners to intervene would grow" (238). American military presence needed to be in a kind of Goldilocks zone to achieve a stabilizing effect on the new and dynamic Eastern European politics, and Bush calibrated it and his own engagements carefully as a result.

It was clear by 1990 that the US would need a new approach to its defense strategy and budgeting. At the same time, the president had to weigh the changes that struck him as dictated by the international political context against the pressures on the defense budget coming from Congress. Attempting to dodge such congressional constraints and to seize the reins of control over military choices, in August at the annual Aspen Security Forum in Colorado, Bush announced the "Base Force," his new defense

Civilian Control after the Cold War   83

strategy for the post–Cold War world. He told the audience of dignitaries and defense intellectuals:

> Our task today is to shape our defense capabilities to these changing strategic circumstances. In a world less driven by an immediate threat to Europe and the danger of global war, in a world where the size of our forces will increasingly be shaped by the needs of regional contingencies and peacetime presence, we know that our forces can be smaller. Secretary Cheney and General Powell are hard at work determining the precise combination of forces that we need. But I can tell you now, we calculate that by 1995 our security needs can be met by an active force 25 percent smaller than today's. (Bush 1990)

Bush went on to explain that a 25 percent cut should not be a blunt exercise, because taking a quarter out of each military unit or capability uniformly would not relate the new force to the new strategic environment:

> The United States would be ill-served by forces that represent nothing more than a scaled-back or a shrunken-down version of the forces that we possess right now. If we simply prorate our reductions, cut equally across the board, we could easily end up with more than we need for contingencies that are no longer likely, and less than we must have to meet emerging challenges. What we need are not merely reductions but restructuring. (Bush 1990)

The speech thus represented Bush's attempt to compel military adaptation through both guidance and budget mechanisms. Bush's Aspen speech was overshadowed by Saddam Hussein's invasion of Kuwait the same day, but the assumptions from the Base Force that informed it stuck, including the assumption that regional threats would become prominent and unpredictable contingencies would demand a range of military capabilities.

This turned out to be so prescient as to almost predict the headlines, because no sooner had the US fought the Gulf War—and then resumed its budget debates as though it had never happened, or as though everything about that war simply confirmed the strategic assumptions they were already making—then war broke out in the former Yugoslavia in the summer of 1991 (Snider 1993). Once again, Bush saw the scene through Gorbachev's eyes. As David Halberstam chronicled, the president and his foreign policy team worried about appearing to endorse national disintegration

84 Chapter Three

at a delicate moment for Moscow (Halberstam 2001). Bush's priority was managing the transition in the US-Soviet relationship, and for Gorbachev domestically. He resisted, therefore, increasing calls by editorial boards and humanitarian activists to send in the Marines.

Bush was backstopped in that position by Colin Powell's strong reluctance to use the military to intervene in the conflict, which he expressed to reporters and in the pages of the *New York Times*, in an op-ed titled, "Why Generals Get Nervous" (Powell 1992). He explained later in his memoirs that he was reacting to interventionists' inability to provide clear objectives, something that was an element of the famed "Powell Doctrine," (originally the "Weinberger Doctrine" after Reagan's secretary of defense, for whom Powell was a military assistant) (Powell 1995). Powell's public advocacy against intervening in Bosnia also reflected the military's post-Vietnam hyperawareness of domestic public support for the use of force. "If we went in," Halberstam summarized Powell's and other senior military leader's views, "who was with us? How far would our allies go? Where was the Congress and where would the media be?" (Halberstam 2001, 39). Powell was playing a welcome role to Bush and his team. Bush always thought the war in the Balkans sounded complicated and risky. Besides, it was an election year, and the possibility of getting into an indecisive, bloody engagement at precisely the moment that he needed to show more attention for domestic issues would not go over well with the American people (Halberstam 2001). Bush wanted no part of it.

But the president did not refrain entirely from using the military for humanitarian purposes in response to public outcry. Failing to be reelected removed the motivation of political survival from his calculus entirely. And Bush had already lost the election when he ordered 25,000 troops into Somalia to participate in the UN humanitarian mission there. The decision to deploy forces to Somalia refracted off the domestic American politics of what was happening in the former Yugoslavia, particularly in Bosnia. Jon Western has shown that Bush and his team—including and especially General Powell—considered a military operation in Bosnia extremely unwise, but also understood that there was mounting pressure from activists and the media to act. They chose to do so in Somalia on the presumption that it would entail less operational risk (Western 2002).[3]

The comparison of the use of force policies toward Bosnia and Somalia demonstrates that despite the energy put into reforming defense spending and finding a strategy to match it, the main purpose of the military without the Soviet threat looming was still unsettled. Initially Bill Clinton's answer to that question was not fundamentally different from Bush's. But he framed it very differently in the context of an election campaign.

Candidate Clinton offered Americans a reprioritization and reintegration of defense as subordinate to and part of domestic economic demands. "While military power will continue to be vital to our national security, its utility is declining relative to economic power," he declared to an audience at Georgetown University in 1991, in a speech crafted in part by Les Aspin. Bush was right to cut defense, Clinton said, but he needed to articulate what the military was for in this "new era." Clinton saw democracy promotion, regional stabilization, and guarding against weapons of mass destruction as the major features of such a vision. And, responding to the domestic politics surrounding defense spending, he claimed he could do it for $100 billion less than Bush had proposed.

Of course, Clinton did not acknowledge that Bush himself had made a similar argument in Aspen in August 1990. Clinton had no military background, but he had been a governor and a lawyer, and knew how to tell a good story to an audience and how to get them to listen. That Bush had a regionally focused strategy already would mean the facts would get in the way of Clinton's story. Besides, Bush seemed to be ignoring a few contingencies that Clinton highlighted. Clinton and his campaign advisors decided to attack Bush's foreign policy bona fides, and the president's hesitant Bosnia approach was the perfect target (Halberstam 2001). "On Bosnia, Clinton Aggressive, Bush Wary," read one headline in the *New York Times*. Over the summer before the presidential election, Clinton stated that he supported a NATO air campaign and lifting the extant arms embargo.

Once in office, however, Clinton found such measures were impossible to implement, in large part because the ideas that appealed to voters in an election year were not always tenable in other political contexts. In Europe, the new president found a variety of opinions among his British, French, and German counterparts. At home, he found a great range of opinions

86   Chapter Three

on the Hill, some of them more forward leaning than his own. As Clinton explained in his memoir,

> My own options were constrained by the dug-in positions I found when I took office. For example, I was reluctant to go along with Senator Dole in unilaterally lifting the arms embargo, for fear of weakening the United Nations (though we later did so in effect, by declining to enforce it). I also didn't want to divide the NATO alliance by unilaterally bombing Serb military positions, especially since there were European, but no American, soldiers on the ground with the UN mission. And I didn't want to send American troops there, putting them in harm's way under a UN mandate I thought was bound to fail. (Clinton 2004, 513)

Clinton had other major constraints on his control over military policy. His lack of experience in uniform or working on military affairs made him rely on endorsements from his uniformed subordinates, and the Democratic Party's split personality on defense matters—personified by the hawkish Nunn and the new HASC chair, Ron Dellums, who wanted a further $100 billion cut across the FYDP—did not help (Weiner 1996). Clinton was deferential to Nunn's views, in part because he perceived Nunn as not only expert, but both tough and fair (Clinton 2004). After the SASC chair demanded a detailed exit plan and other conditions for American military involvement in Bosnia, Clinton acquiesced, restricting American engagement including by levying a requirement that NATO command the operation and that there be a timeline for withdrawing the troops (Sciolino 1994).

Constraints on action alone can often lead to ambiguity, however, and the war in Bosnia dragged on for the first two years of the Clinton administration. Clinton was increasingly exercised about the atrocities being committed there and the effect it was having on NATO's credibility. By 1995, he recalled, "Bosnian Serbs had made a mockery of the UN and, by extension, of the commitments of NATO and the United States" (Clinton 2004, 666). But it was the Serbian assault on civilians in Srebrenica that turned the tide of the entire war—because it turned the tide of domestic politics in the US and finally indicated to Clinton that military-backed action was politically feasible.

If Bosnia suggested that the use of force could be good politics for a president, Somalia seemed to indicate the opposite. When Bush first

Civilian Control after the Cold War   87

announced the deployment in December 1992, Clinton had joined many members of Congress in praising the humanitarian operation. But once the peacekeeping mission shifted to more proactive peace enforcement and violence increased over the summer of 1993, Democrats and Republicans alike began to complain loudly about the lack of White House consultation. Republicans in the House opposed subordinating US forces to the UN, a complaint that particularly resonated with conservative audiences (Hendrickson 2002). When the Battle of Mogadishu occurred on October 3 and 4, the righteous anger and threats to constrain the president rose swiftly and decisively from Congress, with threats to cut off funding and recall the troops immediately.

Clinton's response to these constraints was fundamentally to defer to them, although attempting at the same time to appear more autonomous. His speech to the country on October 7 was a political needle-threading exercise and reveals a great deal about how he evaluated his administration's precarious political position at home and abroad (Clinton 1993). Under intense pressure from the Hill to withdraw—which, as described above, was on its way to becoming a legislative requirement—but not wanting to convey that America could be pushed around by a tinpot warlord, the president appealed to the American people's "conscience" and sense of heroism. "We went because only the United States could help stop one of the great human tragedies of this time," he reminded the audience. He told America it had a choice: "Leave when the job gets tough or when the job is done well." Citing Colin Powell, he said the US couldn't "cut and run" and advocated for American credibility and leadership in the post–Cold War world, "when people are looking to America to help promote peace and freedom." He explained that he would be concluding the mission by March 31, 1994, and sending reinforcements until then, 1,700 more ground troops with an aircraft carrier transporting "two amphibious groups" (Marines) placed offshore. Americans would finish the mission, and then they would come home.

In thinking through whether and how quickly to withdraw, Clinton later wrote, a variety of considerations weighed on his mind. For one, he knew that "Americans were outraged" and the Hill was apoplectic: "There was no support in Congress for a larger military role in Somalia, as I learned in a

88   Chapter Three

White House meeting with several members; most of them demanded an immediate withdrawal of our forces" (Clinton 2004, 551–52). The raid that became the battle was, itself, a mistake to Clinton's mind. "In wartime, the risks would have been acceptable. On a peacekeeping mission, they were not, because the value of the prize was not worth the risk of significant casualties" (Clinton 2004, 553). Finally, like the Bush team before him, Clinton saw the trade space between Somalia and Bosnia: "I had to consider the consequences of any action that could make it even harder to get congressional support for sending American troops to Bosnia . . . where we had far greater interests at stake" (Clinton 2004, 552). What Clinton did with the military was thus a direct result of his estimation of his personal political position and the constraints placed on him by legislative politicians. Coincidentally, as the below section will show, Clinton's deference to his secretary of defense to handle events in Somalia—in part because Somalia had not seemed politically important before October—contributed to the crisis. Much like Bush, Clinton showed that the centrality of political context to civilians' control choices does not correlate with either optimal or suboptimal outcomes for civilians' political fortunes or defense strategy. But it does explain where those choices come from.

The Secretaries

When the Soviet Union began its final process of disintegration in 1991 Richard B. Cheney was fly fishing on the Dean River in British Columbia (Cheney 2011, 228–29). A military coup against the new Russian president, Boris Yeltsin, would fail after a few days, but Cheney was recalled to Washington to help the White House think through possible responses if political leaders in Moscow lost control of their nuclear arsenal. As it happened, the crisis resolved quickly enough that instead of debating plans for loose nukes, the principals met to discuss how to handle the swiftly dissolving ties between Moscow and its satellites.

Just that January in his *Annual Report to the President and the Congress*, Cheney had pointed to another time of uncertainty for American defense leaders, quoting the report to Congress in 1948 from the very first secretary of defense, James Forrestal, who observed that the United States "scrapped our war machine . . . in a manifestation of confidence that we should not need it any longer." Of course, Forrestal had written, the rise of the Soviet Union and the hostilities on the Korean Peninsula (which would later break into a full-scale war) proved them wrong." Current language suggests the Korean War started in 1948, which it did not. It started in 1950. "International frictions which constitute a threat to our national security and to the peace of the world have since compelled us to strengthen our armed forces" once again (Cheney 1991, x). There was no better expression of Cheney's cautious approach and overall perspective on what the end of the Cold War meant for the American military: it was best to wait and see rather than make major, irreversible changes.

Cheney had been in Republican politics for a long time. A staffer for Donald Rumsfeld in the Nixon White House, he had risen to be Gerald Ford's chief of staff, and then was elected as Wyoming's representative in Congress. He was good friends with Brent Scowcroft, who became George Bush's national security advisor, and knew several other close Bush aides well. When the president's first pick for defense secretary, Jim Tower, lost his confirmation vote, the administration turned to Representative Cheney. Cheney's fresh ties to the Hill and his closeness to Scowcroft and Secretary of State Jim Baker were especially helpful to him as secretary of defense, allowing him to win deference from other civilians and to build coalitions to compel military activities. "By virtue of my ten years in the House, my relationship with all the guys up there," he said later, "I could say and do things that nobody else could get away with because I had been a member of the club" (Miller Center 2000, 37). That said, Cheney was also a believer in "executive prerogatives."

> I was of the opinion that the combination of Vietnam and Watergate had significant negative impact on the Presidency and in terms of the balance between Congress and the White House. We ended up with things like the War Powers Act, which I think is a flawed concept, and the Budget Reform Act. . . . I emerged from that experience [in the Nixon and Ford White Houses] a very strong believer in the authority of the President to manage these issues as contrasted with the Congress. I thought Congress had infringed upon executive prerogatives. (Miller Center 2000, 19)

Ideologically hawkish, Cheney believed in maintaining robust military capabilities in case the future was not as bright as the optimism of the

90   Chapter Three

period projected. His views on the mix of his role and the Pentagon overall with politics were complicated. On the one hand, he felt the Pentagon's utility for the president was to help him decide what to do with the military in a technical sense. "Our responsibility at the Department of Defense," he wrote in his memoir, "was to make sure the president had a full range of options to consider. No one else in the government could provide him with these options. He had plenty of people who could give him political advice" (Cheney 2011, 185). But Cheney knew his job was to judge when the options the Pentagon provided were politically feasible, especially with the Hill where he felt he had a comparative advantage within the administration. Balancing between the militarily rational and politically plausible was how Cheney saw his role, making the political context a key part of how he calculated military policy choices.

And Cheney knew that the political context of the post–Cold War period meant that most politicians, including President Bush, were not thinking of the defense budget primarily as a mechanism for controlling the military but as a way to pay bills for domestic programs. At the same time, Cheney's read on the international politics of the Cold War made him cautious about repurposing funds from guns to butter. He didn't believe the Soviet Union's dissolution would be steady or safe for the West and pushed to maintain enough force structure to handle a major security threat (Miller Center 2000; Cheney 2011). This view translated into direction he gave to the chiefs in late 1989, reflecting his desire to constrain other civilians: the Pentagon would not "simply let Congress come along and whack away at the budget" (Miller Center 2000, 89).

Cheney's views on civil-military relations generally conformed to the military's prevailing preference that "civilians approve strategy and generals execute," but he felt it was civilians' prerogative to tell the generals what was included in strategy and grade their execution (Cheney 2011, 216). His mix of delegation to senior military leaders and oversight reflected his view that the secretary had to "assert authority over the military" (Miller Center 2000, 45). Early in his tenure, he publicly rebuked the Air Force chief of staff for negotiating budget matters on the Hill without OSD input as "a very good signal to send around the building . . . a target of opportunity if you wanted to sort of reassert civilian control"

(Miller Center 2000, 44). Cheney later fired that chief's successor outright for making self-aggrandizing and inappropriate comments to the press (Cheney 2011).

But Cheney's actual exercise of control over the military was often more constraining than compelling, sometimes even more deferential, than the reputation he cultivated. Although the CJCS is not in the chain of command under the law, Cheney chose to put Powell there anyway, communicating decisions to the combatant commanders through Powell rather than directly to them. At the same time, he encouraged multiple reporting routes up to him, and used his military assistants as information sources regularly to keep tabs on the services and the deployed force alike (Cheney 2011). This pattern of control suggests that he offered course corrections to military subordinates along with significant autonomy.

The record of who compelled the analysis and writing of the Base Force—and of the Bush administration's defense strategy—demonstrates that Cheney sometimes relaxed his control over the military. Powell takes full credit for the Base Force in his memoir, and many writers have adopted his account of events, which in any case is far more detailed than others. Cheney himself makes much less precise statements about the genesis and content of the Base Force in his memoir and in interviews but does not attribute it to Powell, preferring to focus on the 1992 Defense Planning Guidance—a document that is traditionally not a defense strategy but issues guidance for crafting operational plans given the assumptions and objectives of the strategy. Other analysts have conducted interviews with contemporary Pentagon denizens who claim that the Base Force proposal was Powell's, and Cheney was initially cool to its force structure proposals. Regardless, most accounts agree that one of Cheney's deputies, Under Secretary for Policy Paul Wolfowitz, produced a parallel effort out of the White House-led NSR 12 process. Wolfowitz and Powell collaborated, eventually combining their total of three alternatives, one of which was the Base Force, and presenting them to Cheney. In the end, Cheney concluded that the Base Force was the preferable force structure (Weiner 1996). But he continued to believe that Wolfowitz's strategic vision was an improvement on Powell's—although his description of it in his memoir as "a shift from a focus on the global threat posed by the Soviet Union to defense planning

92   Chapter Three

based on regional threats" is little different from the Base Force (Cheney 2011, 235).

The budgetary implications for the Base Force, as far as Cheney was concerned, were for moderate cuts in both spending and to force structure, especially compared to the counterproposal offered up by Cheney's main congressional adversary on the matter, HASC Chair Aspin. Aspin's "Option C" from his "four alternatives" plan envisioned cutting $41 billion more the administration's proposal over the five years of the FYDP (Gunzinger 1996). Cheney, backed by the joint chiefs, objected strongly (Correll 1992).

Where Bosnia was concerned, Cheney was as skeptical as President Bush, but he knew political pressure at home was building, for which he blamed the ascendant cable news media. "The huge machine is available out there to cover events and have an impact on the debate here at home as to whether or not we want to commit forces," he told an interviewer some eight years later. "It's a very difficult thing for a president to resist the cries to go and deal with the crisis in Bosnia" (Cheney 2000).

As it turned out, the crisis would not be theirs to handle for much longer. Cheney's tenure as secretary ended in January 1993, when he passed the reins of the Pentagon to Bill Clinton's first secretary, former HASC chair Les Aspin. Aspin seemed like a shoo-in for Clinton's secretary of defense. Clinton referred to Aspin's ideas often while campaigning, describing a vision for defense cuts that echoed Aspin's own. In his opening statement for his confirmation hearing, Aspin painted a hopeful picture of American triumph, suggesting threats had been reduced such that nothing imperiled the country's existence. He also echoed Clinton's campaign message that economic and foreign policy were interdependent, and that civilians in the executive and legislative branches could cooperate rather than attempt to compel and constrain each other's actions. "All this then is our context," Aspin declared: "a president eager to work with the Congress to make a better, more prosperous America, and a better, more democratic post–Cold War world."[4] It seemed then like Aspin and Clinton should have been perfect partners, aligned ideologically but with complementary backgrounds and capabilities, Aspin filling in Clinton's substantial gap in military expertise, and Clinton offering Aspin the political star power to propel him into a role he had coveted.

But once he was in the E-ring, it became evident that Aspin's efforts to control the military through the budget process when he was HASC chair had soured many military leaders. He had especially irritated CJCS Powell (Powell 1995). As far as the senior military were concerned, it was like the fox guarding the henhouse. "Something about Les Aspin," wrote veteran journalist of Washington insiders Bob Woodward, "evokes a visceral doubt among some of the brass and the defense cognoscenti" (Woodward 1993). The Air Force Chief of Staff, General Merrill A. McPeak, had openly criticized Aspin's force structure proposals, calling them "a recipe for military disaster" and saying they would have made Desert Storm, "Desert Drizzle" (Carroll 1992).

For backup, Aspin brought in several close aides, tackling the BUR as a first order of business. But he couldn't seem to get traction with the president. The likely culprit was the disastrously failed effort to lift the military's ban on gay and lesbian Americans from serving in uniform. The most the administration could get Congress to concede was a compromise policy called "Don't Ask, Don't Tell," whereby gay and lesbian people could serve but not openly. Not a single person important to the president's political context was happy. The military and its congressional allies remained angry about the way the president attempted to simply compel the military to implement the policy, and the gay community felt betrayed when the administration deferred to congressional control (Clinton 2004). Aspin had not helped the president out of the lose-lose situation. Perhaps the worst moment was when he appeared on the Sunday talk show *Face the Nation* and seemed entirely ambivalent about the president's policy: "If we can't work it out, we will disagree and the thing won't happen," he said (quoted in Schmitt 1993a). The experience demonstrated that although Aspin had understood politics on the Hill, he was much less capable of evaluating the political context for a president—or, therefore, for himself as an executive administrator. It cost him. In the wake of Don't Ask, Don't Tell, the White House lost faith in Aspin, often discounting his views and sometimes not returning his phone calls—most disastrously in the case of the Battle for Mogadishu.

Aspin's first priority had always been the BUR, and he was probably glad to get back to it in March 1993. He picked up where his force structure

94   Chapter Three

work on the HASC left off, where he had argued that the force needed to be rebuilt "from the bottom up." He also imported the "two major regional conflicts" model to determine the necessary size of the military from his own work and the Base Force. "2MRC" is a concept for determining force structure used by the Pentagon into the 21st century.[5] His aim was to finish major parts of the review in time to influence the FYDP beginning in fiscal year 1994 (Gunzinger 1996). In mid-June, after four months of work, he tested the main premises for the emerging force structure in a public speech at the National Defense University. One such premise was what he called the "win-hold-win" scenario, where instead of fighting two wars simultaneously, the US could fight one full-scale "major regional contingency" while halting an invasion elsewhere, then defeating the invaders at a later date. But reporters found critics of the approach in the military services and among major allies like South Korea (Gunzinger 1996). Aspin responded by deferring to these concerns and reverting to the two-simultaneous-wars construct, not because he agreed with the resistance but because he knew when to compromise.

When it came to the actual use of force, however, Aspin wanted guidance from the White House, and he was unable to get it. At a fateful principals committee meeting, Aspin explained that his ground commander in Somalia had requested more forces and equipment to support the mission to hunt down Aideed. The political advisors in the room balked. The troops were supposed to be coming home, not going back out. Aspin concluded his political guidance was to minimize the deployment, and so he denied the request (Halberstam 2001). It was a consequential decision, one that made him look responsible for the disaster in Mogadishu that came just days later. That this judgment was, at best, harsh, made little difference. Aspin had lost Clinton's confidence long ago, and someone had to be held accountable for the tragedy. In early December 1993, Aspin resigned at Clinton's request.

Clinton chose his next secretary of defense after a false start in naming retired Vice Admiral Bobby Ray Inman, who subsequently withdrew. Eventually, Clinton turned to Deputy Secretary of Defense Bill Perry. Perry was a career administrator, the former under secretary of defense for research and engineering in the Carter administration. He had two degrees from

Stanford University and a PhD in mathematics from Penn State. He had served in the enlisted ranks in the Army at the very end of WWII. Between the Carter and Clinton administrations, he remained active in defense matters, serving on the Defense Science Board and the Packard Commission, the latter an effort to reform the Pentagon's acquisitions process. At the beginning of the Clinton administration he was a professor at Stanford and an investment banker, content with his life and treating international security as a "hobby." In January 1993, days before Bill Clinton took the oath of office, Les Aspin called Perry, who happened to be at a Carnegie Corporation–sponsored conference with several members of Congress. Aspin asked Perry to become his deputy. Perry later recounted that although he told Aspin he wasn't interested in the job, Senators Nunn and Dick Lugar "backed me up in a corner for the rest of that meeting and told me that 'no' was the wrong answer to the question" (Perry 1998a, 7). Now it was less than a year later, and President Clinton was asking Perry to become secretary. Again, he said no. He later explained that he felt it was possible to perform jobs below the level of secretary "on an apolitical basis," but that he "would be unable to avoid being drawn into partisan political issues as a cabinet officer" (Perry 2015, 87). Perry saw himself as a technocrat, a mathematician who loved the substance of defense challenges. After a full-court press from the administration, including Vice President Gore who assured him that the White House would respect his desire to keep defense policy as nonpartisan as possible, Perry accepted the job (Perry 2004).

Perry later told interviewers that he had three main concerns when he walked into the secretary of defense's E ring suite for the first time: the determinants for the use of force, reforming the acquisition system, and addressing the sudden decentralization of control of nuclear weapons "in the nations of the former Soviet Union that were in a state of social and economic turmoil" (Perry 1998b, 8). The chaotic politics of Eurasia struck Perry as a major source of American insecurity. At the same time, he acknowledged, determining the role of the use of force in the Balkans and elsewhere demanded immediate resolution because "if you don't get that right, nothing else is going to work" (Perry 1998b, 7).

Perry had a fourth concern when he became secretary, and that was the national security strategy. By this, Perry did not mean a strategy for the

DoD, but for the entire government—and in his view, that required close collaboration between DoD, the State Department, and the White House (Perry 1998b). Such collaboration was yet another point of contested control between the president and his military bureaucracy. The White House had produced its first National Security Strategy with input from the BUR process—because the two documents were supposed to nest together and because the publication of the BUR preceded the writing of the National Security Strategy, the White House's document had to defer to the Pentagon's predeveloped vision for defense activities. Perry was now in a position to refine both documents and implement the defense strategy.

Perry saw strategy as a control mechanism for a control mechanism—a way to "guide" the budget (Perry 2004). As deputy secretary he had been Aspin's budget guru and had helped ensure planned defense programs were consistent with the objectives the BUR laid out. At the press conference where Clinton announced his nomination, Perry acknowledged the difficulty of implementing the BUR: "In order to carry out the Bottom Up Review," he told reporters, "we will have to manage the Pentagon very well. We will have to have real acquisition reform. We will have to have careful planning and management of our programs. We have to do all of this while we are maintaining a very high level of readiness."[6] Like Aspin before him, Perry believed in the power of analysis. Unlike Aspin, he had extensive managerial experience at the Pentagon and in the private sector, and he knew that analysis meant little without implementation.

But he was secretary now, and being secretary meant exactly what he had feared: deep involvement in the political contexts that drive civilian control choices. And in that regard, Perry's initial days as secretary were, as senior political officials often quip about taking on administrator roles in government, "like being shot out of a cannon." Just twenty-four hours into the job, he left for the Munich security conference, the annual gathering of Western ministers of defense and many heads of state and other functionaries to discuss international security matters. The US ambassador to Germany, Richard Holbrooke, met Perry's plane when it landed and told him about the massacre at the market in Sarajevo and also told him he had set up a press conference for Perry to address the attack. Perry spoke with the press about events in Bosnia just an hour later, then attended the security conference, and then turned around to fly back to Washington in time to testify on the Hill about the defense budget (Perry 2015). As had been the case for several years, the debate on the latter was still over how deep to make the cuts and how quickly they should be implemented (Schmitt 1994). Perry's first week as secretary showed him how the international and domestic levels of political context arrayed the issues and people that he had to consider when exercising—or trying to respond to—civilian control.

The budgetary debates and the war in Bosnia persisted as essential issues for Perry's time on the E-ring. A press conference he held ten months into the job covering the defense "topline" (total budget authority), modernization investments, weapons system cancellations, and a statement on the policy toward Bosnia was a case in point. Perry announced that Clinton had decided to restore $25 billion to the defense budget over the six years beginning in fiscal year 1996, a decision that eased cuts to modernization. Perry explained that many of the acquisitions and modernization choices involved delays, restructured programs, and other adjustments to "protect our technology base . . . at a rate that we can afford."[7] The announcements showed a clever blend of logical management and political palatability on the Hill, canceling just two major programs and merely shifting or spreading costs for others, meaning parochial interests would not suffer too greatly.

Perry then shifted to speaking about Bosnia. Administration decision making about Bosnia had dragged out over the course of 1994. Privately and publicly, Perry evaluated the options in Bosnia like a technocrat, and he concluded that an American mission with ground forces would be the most effective way to protect Bosnian Muslims and stop the fighting (Perry 2015). But his analytical orientation did not mean he was ignorant or unskilled about evaluating the political context. In addition to the relevance of European allies' preferences and Washington's diplomatic positions at the UN, Perry understood the long shadow the disaster in Somalia cast over domestic opinion about military interventions. "The president was very limited in what he could have done in Bosnia," Perry explained later, "given the debacle that occurred just a few months earlier in Somalia" (Miller Center 2006, 85–86). Aides to President Clinton preferred a "lift and

98   Chapter Three

strike" policy, which advocated lifting the UN arms embargo on parties to the conflict and conducting airstrikes on Serbian positions, much as candidate Clinton had advocated during the presidential campaign. To garner domestic political support, or at least avoid opposition, the White House wanted NATO to implement the "strike" portion of the policy, not the UN. Yet the NATO allies were reluctant to abandon the UN intervention. Perry perceived all these political winds, many of them countervailing, and mixed a technocrat's logical answer with political pragmatism when asked about his views: effective intervention would require a major US ground operation, but he just didn't see that happening (Gordon 1994).

Back at the press conference, he recalled for the gathered reporters that Clinton had decided early in the term not to send American forces to participate in UN operations in Bosnia. But, Perry shared, he had recommended to the president that the US support any NATO efforts to extract the UN forces from Bosnia. His reasoning was more about NATO than the conflict: the US had always supported NATO actions and should not break that tradition now. In response to a reporter's question, Perry said he expected that if an extraction operation were to happen, the US would make up a substantial proportion of the overall force. "This will involve a significant commitment of the US" of several brigades (tens of thousands of soldiers) he said.[8]

The press conference illustrated Perry's political context and control choices. NATO membership applied unique pressure on the US to participate in the alliance's military actions, and Perry advised the president to deploy American forces accordingly, using a force management decision to exercise civilian control over the use of force. The reporters' questions also reflected the kind of domestic political risks the administration—and Perry himself—faced. What size of commitment would the US have to make if it intervened militarily? Would troops be in combat? Would the administration seek congressional approval? Perry took these in turn, reassuring his domestic audience that the US would avoid becoming entangled in a foreign war, and would ensure American soldiers were strong enough to protect themselves. "I am clear on one point," he said. "If we go in on this operation . . . we're not going in with a token force. We'll want to go in with a strong enough force that will command respect." He emphasized that the US would not be taking sides in the war, but, he continued, "we will be prepared for combat operations if we go in." Regarding legislative branch approval, Perry said, "We will have full consultation with the Congress on this, at high levels and at committee levels."[9] Whether consultation meant deference to members of Congress or attempting to constrain or compel their actions (such as by persuading them to pass a resolution condoning the deployment) was unclear from Perry's remarks, but he publicly signaled his recognition of the political and legal importance of acknowledging Congress's role in making use of force decisions.

What finally made NATO allies willing to intervene directly, Perry later recalled, was the massacre at Srebrenica in July 1995. "The whole problem was getting the Europeans to agree to do it, and to get that to happen, the Srebrenica [attack] was the triggering event," he explained (Miller Center 2006, 54). The key to American use of force was not the threat to European stability, or American national interests per se, but the political possibility of multilateral action. To Perry, that was the "trigger" to deploy military forces. Could the United States have acted sooner, unilaterally? Of course. But the administration—Perry included—strongly preferred international endorsement. Like Cheney, Perry had been skeptical about facile-sounding bombing campaigns without the use of overwhelming force. The horrors of Srebrenica overcame everyone's hesitancy, but that also meant that a larger force package was suddenly more acceptable to the Europeans—and to Americans. Perry's old friend Vice President Gore was an especially impassioned advocate (Halberstam 2001). After Srebrenica, executive politicians and administrators aligned to send American troops to Bosnia, exercising compelling control over the military with a force management decision.

The exercise of civilian control over military action in Bosnia was easier for Perry than it might have been, given that General John Shalikashvili was now CJCS. Shali, as he liked to be called, was much more open to using force for humanitarian goals than General Powell had been. The son of a Soviet Georgian father and a German-Polish mother, Shali lived in Warsaw through WWII and immigrated to the US from Poland at age sixteen. He had witnessed atrocities and the lives of ghettoized Jews. After he graduated from high school in Illinois, he joined the Army, served in Vietnam,

100   Chapter Three

and moved up the ranks. He impressed Powell during the Gulf War, and afterward had run Operation Provide Comfort to save the Kurds of northern Iraq from Saddam Hussein's persecution. After that, Powell brought Shali, now a three-star general, back to Washington to be his top aide (Halberstam 2001). Shali's initial views on Bosnia were not so different from Powell's, but they were less doctrinaire. Much like Perry, he calculated the operational difficulty of any intervention but wasn't ideologically opposed to it, simply cautious of deploying forces under an imprecise policy backed by a weak commitment. He, too, felt the shift after Srebrenica. It was Shali who finally endorsed the idea of a massive air campaign. He, Perry, and Secretary of State Warren Christopher convinced the Europeans to endorse a NATO-run air operation to deter and punish the Serbs if they conducted further attacks on Bosnian Muslim areas, with the goal of forcing them to negotiate (Halberstam 2001). NATO's bombing operation began at the end of August, after the Serbian shelling of the marketplace in Sarajevo. By the end of September, the Serbs signaled they were willing to negotiate.

Perry described the Bosnia policy and eventual settlement as an example of the kind of civilian unity and civil-military coalition necessary to the successful use of force. It "was a very close collaboration between [Secretary of State Warren] Christopher and me, between [Special Envoy] Holbrooke and me, between Holbrooke and Shalikashvili; all of us worked together quite harmoniously in putting [the eventual peace deal] together" (Perry 1998b, 12).

Echoing the value he placed on interagency collaboration at home, Perry shared the entire administration's emphasis on multilateralism in Bosnia, believing it was not possible for the United States to force a cessation of hostilities and then enforce a peace agreement without the validation of international institutions. He went so far as to conduct extensive diplomacy with the Russians to get them to contribute an armored brigade to the mission (Miller Center 2006).

Much as he did not let his technocratic nature dismiss the importance of politics, Perry also knew there was an ethic to being a civilian controller. For Perry, the civilian ethic was neither technical nor political, but was part of the consequences of control decisions. "To me it was important," he told the OSD Historical Office in 1998, "on the one hand to make the decisions about whether people should go on missions as objectively as possible." But, he continued, "when the people were actually killed on a mission," he had "to be very subjective about it,"

> to meet with the families [of fallen personnel] so that I could feel the consequences personally. It's a balance that every secretary has to make. Having made that balance, it allows one to look both at the objective policy reasons for sending 25,000 troops into Bosnia as well as to relate to the subjective aspect of the risks involved and what the personal losses were going to be. . . . If there was a large deployment, involving many thousands of troops, the president had to be involved and had to make the ultimate decisions. But I was the one who signed the orders to send the troops out there. (Perry 1998b, 5)

Conclusion: Framing Variation in Civilian Control

Perry's reflection on the responsibility he shared with the president for putting American servicemembers at risk captures the integration of politics, values, and civilian control. Debates about what and who is important, and how to prioritize them in terms of government action, drive civilians' choices about how much control to exercise over military affairs and when. Civilian controllers see the world through the lenses of their professional backgrounds and positions, and those who last in government roles do so because they are able to understand the relationship between the political context and their own choices. That the objects of their control efforts—other civilians and the military—are themselves actors in political contexts only makes their decisions more complex. Exercising control, then, takes tremendous willpower but also flexibility; deference is often more beneficial politically. Moreover, when deference helps to forge unified positions among civilians, they are better positioned to compel the military to take action.

FOUR

Civilian Control and the War in Afghanistan

THE PREVIOUS CHAPTER DEMONSTRATED HOW different types of civilians controlled the military and each other through strategy, budgeting, and force management in an era of major international change. This chapter focuses more narrowly on force management in the context of a single war across multiple presidential administrations and congresses.

For almost twenty years conflicting pressures from politics at the international and domestic levels prevented civilian controllers from maintaining a stable number of troops in Afghanistan. Domestic constituencies demanded a swift end to the war, while Afghan, regional, and NATO politics precluded political equilibrium in Kabul or a decisive military victory for the Afghan government. The American troop presence started with approximately 1,500 special operators in October 2001, surged to 100,000 at the peak of the occupation in May 2011, and finally dwindled to 2,500 at the start of 2021, the final year of the war (CRS 2017; Blanton et al. 2021).[1] Successive presidents raised and lowered troop numbers as a function of these countervailing political pressures, while armed services chairs reflected public opinion with calls to scale back or scale up commitments, and secretaries of defense tried to balance politicians' concerns with general officers' requests for troops.

This chapter focuses on civilian force management decisions for Afghanistan: whether to increase the level of forces, and when, how, and how quickly to draw down the American presence. I examine how the political contexts and civilian types shaped the control choices nine civilian controllers made about the military mission in Afghanistan: Presidents George W. Bush, Barack Obama, and Donald Trump; SASC Chairs John Warner, Carl Levin, and John McCain; and Secretaries of Defense Donald Rumsfeld, Robert Gates, and James Mattis.

The Political Context

Operation Enduring Freedom, the American military mission in Afghanistan, began on October 7, 2001. The US launched the invasion to retaliate against al Qaeda, a transnational terrorist group that hijacked commercial airliners and crashed into the World Trade Center in Manhattan, the Pentagon in Arlington, Virginia, and a field in rural Pennsylvania on September 11, 2001. Millions of Americans watched the second plane fly into the south tower of the World Trade Center live on television, and then watched both towers collapse. The nineteen attackers killed almost three thousand people.

It was one of the rare times in American history when the use of force in response to an event was beyond question in almost any context that mattered to civilian controllers. Condemnation of the attacks and expressions of solidarity with the US came from around the world. A day after the attacks and for the first time in its fifty-year history, NATO invoked its collective defense. Meanwhile, domestic US support for the operation was very strong. The Gallup polling organization found that the number of participants in their "Social Series" survey who called the war "not a mistake" actually went *up* from November 2001 to January 2002, when it peaked at a staggering 93 percent.[2] Beginning on September 12, executive branch lawyers and the leaders of the Democratic and Republican parties in the House and Senate worked out language for a resolution on the use of force against any person or nation who planned, or harbored the planners of, the 9/11 attacks. Congress passed the authorization (later referred to by its acronym, the AUMF, which stood for the generic "authorization for use of military force") on September 14, and the president signed it into law on September 18.

104   Chapter Four

Because Afghanistan, the mountainous country in South Asia sandwiched between Pakistan, Iran, and the countries of central Asia, harbored Osama bin Laden, the head of the al Qaeda organization that had launched the attacks, the George W. Bush administration demanded the ruling Taliban regime relinquish him into American custody. If they would not give bin Laden up, the president would invoke his new AUMF and use the US military to depose the regime. The Taliban refused, and the United States invaded. Taliban forces retreated south to Kandahar and Pakistan. The US then supported a national political process to form a government in Kabul, favoring a Pashtun man named Hamid Karzai as chairman of the Interim Administration, then as acting president. In 2004 Karzai was elected president of Afghanistan.

Beginning in 2002, perceiving politics in Afghanistan as stabilizing, the Bush administration took military assets—and civilian expertise, including from the intelligence community—out of Afghanistan to wage the invasion and occupation of Iraq. The effect on Operation Enduring Freedom was arresting. Over the next two years, the Taliban began taking back territory and seized control over the black market for opium, signaling to Afghans that Talibs were committed to outlasting NATO forces and to controlling the country (Sanger 2009). In 2006 the Taliban launched a major offensive to regain even more territory in the east and south of the country. Meanwhile, the effort in Iraq was also stalling, and President Bush ordered troop surges in both countries to regain control, with the balance of forces going to Iraq.

In 2008, the United States housing market crashed, and the country began to suffer a major financial crisis. The presidential campaign became a referendum on the American economy and on anything that diverted resources from domestic programs—foremost the wars in Iraq and Afghanistan. In his campaign, presidential candidate Barack Obama argued that the war in Iraq had squandered lives and treasure when it was Afghanistan that truly implicated the nation's security. Senator John McCain, Obama's opponent in the election and one of the SASC chairs examined below, could not overcome public discontent with the economic and foreign policy records of G. W. Bush, his copartisan, and lost the election to Obama. Once in office, Obama reviewed progress in Afghanistan regularly, issuing revised strategies and increasing the military presence to 100,000 troops and then beginning a steady draw down of forces in 2011.

In 2016, Donald J. Trump was elected president. He called for an end to the war in Afghanistan, although he moderated his campaign rhetoric somewhat after the primaries, when he became the GOP nominee for the general election. Once in office he attempted to follow through on his calls for withdrawal at both the beginning and the end of his administration. He believed the American people were opposed to continuing the war and that ending it would benefit him at the ballot box. For approximately eighteen months, his military and civilian advisors convinced him that it would be far too dangerous to leave Afghanistan vulnerable to becoming another base for terrorist attacks on the US homeland. But as the 2020 elections drew closer, Trump rejected that argument.

The international politics of Afghanistan involved allies, adversaries, and proxies. All added variables to civilians' calculations about the context and what it meant for military policy. On its own, the NATO mission involved so many different countries that coordinating among them at all levels—diplomatic to tactical—was convoluted. The variety of allies to keep motivated, committed, and communicative required a full-court press from as many US officials as possible, civilians and military, meaning that coordination among the allies was refracted through coordination among different Americans. Then there were Pakistani, Chinese, Indian, Iranian, and other activities, overt and covert, affecting conflict dynamics in Afghanistan. The likely impact of outside countries and their proxies of American military operations had to be integrated into strategy, and managed diplomatically and militarily.

THE PRESIDENTS

The president's control choices reflect the tension between battlefield needs and domestic politics. All four presidents exhibited the desire to both be frank with the American people about the difficulty of the military mission in Afghanistan and garner their support. The latter desire resulted in a persistent narrative across administrations that the US, its allies, and the Afghans themselves were progressing toward a range of objectives in the interests

106   Chapter Four

of American national security. Behind the scenes, the presidents resented Afghan president Hamid Karzai, received reports about the uneven performance of Afghan forces, and saw intelligence about Pakistani duplicity. In public, presidents were optimistic. In private, they increasingly doubted America's power to win the war, or, in Trump's case, the point in doing so.

Reviewing each president's thoughts about when and how to use military force to achieve objectives in Afghanistan also reveals something like a dialogue among the three men about how they saw their respective political contexts and how those contexts differed from each other over the years. Bush believed it was important for the United States to show resolve, reflecting his post-9/11 international and domestic political situation, whereas Obama suspected focusing on resolve was less salient to a public fatigued by the war in Iraq, and that results were more important. Trump reflected the public's indifference toward even results in Afghanistan, arguing that they simply wanted to be rid of the war. The three presidents differed less on the prospects for stability in Afghanistan, although they were progressively less optimistic. Obama sensed by the end of his presidency that the probability of an outside force imposing political stability in the region was low. Both Bush and Obama believed that the Taliban's will to fight could be broken and its political leaders would stamp out corruption, that Pakistan could be persuaded to expel al Qaeda and stop using extremists to menace India. Trump was pessimistic about the region's politics but thought about them mainly through the lens of his own domestic political viability.

All three men constrained the size of the military presence in Afghanistan because of their readings of American domestic politics—either the political impacts of the Afghan war itself, or because it was a lower priority than Iraq or other issues. Obama judged American voters would not tolerate an open-ended commitment and an unrestrained flow of money after so many years of indecisive war and, as he put it, the worst financial crisis since the Great Depression. But he also wanted the benefit of military credibility, and an outright failure in Afghanistan, especially if associated with his rejecting the military's advice, would erode his national security standing. He mixed these political judgments with a sincere belief in the threat posed by al Qaeda, and the ongoing risk of a terrorist attack on American territory. That risk itself threatened both American security and Obama's political power. Trump was skeptical from the beginning but allowed himself to be persuaded that a presence in Afghanistan prevented further attacks on American soil.

When it came to domestic politics, however, presidents' judgments were accurate. Bush, Obama, and Trump sensed the country's moods well. Bush knew Americans expected retaliatory action in the weeks after 9/11, Obama realized the public experienced war fatigue and no longer understood the purpose in Afghanistan, and Trump understood that support for American occupations abroad was gone. Each president suspected that American voters would not remove them from office if they kept US forces in Afghanistan but might do so if they withdrew the military and another 9/11-like terrorist attack ensued.

George W. Bush was unique among the presidents in this volume because he had watched his father, the forty-first president of the United States, do the job first. In his memoir, Bush recalls studying the emotional toll deploying troops took on his father (Bush 2010). George W. Bush also saw the world in abstract moral themes. His writings and speeches are filled with words like "justice," "righteous," and "evil." His military background consisted of service in the Texas Air National Guard during the Vietnam War, and his record of not being in combat was controversial during both presidential campaigns in 2000 and 2004. He confessed that as president, he was initially intimidated by military officers. He adopted the attitude that the president should delegate the details of planning to the military. "My instinct was to trust the judgment of the military leadership. They were the trained professionals; I was a new commander in chief" (Bush 2010, 194).

This bias toward deference likely informed his decision making in the wake of the 9/11 attacks. Moreover, collective outrage at the attacks pressured Bush to act swiftly, which meant he also evaluated the political context in haste. In some ways, the clarity of national sentiment obviated any need for political interpretation.[3] Near unanimity among congressional politicians reinforced this sense. Only one member of Congress (Representative Barbara Lee of California) voted against the AUMF. Consensus in almost every corner of the country was that al Qaeda provoked the United

108   Chapter Four

States, and the United States should retaliate. The political context made what Bush had to do obvious to him; his choice was mainly how to do it, and how swiftly. And in his view the first phase of the military operation had to occur on a very short timetable (Woodward 2002).

Although there were several NSC meetings in the days after 9/11, the president held his first meeting to plan the invasion of Afghanistan on September 15 at the presidential retreat at Camp David. At the meeting, the president took briefings about CIA, State Department, and DoD preparations to strike al Qaeda targets and topple the Taliban regime, plans that had been developed quickly in response to Bush's queries during the week (Shelton 2010). The CIA proposed bolstering the Northern Alliance, the Taliban's domestic adversaries. State's diplomatic efforts focused on international solidarity and practical contributions to American-led counterterrorism activities, especially Pakistani support. Islamabad had a history of assisting the Taliban, and the mountainous, barely defended border between Afghanistan and Pakistan provided al Qaeda and the Taliban places to evade capture. Pakistan's president, Pervez Musharraf, had agreed to cooperate with the invasion, but Pakistan's domestic politics drove suspicion of the US and ongoing support for the Taliban (Coll 2018). Nevertheless, in the immediate aftermath of the attacks, Bush focused on securing Musharraf's personal support rather than worrying about the depth, reach, or sustainability of his commitments. In a way, Bush thought about the implications of the international component of the political context for near-term military action, but not for long-term military success. The civilian control question to his mind was whether he could launch an invasion, not succeed at an occupation.

In that spirit, CJCS Hugh Shelton presented three off-the-shelf options involving progressively larger numbers of military personnel: missile attacks alone, missile attacks plus an air campaign, and missile attacks with an air campaign and ground force elements (Cheney 2011; Bush 2010). The plans were no more than sketches, but they triggered debate about what kind of military operation it would be, and how many forces it would take. Here, Bush already thought that international audiences were more impressed by overwhelming force, and he connected that view to his control choices. In his memoir, citing previous terrorist attacks in Lebanon,

Tanzania, Kenya, and Yemen, Bush argues that the American responses were too muted, seeking deescalation rather than punishment or deterrence. Bush believed that Osama bin Laden, and others like him, had been emboldened by American forbearance. "After 9/11, I was determined to change that impression. I decided to employ the most aggressive of the three options General Shelton had laid out" and send in ground forces to convey America's seriousness of purpose. Moreover, Bush determined that he would "keep them there until the Taliban and al Qaeda were driven out and a free society could emerge" (Bush 2010, 191). He did not attach force levels or timelines to this latter idea, and instead focused on launching an operation that would signal American power and the consequences of challenging that power. That did not necessarily mean the force numbers had to be large, simply that they had to communicate destructive power and deliver convincing punishment—a debate explored more below. For Bush, who believed in delegating details, the main point was to use force to communicate resolve.

In public, Bush spent the three weeks between September 11 and October 7 expressing combinations of comfort and resolve and promising swift justice. At the remembrance service at the National Cathedral three days after the attacks, the president said, "We are here in the middle hour of our grief. So many have suffered so great a loss, and today we express the Nation's sorrow." In the next phrase, he pivoted: "Our responsibility to history is already clear: to answer these attacks, and rid the world of this evil" (Bush 2001a). The same day he spoke at the National Cathedral, he flew to the World Trade Center site and in spontaneous remarks told rescue workers, "The people who knocked these buildings down will hear all of us soon" (Bush 2001b). In his address to Congress on September 20, he said, "We are a country awakened to danger and called to defend freedom. Our grief has turned to anger, and anger to resolution. Whether we bring our enemies to justice or justice to our enemies, justice will be done" (Bush 2001c). He saw the political moment as driving an undeniable public and moral demand for the use of force.

Politics at all levels infused Bush's thinking about his choices. Beyond Pakistan, he considered the ways to ensure international support for the military campaign, and he personally reached out to the president of the

110   Chapter Four

Russian Federation Vladimir Putin to secure overflight rights and for help with access to Uzbekistan and Tajikistan (Bush 2010). Meanwhile, domestic political pressures and anxieties shaped how he thought about the war's purpose and management. Saving American lives from future terrorist attacks was the primary benefit of the war policy, but Bush was also aware of the scrutiny he was under, and the relationship between Americans' evaluation of his leadership and their sense of security. In a passage that both described his situation and presaged that of his successors, he wrote: "I knew the public reaction to my decisions would be colored by whether there was another attack. If none happened, whatever I did would probably look like an overreaction. If we were attacked again, people would demand to know why I hadn't done more" (Bush 2010, 180). Doing more, then, posed less risk to Bush's political survival. Also weighing on his mind was the ethic of civilian control of the military: the inevitable loss of American lives and the moral implications of being the one who made the decision that led to their violent deaths. "I felt the gravity of the decision," he wrote. "I knew the war would bring death and sorrow. Every life lost would devastate a family forever" (Bush 2010, 184).

Cognizant of these risks, Bush's address to the country announcing the start of the air campaign on October 7, 2001, was an exercise in persuasion and legitimation, a recognition that the use of the military instrument had to be consonant with domestic and international political contexts. His first point after stating that air strikes had begun was to illustrate international support for the operation. Bush explained that the United Kingdom was taking part in the operation, that other Western allies promised to provide military forces later, and that forty other countries had given permission for the US to use their airspace and logistical facilities. "We are supported by the collective will of the world," he asserted (Bush 2001d). He also reminded his audience that he had given the Taliban regime a series of ultimatums as a way out of war, but the Taliban had not met them. Nevertheless, the US would be discriminating in its military strikes, only hitting "military targets," and extending aid and friendship to "the starving and suffering men and women and children of Afghanistan." The operation in Afghanistan would rout al Qaeda and facilitate humanitarian relief at the same time (Bush 2001d).

Bush also worried about foreign publics' views of American operations. This especially constrained military activities vis-à-vis Pakistan. Early in the war, Bush expressed concern to Musharraf that Taliban fighters were hiding safely on Pakistani territory. Musharraf warned that American military operations on Pakistani soil could enflame domestic sentiment so severely that "his government would probably fall. The extremists could take over the country, including its nuclear arsenal" (Bush 2010, 213). Bush subsequently chose not to court such a disaster as a policy (a choice Barack Obama also made until the Osama bin Laden raid in Abbottabad, Pakistan, in 2011). But keeping Pakistan onside required managing the appearance of American favoritism between Pakistan and India and balancing the power between the leaders of the two countries and Afghan president Hamid Karzai. As he had with Putin, Bush put a premium on personal diplomacy and was highly influenced in his political assessments by the judgment of other leaders and advisors, later calling Musharraf's judgment about South Asian politics "well-founded" (Bush 2010, 217).

By early 2002, Bush realized the scope of the political and economic development needed to match his vision of a "free society" for Afghanistan was far greater than he originally appreciated. Though he had opposed nation building when he ran for president, Bush admitted, "I changed my mind. Afghanistan was the ultimate nation building mission" (Bush 2010, 205). Yet Bush wanted to minimize force numbers. "We were all wary of repeating the experience of the Soviets and the British, who ended up looking like occupiers" (Bush 2010, 207). The force level the NSC and the Pentagon agreed to was 13,000. Other elements of national power—diplomacy and development—and international partners would take the lead, to Bush's mind.

The speed with which Bush reduced the military's role in Afghanistan was motivated not just by domestic political pressures for swift action and regional sensitivities to a lasting American presence, but also by his broader sense of global political momentum. From the first days after the 9/11 attacks, the president began referring to terrorism as a global phenomenon that would require a global war (Woodward 2002). It was partly this perspective that drove him to invade Iraq in 2003.[4] The full context of that war is beyond the scope of this case, but the fact of the Iraq invasion limited what the US military could do in Afghanistan. Bush and his advisors dedicated the balance of military capacity, and their own time, to the military operation, civil war, and counterinsurgency in Iraq. Until 2006, Afghanistan's progress toward security, political liberalization, and economic development shifted below Iraq on Bush's priority list. By 2006, the Taliban had clawed back a large amount of territory. Frustrated by events on the ground but not wanting to add the perception of failure in Afghanistan to his domestic difficulties concerning Iraq, Bush ordered a "silent surge" of forces, boosting troop levels to 31,000 from 21,000 (Bush 2010, 211).

But Afghanistan never broke through to become politically salient enough again to provoke Bush into anything more than a holding action. By the end of his two terms as president, the general consensus was that the early political and security gains in Afghanistan were sliding away. Democratic presidential candidate Barack Obama seized on the lack of resolution in Afghanistan during the 2008 campaign, calling it the "war of necessity" and blaming Bush for trading success in Afghanistan away to invade Iraq.

Obama exemplified the professional politician: vigilant about public sentiment and all the factors that informed it, and how they impacted how much control he could exercise. He explained the kind of situation that presidents in particular dread and try to avoid: "The negative stories [in the media] don't let up, which leads to a drop in your popularity. Your political adversaries, smelling blood in the water, go after you harder, and allies aren't as quick to defend you" (Obama 2020, 519). Eventually it can get so bad, he wrote, that a president loses control of the situation, like riding in a barrel over Niagara Falls, just hoping to survive the descent. Obama's presidency was sometimes "in the barrel." His approval ratings would drop, unemployment was still high and mortgage foreclosures still loomed, his effort to pass health care reform spurred controversy, and "press coverage became more critical," including on his "decisions to send more troops into Afghanistan" (Obama 2020, 519). Time and again in his memoir and interviews, he acknowledged that he did not want to make military policy to avoid personal political consequences, but he did think other political consequences were reasonable factors in decision. About the idea of a no-fly zone over Libya in 2011, he told the writer profiling him for *Vanity Fair* that he worried if he "announced a no-fly zone and if it appeared feckless, there would be additional pressure for us to go further" (Lewis 2012). In other words, Obama believed politics could compel suboptimal military policy.

In his memoirs, Obama reveals the private thoughts he wrestled with in 2009 as he and his national security team debated whether to grant General McChrystal's request for 40,000 more troops in Afghanistan. "I felt the weight of the office more than at any other time since I'd been sworn in," he wrote (Obama 2020, 438). He pondered the difference between the "real but not existential" threats the United States faced in Afghanistan, and those that presidents faced during the Civil War and World War II. The Taliban and al Qaeda did not pose a threat that made policy choices obvious, and Obama believed that "to insist that our safety and standing in the world required us to do all that we could for as long as we could [in Afghanistan] was an abdication of moral responsibility" (Obama 2020, 439).

At the same time, doing nothing was not feasible. As Carter Malkasian (2021) points out in his history of the American war in Afghanistan, at no point in 2009 did the president seriously consider scaling the troop commitment down, which contemporary reporting confirms. After all, he had just approved 17,000 additional forces. What he wanted to do was manage the costs and risks—in terms of lives and politics—and conclude the war without the appearance of losing.

The reason for this had to do with the key people in Obama's political context. His then CIA director, Leon Panetta, who had over forty years of experience in Washington politics, explains in his memoir that although the president had an antiwar constituency and a Congress impatient with the mounting human and financial toll of Afghanistan, they were offset by an even more powerful set of actors: "Obama was a new president, a Democrat without military experience. For him to defy his military advisers on a matter so central to the success of his foreign policy and so early in his presidency would have represented an almost impossible risk" (Panetta 2014, 254). At the same time, many of his fellow Democrats wanted to fall in line behind him, and powerful Republicans on the Hill supported troop increases. One news article in October described his political position well: Obama's engagements on the Hill "underscored the perilous crosscurrents" in national politics. "While some Democrats said they would support whatever [Obama] decided, others challenged him about sending more troops. And Republicans pressed him to order the escalation without delay" (Baker and Zeleny 2009). Meanwhile, the power of military and military-supporting actors echoed Panetta's evaluation. Veterans' advocacy groups organized petitions and lobbied Congress, saying the president should "listen to the commander on the ground in Afghanistan" (Dreazen 2009).

Obama's final policy was a compromise driven by those crosscurrents and the tension with his military advisors and those who supported them. In his speech at West Point on December 1, 2009, the president laid out the terms of the agreement he had made with DoD: he would commit 30,000 additional military personnel, fewer than McChrystal requested but more than his White House team and some far-left Democrats wanted, bringing the total number of deployed troops close to 100,000, the highest level of the entire war. He would, however, limit the time frame during which the number of troops would be so high. The US would take another eighteen months to train Afghans to provide their own security against the Taliban, so the US could complete its core mission: to "disrupt, dismantle, and defeat al Qaeda." He would start to bring forces home in the summer of 2011, because as president, he had to husband resources to protect prosperity at home. "Our troop commitment in Afghanistan cannot be open-ended—because the nation that I am most interested in building is our own," he said (Obama 2009).

Obama's description of his thinking about Afghanistan illustrates the way an executive politician refers to national values and priorities to make control decisions about the military. Obama wrote that he thought the president's job was "to weigh the costs and benefits of military action against everything else that went into making the country strong" (Obama 2020, 436). Again, risk was a factor, and military risks were also political risks. The president viewed with skepticism risking more lives and spending more treasure on an effort with dubious security benefits. He was willing to try one more time because of domestic pressures, but he also constrained that effort because of countervailing domestic politics.

Over the course of his eight years in office, Obama increasingly acknowledged the sense of war fatigue among the American people. By 2015, following the planned drawdown in forces, just under 10,000 troops remained in Afghanistan. The new Afghan president, Ashraf Ghani, the first politician to replace Karzai since 2002, requested a pause in troop reductions, and Obama agreed (Lee and Nelson 2015). In his final address about Afghanistan over the summer of 2016, he said, "When we first sent our forces into Afghanistan 14 years ago, few Americans imagined we'd be there—in any capacity—this long" (Obama 2016). He layered consolations onto this sentiment, assuring his audience that the combat mission was over, that Afghans were fighting for their own country, that American forces had largely come home, that Afghanistan wouldn't be perfect, but it would be better than it was under the Taliban. But he couldn't mollify Americans with a sense of real accomplishment in the form of victory. He couldn't say the US and its partners defeated the Taliban. The best he could do, as in Iraq, was to call drawing down American troops in Afghanistan "responsible."

Donald Trump was more sensitive to the domestic political context than either of his two immediate predecessors. He cared very little about international politics, except to the extent that engaging with them burnished his image as a tough negotiator and a wielder of American power. His political sense had little substantive ballast—it was almost exclusively reliant on optics, on what things looked like to his audiences and to how much they were looking at him. He was not concerned with policy and was dismissive of facts that prevented him from getting what he wanted or made him look bad. He exercised control over the military and other civilians with the goal of guaranteeing his reelection and boosting his ego, which were generally coterminous ideas.

Trump also brought a deep skepticism of the war in Afghanistan into the Oval Office. "We should have speedy withdrawal," he wrote on his Twitter account before he was elected. "Why should we keep wasting our money—rebuild the US!" (Gordon, Schmitt, and Haberman 2017). Although expressed in more crude language, it was an echo of Obama's call to nation build at home, demonstrating how similar things can look to different civilians of the same type. At his inauguration, Trump laid out a protectionist foreign policy. Although he did not mention Afghanistan by name, he criticized the sorts of efforts the US had been making there for sixteen years. He said that Washington had "subsidized the armies of other countries while allowing for the very sad depletion of our military . . . and spent trillions of dollars overseas while America's infrastructure has fallen into disrepair and decay" (Trump 2017b). At the time, the US troop presence in Afghanistan stood at about 9,000.

Meanwhile, the Taliban had regrouped. The commander in charge of Afghanistan in 2017 when Trump took office, General John Nicholson, told the SASC just three weeks after Trump's inauguration that the war between the Afghan government and the Taliban was at a "stalemate" and more American trainers could help turn the fighting to the Afghans' advantage (Gordon 2017a). In the months that followed, Nicholson, Secretary of Defense Jim Mattis, and National Security Advisor (and active-duty Lieutenant General) H. R. McMaster worked to convince Trump to change his mind about withdrawing from Afghanistan.

It was a high bar for the internationalists on Trump's national security team to clear. Trump had run for office pledging to put "America first" and to make all major decisions in reference to whether it would help or hurt Americans.[5] Trump's views on Afghanistan were consistent with his larger perspective: the US was propping up a government in partnership with allies at a high cost with no discernible benefit. As journalist Peter Bergen wrote in his book about Trump's foreign policy choices, "For Trump, mutual defense alliances such as NATO were largely worthless. The real estate developer from New York City saw relations with other countries as transactions . . . and he fervently believed that the United States was getting stiffed by some of its closest allies" (Bergen 2022, 10). Taking a careful approach with allies had prevented previous presidents from precipitous actions regarding the American troop presence in Afghanistan, but such a sensitivity did not enter Trump's calculus.

Determined to change the president's mind, Trump's national security team conducted a strategic review of Afghanistan through the spring and summer of 2017. In this effort, McMaster, Mattis, CIA Director Mike Pompeo, and Secretary of State Rex Tillerson were arrayed against the president and his inner circle of advisors, especially Senior Counselor Steve Bannon. The intra-administration power politics dominated the process for several months, and casual outside observers believed that the multiple active duty and retired general officers on the president's national security and White House teams were persuasive because Trump had evinced such admiration for, and therefore deference to, them. In fact, their underlying values were highly divergent, and Trump's cosmetic admiration of men in uniform curdled quickly over the course of the Afghanistan strategic review.

In the end, it was the domestic politics of counterterrorism, not an affinity for military advice, that convinced Trump to send more forces to Afghanistan rather than pull them all out. In a briefing in mid-August, CIA Director Mike Pompeo compared the potential withdrawal from Afghanistan to President Obama's 2011 withdrawal from Iraq. Trump had been publicly critical of the precipitous withdrawal, which he believed gave rise to ISIS. Pompeo and his briefing team now told the president that the main way to prevent an Iraq-like outcome in Afghanistan was to keep training the Afghan forces so they could repel the Taliban, a policy that required an American military presence (Bergen 2022). At the final decision meeting at Camp David a few weeks later, Trump acquiesced not only to keep forces in Afghanistan for the foreseeable future but also to a modest increase of around 4,000 troops. In a televised address on August 21, 2017, Trump drew the parallel that had been the final factor in his decision: "As we know, in 2011, America hastily and mistakenly withdrew from Iraq. As a result, our hard-won gains slipped back into the hands of terrorist enemies" (Trump 2017a).

But Trump had no conviction to his decision. Although he used the speech to align himself with the noble reputation and "heroic example" of the American military, his deference to the Pentagon (and the CIA) was driven more by political risk aversion than by strategic logic. Trump never stopped resenting the costs of the war and America's inability to win it, nor did he stop seeing the political benefit of getting the US out of "a bad deal." Shortly after the midterm elections in 2018, where Trump's Republican Party lost the majority in the House of Representatives, Trump again ordered the Pentagon to reduce the troop presence in

118   Chapter Four

Afghanistan. American forces in Afghanistan had spent the year fighting an increasingly lethal ISIS front, Secretary Mattis had just resigned from the administration, and Trump expressed exasperation with the strategy he had approved in 2017 (Malkasian 2021). Trump directed Pompeo, now the secretary of state, to engage in talks with the Taliban to negotiate a peaceful end to the American military occupation in exchange for Taliban concessions regarding al Qaeda and the government in Kabul.

Trump connected international negotiations directly to domestic opinion, and was explicit that the way he intended to control the military via troop levels was a direct result of his domestic political calculations. Mattis's eventual successor as secretary of defense, Mark Esper, reports in his memoir that at a 2019 NSC meeting about Afghanistan, "Trump said he wanted any public statement we might release about the peace deal to say that the US would be at 'zero [troops] in October' 2020, just before the election. November 3, 2020, was the lens through which he viewed the agreement" (Esper 2022, 223). Trump held this perspective throughout 2019 and 2020, and as "November 3 neared, getting all (or at least most) of our forces out of Afghanistan sooner rather than later became Trump's singular focus" (Esper 2022, 223). On October 7, 2020—less than a month before election day—Trump tweeted, "We should have the small remaining number of our BRAVE Men and Women serving in Afghanistan home by Christmas!"[6] Trump was making a control choice using the force management mechanism to benefit his electoral fortunes.

THE CHAIRS

The prominence of the domestic electoral political context for members of Congress is exemplified in the cyclical promotion and demotion of SASC chairs and ranking members. Senator Carl Levin was SASC chair from 2001 until January 2003, when the new Congress brought Republicans back into the majority and put John Warner in the chair. Four years later, Levin and the Democrats were back on top again, where he and they remained until January 2015, when Levin retired from the Senate and Republican Senator John McCain became chair. This waxing and waning of power per nationwide elections meant that electoral prospects were never far from any

SASC chair's mind. (John McCain had the additional experience of running for president in 2008.) The partisan identity of the chair often amplified or muted their divergences with presidents, with copartisans trying to support their party's leader in the White House and counterpartisans using Afghanistan to undercut presidents. At the same time, Republican and Democratic chairs alike believed there should be a national consensus over rhetorical and fiscal support to the military, which had the effect of muting differences among SASC members over troop levels in Afghanistan. And as the war went on, each chair became progressively more vigorous in exercising skeptical oversight of the war, regardless of partisanship.

As was also the case in the executive branch, the chairs spent more time in the hearing room considering policy toward Iraq than toward Afghanistan, making discussion of Afghanistan strategy and force deployments shallower and more episodic than they otherwise might have been. The dynamic was self-perpetuating: because the American military presence in Iraq was far larger, it got more media and public attention, and because the SASC wanted to work on issues that reflected the public's priorities, the chairs focused on Iraq more than Afghanistan. The nature of congressional oversight is also episodic relative to the persistent attention presidents and secretaries of defense are able to pay to military operations. Levin, Warner, and McCain each traveled to Afghanistan many times and sat through hours of hearings, but there were still wide gaps in the time they spent on Afghanistan, often tuning back in when a surge or drawdown was on the table.

Senator Carl Levin of Michigan had been chair for almost exactly four months when the war in Afghanistan began. He had been a US senator since 1979, having entered politics through the legal profession, serving on the Michigan Civil Rights Commission and for the state's attorney general before becoming a council member in Detroit (Johnston 2014; McFadden 2021). He became a member of the Armed Services Committee in his first term and rose to the senior-most committee position for the minority party, ranking member, in 1997. After two decades, he knew his committee and its business well, and he had a reputation for honesty, pragmatism, and keeping his promises. Republican colleagues appreciated his style and integrity, even if they frequently disagreed with him.[7]

120   Chapter Four

Levin saw his role as SASC chair squarely as one of oversight, not policy-making. In fact, oversight was his brand and his legacy—the Levin Center at Wayne State University Law School in his home state of Michigan is focused on best practices in bipartisan oversight (Stanton 2021). He could be very critical of the policies successive presidents and secretaries of defense proposed, but he waited for them to initiate ideas. He was also proud of the SASC's reputation for bipartisanship, something he saw as a result of the nationally unifying character of the military itself (Levin 2021).

Levin's role in authorizing military action in Afghanistan was deferential to other civilians; the party leaders in both chambers of Congress led legislative action in the post-9/11 rush. Lawyers at the White House and Justice Department offered draft language to the Hill on September 12, which the majority and minority leaders in the two chambers then revised and approved through their party caucuses. Even in the haste of the moment, Congress exercised some control over the executive, striking out a capacious clause that would have given the president the authority to strike all terrorists anywhere, regardless of their affiliation with the attacks of 9/11 (Murray 2014).

From the start of operations in Afghanistan, Levin was optimistic about defeating the Taliban and about the long-term viability of the government in Kabul. He and ranking member Warner first traveled to Afghanistan in late November 2021, a trip that encouraged Levin's sense of Afghans' commitment to expelling the Taliban. He also applauded the light footprint approach to US military operations. In his opening statement during the SASC's first hearing on Operation Enduring Freedom, Levin praised the combination of "innovative techniques and revolutionary technologies" including "warriors on horseback . . . calling in precision air strikes" (SASC 2002). He wrote in his memoir that he always thought the primary US mission should have been training Afghan soldiers, not fighting the Taliban directly (Levin 2021).

Levin also believed international political support for the American presence in Afghanistan, especially among Muslim-majority nations, was necessary for operations to succeed (Levin 2021). His desire for international solidarity extended to NATO participation in stabilization operations as well. In these ways, Levin did not depart from Bush administration views or policy, and he showed deference to the military's use of force in Afghanistan during his visits and public remarks.

In 2003, the Democrats lost the majority on the Hill, and Senator John Warner took over as the SASC chair. Warner had been chair before, from 1999 to 2001, when he developed a reputation for being proactive and well connected with Pentagon leadership, especially the secretary (Schmitt 1999). His early life involved service in the Navy in WWII and the Marine Corps in Korea, interspersing these experiences with college and law degrees. He was a law clerk and assistant US attorney, and became undersecretary and then secretary of the navy for President Nixon (Hulse 2021). He became a senator in 1979, the same year as Carl Levin, and developed a reputation as an independent actor with an ideologically moderate legislative record.[8]

Warner's second term as SASC chair began just two months before the US invaded Iraq, and the politics of the added war overshadowed Afghanistan for Warner and the committee. A profile of Warner for *Roll Call*, a periodical focused on congressional activities, a few weeks after he reclaimed the SASC chair in January 2003 explained the domestic and international pressures he felt. It also demonstrated his desire to help the president navigate the political terrain: "Warner considers himself most on-guard these days about the public's mood with the nation on the brink of war. He worries that European allies are hesitant to support Bush and Congressional Democrats are ready to pounce, while Americans at large aren't sure what to think. 'It's just not coming together for this president,' Warner said" (Kane 2003). Managing the political risks to the president and the Republican Party, the prerogatives of the Senate, and the soundness of military operational planning for Iraq left Warner far less time for Afghanistan, driving him into deference to the administration by default. It also appeared, by 2003, that the major combat phase of operations against the Taliban was over, while the scale of military activities in Iraq was ramping up. Warner concluded that his energy and the bulk of military capacity should aim for Iraq.

A case in point is the series of three public hearings Warner organized in 2005 on "US Military Operations and Stabilization Activities in Iraq and Afghanistan." Afghanistan was only a topic for the first hearing, and senators largely directed questions about it to the State Department witness, reflecting their assumption that military policy had become less relevant there (SASC 2005). During his chairmanship between January 3, 2003, and January 3, 2007, Warner held only one hearing that covered Afghanistan alone. Four additional hearings covered both Afghanistan and Iraq, and another five covered just Iraq.[9]

As noted above, because it consumed attention Iraq consumed troops, exemplifying the relationship between politics and the degree of control civilians exercised via force management. For the president, the low force level was a constraint on the military, but to Congress it reflected deference to the president. Afghanistan was an afterthought, and Warner, like many civilians, looked for ways to economize and improvise force levels there. Like Levin, he often focused on transferring security burdens to Afghans and allies. At that first SASC hearing on Afghanistan in 2002, Warner, then ranking member, said in his opening statement, "We are not going to be an occupation Army. We, working with our allies, are to 'turn that land over to its people.'" (SASC 2002, 4). Four years later, at Gates's confirmation hearing, after discussing Iraq and a variety of other DoD management issues, Warner asked about Afghanistan, "What do you think about the level of forces over there?" (SASC 2006). Although Gates acknowledged more may be necessary to keep the Taliban at bay, he and Warner turned to NATO forces as a solution.

By 2007, the tide had turned for Democrats on the Hill, and Levin was SASC chair once again. During the following eight years of his chairmanship, Levin convened fifteen hearings that covered Afghanistan as a main topic, nine of which were solely about the country. Levin's optimism about the average Afghan's commitment to the new government had not wavered (nor did it for the rest of the war—he died just a month before the final US withdrawal in August 2021, having recently published a memoir that restated his long-held position). He was just as likely to ask presidents, secretaries of defense, and other DoD leaders about increasing the number of Americans training Afghans as he was to debate the overall troop numbers. His focus on training Afghans came from his read of the domestic political context, which was similar to how successive presidents read it. He evinced less concern than presidents and secretaries of defense for the military's own preference to boost troop numbers. He expressed his preference to train Afghans rather than surge Americans during the two rounds of debate over troop levels in Afghanistan in the first year of the Obama administration. "I think we should hold off on a commitment to send more combat troops until these additional steps to strengthen the Afghan security forces are put in motion," he told reporters in September 2009 (Schmitt and Sanger, 2009). His position as SASC chair provided him the platform to keep pressing the point. "What is disturbing and hard to comprehend," he told two DoD witnesses at a hearing in 2010, "is that the training mission still does not have enough trainers to process all the Afghan recruits who are signing up to join in the security forces" (Shanker 2010).

Levin's interpretation of domestic Afghan politics fueled his position. He believed an Afghanistan that could defend itself from the Taliban would reinforce the political legitimacy of the regime in Kabul, making for a more stable and sustainable situation. He once told Obama that "withdrawal of US troops [as planned in 2011] and a stronger Afghan army would mean that the Taliban would hopefully be losing both the military battles and their propaganda argument that they are fighting to remove foreigners from Afghanistan" (Levin 2021, Kindle 2582). He said the same in open hearings, adding that the Afghan army's legitimacy would itself pick away at the Taliban's strength. "As support for the Afghan army and police grows, lower-level insurgent fighters are slowly beginning to reintegrate into Afghan society," he said in the hearing to consider the DoD's fiscal year 2012 budget (SASC 2011, 7). Altogether, domestic American and Afghan politics convinced Levin that lower American troop numbers were both preferable and viable.

Levin, like Panetta, suspected that Obama "felt politically vulnerable" because he had no military experience (Levin 2021, Kindle 2567). Levin wanted to shore up that vulnerability for his fellow Democrat, and he pressed to give Obama some space to make his decision. Appearing on the PBS *NewsHour* in September 2009, he minimized the discussion of troop numbers and focused on the strategic questions behind McChrystal's report. He also made a distinction between "combat forces" and trainers, saying he preferred not to increase the number of troops whose mission would be to fight the Taliban (Public Broadcasting Service 2009). At the same

124   Chapter Four

time, Levin had his own committee politics to manage, most vocal among them ranking member John McCain. As Obama began considering the McChrystal review, McCain published an op-ed in the *Wall Street Journal* with two Senate colleagues praising McChrystal and declaring "the team on the ground . . . can win this war," provided it was given "the resources it needs to succeed—including a significant increase in US forces" (Graham, Lieberman, and McCain 2009). Meanwhile, the Democratic caucus was divided, with some like Senators Russ Feingold, Diane Feinstein, and Barbara Boxer calling for withdrawal, while others were unenthusiastic about either expanding or eliminating the troop presence in Afghanistan (Dreazen, King, and Spiegel 2009). Levin did his best to give his copartisans on the Hill space to exercise independent oversight while ultimately closing party ranks with the president. As one news article captured it:

> Democrats say tough oversight from the president's own party—something Mr. Bush escaped in the build-up to the war in Iraq—can only help Mr. Obama by improving his policies. Although the flak may be frustrating for the president, "he's better off to have questions asked by people who are in fundamental agreement with him," says Senator Carl Levin, the Michigan Democrat. (Lakshmanan 2009)

But Levin was sincerely skeptical about sending additional American forces and joined colleagues in both chambers asking for General McChrystal to testify on his recommendations. Hearing directly from McChrystal before the president made any decisions would have amplified Congress' ability to influence Obama, effectively using a military officer's expertise to control the executive. Secretary Gates blocked the testimony, explaining through the Pentagon spokesperson, "Secretary Gates still believes Gen. McChrystal's focus right now should be on managing the war in Afghanistan rather than wading into the debate about it back here in Washington" (Dreazen, King, and Spiegel 2009). Eventually, Levin supported the president's decision to send 30,000 more troops to Afghanistan, a position that happily aligned him with his ranking member.

It wasn't until 2015 that McCain himself became chair, a position he held for the last two years of the Obama administration and the first twenty months of the Trump administration. McCain had national security credentials unusual for legislative politicians. A Vietnam war veteran, he had

Civilian Control and the War in Afghanistan 125

been a prisoner of the North Vietnamese for five and a half years, enduring brutal conditions, torture, and severe injuries that affected him for the rest of his life. His experiences led him to be a career-long advocate for humane treatment of detainees, especially in Afghanistan and Iraq.[10] In his memoir, McCain explained that he viewed his role as a politician as different from military leadership. "I was a politician, and I had other responsibilities, one of which was to make certain there was a valid purpose for ordering Americans into harm's way" (McCain and Salter 2018, 107). McCain's career as a legislative politician began in 1987 when he joined the Senate representing Arizona. He grew into a leader in the Republican Party, eventually running for president in 2008 as the GOP nominee—and losing to Barack Obama. Six years later, he became SASC chair, in time to oversee the last two years of Obama's management of the war in Afghanistan.

McCain paid more attention to Afghanistan than almost any other senator—but still far less than he paid to Iraq, especially during the initial years of the war in the latter country. His first visit to Afghanistan was in January 2002, while Americans were still fighting remnants of the Taliban in the south. He met with Hamid Karzai, "clearly the US and Britain's preferred choice for the national government's leader," McCain later wrote (McCain and Salter 2018, 106). He left the country after that first visit with a sense of optimism, much like Carl Levin's. Like many of his colleagues, he understood Afghanistan in comparison to Iraq, and knew that force level decisions for Afghanistan were a function of decisions on Iraq. Writing about the first four years in Afghanistan, which overlapped with the first two years in Iraq, McCain said:

> By 2005, I had become single-minded in my advocacy of a revised strategy in Iraq, and a big increase in the number of troops there. I knew what that meant for Afghanistan. We would have to maintain our position there with less force than desirable. That wasn't fair to the soldiers who were holding the line in Afghanistan. But there wasn't much of a choice. As tough as it was there, it wasn't as bad as Iraq. We would have to muddle through until we had salvaged the disaster that Iraq had become. (McCain and Salter 2018, 117)

Over time, however, as conditions improved in Iraq, McCain and his SASC colleagues were able to focus far more attention on the war in

Afghanistan. McCain liked the troop increases in 2009, but he did not like President Obama's policy of timeline-based drawdowns. "What concerns me greatly," he said in a statement issued shortly after Obama's December 1 announcement, "is the President's decision to set an arbitrary date to begin withdrawing US forces from Afghanistan" (McCain and Salter 2018, 143). McCain believed that announcing a time to leave, divorced from the state of play on the battlefield, was a recipe for defeat. He also thought that Obama's interpretation of the politics of troop numbers "was dubious. Whatever criticism you got from opponents of the war for increasing the force level, it wouldn't be appreciably more or less if you deployed forty thousand rather than thirty thousand" (McCain and Salter 2018, 144). By the time the Obama administration was drawing down the troop presence as promised, McCain told Leon Panetta during his nomination hearing for secretary of defense, "any drawdown should be modest so as to maximize our ability to lock in the hard-won gains of our troops."[11]

Eight years later, when Donald Trump was sworn in as president, McCain had been chair for two years and was still pressing for more troops and more time to ensure the Afghan security forces were capable of defending the country before the Americans withdrew. At a hearing on February 9, 2017, he said, "In recent years, we have tied the hands of our military in Afghanistan, and instead of trying to win, we settle for just trying not to lose. Time and again, we saw troop withdrawals that seemed to have a lot more to do with American politics than conditions on the ground in Afghanistan" (SASC 2017, 3). McCain generally believed in withstanding domestic political criticism if it meant military success. Although that principled belief was sincere, it was also not a position that challenged his political survival as a pro-military Republican war veteran popular with his constituents.[12] It was therefore politically safe for McCain to push presidents to make military policy decisions that were risky to them.

THE SECRETARIES

Donald Rumsfeld was George W. Bush's first secretary of defense, and Gerald Ford's last. His return to the E-ring—which he had last occupied in 1977 after being Ford's White House chief of staff—made Rumsfeld think of himself as the elder statesman of the Bush administration. In his memoir he recalls dispensing advice to other cabinet officials and questioning the wisdom of their choices, with frequent references to his experiences with previous occupants of their positions. He often sent memos to his colleagues telling them what they ought to do, a practice that did not endear him to many people. He also had strong views on his own role, which he saw as a balance between imposing the president's policies on DoD and representing the department's views to the president. Either way, the secretary acted as a translator. "As secretary of defense it was my job to advise the President, but also to interpret his guidance and ensure that it was implemented," he wrote in his memoir (Rumsfeld 2011, 346).

His attitude toward civil-military relations mixed an emphasis on civilian dominance of policymaking with leveraging—but often challenging—military expertise. He wanted to be "closely linked" to the CJCS (Rumsfeld 2011, 368) and urged his civilian undersecretaries to communicate openly with their uniformed counterparts as well, yet he had a pugnacious reputation with senior military leaders. CJCS General Hugh Shelton referred to Rumsfeld in his own memoirs as "a little pit bull" (Shelton 2010, 448). When it came to planning the Afghanistan war, he emphasized the senior military leadership's role in generating the plans although he continued his "habit of asking probing questions" (Rumsfeld 2011, 369). Nevertheless, he tended to step back and let the CJCSes during his tenure, Hugh Shelton and Richard Myers, brief the president. He endorsed Central Command's commander Tommy Franks's battlefield decisions. Whether or not it was an accurate view, Rumsfeld wrote of himself that one "criticism would have been that I too often deferred to the views, opinions, and decisions of the generals who were in charge" (Rumsfeld 2011, 705).

Donald Rumsfeld began his long public service career as a pilot in the US Navy, having attended Princeton on an ROTC scholarship. At the age of thirty-one he was elected to the US House of Representatives from Illinois. After three terms he transitioned from politician to administrator to work for the Nixon administration. His time as an elected official and in the White House gave him a feel for national politics, and his evaluation of the political context after 9/11 incorporated public sentiment, economic factors, and media coverage. "Across the United States," he wrote, "Americans

128   Chapter Four

expressed anger and sadness. They also voiced fear of further attacks" even as the stock market plummeted (Rumsfeld 2011, 349).

Rumsfeld's evaluation of the international political context revolved around ideas about sovereignty. He judged that al Qaeda's public opposition to American forces' presence in the Middle East was more for publicity, and that their real goal was to return the territories of modern countries to "an ancient caliphate . . . one pan-Islamic state, much like the Taliban's rule in Afghanistan." At the same time, al Qaeda and other terrorist groups were "present in numerous countries with which we were not at war" (Rumsfeld 2011, 354). Getting access to those countries was a delicate political challenge. But his evaluation of international political contexts was often simplistic. His June 25, 2002, memo about Pakistan, according to scholars at the National Security Archives at George Washington University, revealed "how naïve top American officials were about Pakistani motivations" (Blanton et al. 2021). The memo, addressed to Undersecretary of Defense for Policy Doug Feith, was only three lines and suggested buying Pakistani president Musharraf's compliance with American counterterrorism policy.

More important for Rumsfeld's effectiveness, he did not align himself well with other civilians, most importantly President Bush, failing to incorporate the president's evaluations of the domestic and international political contexts into his own thinking or actions. Instead, he frequently disputed the president's views, and argued with or corrected other cabinet officials and presidential advisors. He was also aggressive with other members of the administration and alienated many potential political allies, giving him far less influence over the thinking of other civilians.

Right or wrong, his judgments about national politics informed his force management decisions. He agreed with the president's view that swift military action was the only viable option politically. To Rumsfeld, the low initial force levels used in the invasion connected logically to the desire for speed. Rumsfeld later wrote that a larger presence would have taken several months to deploy, and "delay might have eroded popular support at home and abroad for the President's counterterrorism strategy" (Rumsfeld 2011, 377).

By August 2002, Rumsfeld was convinced that Afghanistan did not present a security challenge so much as a "civil" challenge. By this he meant the domestic politics of Afghanistan. Hamid Karzai, the president of Afghanistan, needed to "develop political strength in the regions" of the country. "He needs to be able to show the Afghan people that he is delivering for them and that it is in their interest to help keep the Taliban out" he wrote to President Bush in August. In a prescient line, he added, "In any event, without successful reconstruction, no amount of added security forces would be enough. The Soviets had over 100,000 troops [in Afghanistan during their occupation of it in the 1980s] and failed" (Rumsfeld 2002b). Rumsfeld's political analysis also motivated his desire to keep US military deployments to a minimum in Afghanistan. Afghanistan's regional political context, where neighboring governments distrusted each other and were aligned with opposing groups inside Afghanistan, primed the country for a proxy civil war. He also believed that Afghans should rule with political skills, not military might. "If Karzai could not prevail against local forces without American military assistance," he later wrote, "I felt he could not survive politically anyway" (Rumsfeld 2011, 407). He recommended to President Bush that the "the critical problem in Afghanistan is not really a security problem" (Rumsfeld 2002a), and he maintained this perspective even as the Taliban began to regroup and retake territory in 2006, urging an increase in the number of Afghan National Army personnel but not in the number of deployed Americans (Rumsfeld 2011). When Rumsfeld left office in 2006, there were approximately 20,400 American "boots on the ground" in Afghanistan, about a seventh as many as the number in Iraq (Belasco 2009).

Rumsfeld left office because President Bush asked him to step down. There was by then a widespread perception that neither war was going well for the US and that new leadership at DoD was needed to reverse course. The proximate excuse was the GOP losses in the 2006 midterm congressional elections, but Rumsfeld was already facing too many political headwinds in the media and inside the administration. Only Vice President Cheney advocated for him internally (Gates 2014). He had failed at the art of deferring to other civilians from time to time, instead following his impulse to compel his preferred actions out of colleagues and the military alike. Without alliances with other civilians, he controlled very little in the end.

130   Chapter Four

To replace him, Bush asked former director of the CIA Robert Gates to serve. Bob Gates had retired from government service, he thought for good, and had become president of Texas A&M University. Growing up with a "rock-ribbed Republican" father and a Democratic mother, Gates concluded early in life that bipartisanship was "sensible" (Gates 2014, 14). Expressing that sensibility, he had chosen a career as a government staffer who started in the Air Force as part of a CIA recruiting program, then rose to the level of executive administrator. In his office calls with senators that are typical of the preconfirmation process, he was alarmed by the partisanship and parochialism they expressed, and the personal acrimony they directed at the president and leaders at DoD. "Washington itself had become a war zone" he thought (Gates 2014, 13). Although Gates didn't see himself as a political actor, he realized he had taken a role that required him to interact with those who did, and with partisan and inter-branch politics.

Having been through three previous confirmation processes (one ending with his withdrawal amid the Iran-Contra scandal), Gates sensed that the conditions this time around—a politically unpopular secretary preceding him—smoothed his confirmation. News analysis at the time corroborated this view. The *Financial Times'* Edward Luce wrote, "given Mr. Rumsfeld's deep unpopularity and the fact that Capitol Hill is desperately seeking someone to offer hope that Iraq can still be pulled back from the brink, senators might well smother Mr. Gates with praise" (Luce 2006). But Gates harbored concerns about his professional survival after confirmation. He admitted to his wife that the George W. Bush administration "was held in pretty low esteem across the nation. I told her, 'I have to do this, but I just hope I can get out of this administration with my reputation intact'" (Gates 2014, 8).

As he transitioned into the Pentagon, Gates cultivated goodwill among Washington power brokers. He had learned that to lead large organizations toward big objectives—like winning wars—it was necessary to get "buy-in" from people in positions to facilitate or obstruct progress (Miller Center 2013). Reinvigorating his network began with the Hill during his confirmation process, aided significantly by his friendship with the outgoing SASC chair, Senator Warner. (Shortly after his confirmation the Democrats assumed the Senate majority, and Senator Carl Levin became chair.) Within the administration, he knew he needed the trust of the president above all, and he worked to build good relations with the other national security leaders who advised the president, too, emphasizing the secretary of state. And within the Pentagon, he focused on repairing civil-military relations. He also asked Colin Powell, a friend from their days in the H. W. Bush administration, to smooth the way for him among military officers (Gates 2014, 21–23). He kept all the civilians already working for the secretary, choosing the institutional knowledge (and internal connections) of those already there. His purposeful cultivation of allies, advocates, and insiders produced a network he used to devise, defend, and implement military policy. "In short," he wrote, "despite the tremendous power inherent in the job, the secretary of defense must deal with multiple competing interests both within and outside the Pentagon and work with many constituencies, without whose support he cannot be successful" (Gates 2014, 83).

Gates also relied on his own substantive knowledge about Afghanistan. When he was deputy director of the Central Intelligence Agency in the 1980s, CIA analysts wrote products for policymakers about the Afghan insurgency against the Soviets, the Soviet's efforts to train the Afghan army, and the morale and effectiveness of Soviet troops (US Senate Select Committee on Intelligence 1991, 31). In Gates's first meeting with President Bush, he "expressed my deep concern about Afghanistan and my feeling that it was being neglected, and that there was too much focus on trying to build a capable central government in a country that essentially had never had one, and too little focus on the provinces, districts, and tribes" (Gates 2014, 7). In other words, Gates felt that the administration wasn't assessing the roots of Afghanistan's political instability correctly. His initial review of the situation in Afghanistan deepened his concern. During his first trip to the country as secretary in January 2007, Gates learned about the increasing rate of Taliban attacks, the haven they enjoyed in Pakistan, and the difficulties American and NATO forces had operating safely given their different national rules of engagement. Meanwhile, the CIA's prognosis of the Kabul government's survival was pessimistic whereas the American military commander, General Dan McNeill, reported steady security progress (Coll 2018). Gates had to chart a course given conflicting information.

132   Chapter Four

Many of the differences in perspectives among the main actors co-alesced around the level of troops deployed to the country. The optimal number of forces was different depending on whether American domestic politics, NATO alliance politics, popular Afghan sentiment, or battlefield effectiveness was the priority. During the transition period between Rums-feld and Gates at DoD, President Bush approved a new NSC strategy for Afghanistan that included an increase in the number of American troops (Coll 2018). At the time, approximately 21,000 American military personnel were deployed to Afghanistan. Gates thought it was likely more forces were needed, and he said as much to Senator Warner during his confirmation hearing—although he noted that NATO allies might be able to supply the additions (SASC 2006). He was concerned about the strain on American troops, many of whom were deploying to Iraq and Afghanistan for unusu-ally long periods and not getting sufficient rest time at home.[13] As an in-terim solution once he was confirmed, Gates approved an internal DoD proposal to increase the "end-strength" or total numbers of active-duty forces for the Army and Marine Corps. Congress would have to approve the proposal, which would take years to implement in any case. So, in the immediate term Gates used his sole authority to lengthen deployments to fifteen months, a decision that provided coverage of both Iraq and Afghan-istan but strained soldiers, Marines, and their families, and contributed to discontent with the wars at home (Gates 2014, 203). Although Gates be-lieved that the president (both Bush and later Obama) could sustain suffi-cient political support for the war despite its unpopularity, he recognized that the public needed to see progress and "that an end was in sight" (Gates 2014, 342).

As Gates and Warner had discussed, another solution to the strain on the US military was to ask NATO militaries to "do more," but making such a request involved engaging European leaders in conversations about the best strategy for Afghanistan, conversations that led to disagreements about counterterrorism versus nation building. Nevertheless, Gates made a campaign of appeal at the NATO ministerial—a gathering of ministers of defense from NATO countries—in a public address to Europeans at the annual Munich Security Conference, and again at the NATO summit in April 2008, where he attempted to persuade allies to send more troops by promising a significant increase in American force and signing up to a "vision statement" that emphasized improving governance in Afghanistan. The campaign did persuade several NATO countries to send more troops. But eliciting growth in NATO force presence "committed us to broad, ambitious goals that I and other US officials were increasingly coming to see as unachievable in wartime" (Gates 2014, 216). To get more boots on the ground, Gates had to trade away the strategic focus he preferred.

Politics on the ground in Central and South Asia were just as fraught. Most officials examining the situation agreed that the Taliban's sanctuaries in Pakistan were essential to their success, but Gates could achieve very little in the bilateral relationship because the military wielded far more power in Islamabad than civilian leaders. To get the Pakistanis to do more to suppress Taliban cross-border movement, Gates ceded management of the defense relationship to CJCS Admiral Mike Mullen (Gates 2014). Gates also worried about the American image among Afghans. In his memoir, he writes repeatedly that he feared troop levels would get so high that the US looked like an occupation and alienate the population, driving them to support the Taliban instead of their own government. This perspective about Afghan public opinion vis-à-vis the US drove his preference for a smaller footprint, counterterrorism-focused strategy (Gates 2014).

Gates also had to manage conflicts between senior military leaders and the White House over the former's requests for more resources, including more forces, for Afghanistan. McNeill and his replacement, General David McKiernan, regularly asked for more troops, and CJCS Mullen frequently irritated President Bush by claiming in the press and before Congress that Afghanistan was of distinctly secondary concern to the administration compared to Iraq. Meanwhile, like everyone else the commanders of Central Command, to whom the commanders in Afghanistan were subordinate, were focused on Iraq.

Because president-elect Obama asked Gates to stay on as secretary, Gates participated in the final G. W. Bush administration strategy review of Afghanistan and the Obama administration's first such review. Once again, force management dominated discussion and acted as a proxy for different strategic approaches. Team Bush had decided that another troop increase was necessary, and General McKiernan had made a formal request for

134 Chapter Four

30,000 more forces in the fall of 2008 (including by making the case to Vice President-Elect Joe Biden during his visit before the inauguration) to deal with the summer fighting season and to provide election security during Afghanistan's elections that coming August. Gates ordered "preparations" to deploy two more brigade combat teams to enable the Obama team to act swiftly if they so chose (Coll 2018, 347). The move was prudent from a technocratic perspective, allowing the two teams time to train and organize their affairs before shipping out. But it also shifted momentum toward additional deployments before the commander-in-chief decided what to do. The new Obama administration discussed McKiernan's request at its first NSC meeting on Afghanistan on January 23. Making decisions about troop levels before completing their own strategic review struck several at the table as backwards (Gates 2014).

Once again, Gates mediated tensions between the White House and military leaders over troop levels. The "pressure for an early decision on a troop increase in Afghanistan," Gates wrote, "had the unfortunate effect of creating suspicion in the White House that Obama was getting the 'bum's rush' from senior military officers, especially Mullen and [Central Command commander David] Petraeus, to make a big decision prematurely" (Gates 2014, 338). In the end, the NSC recommended, and Obama approved, an increase of 17,000 troops before the strategic review was completed. The ensuing strategic review endorsed that number, plus another 4,000 to train Afghan soldiers.

But that wasn't the end of troop requests for Afghanistan. Shortly after President Obama announced his new strategy, Gates recommended replacing McKiernan with Stanley McChrystal, who had been successful in counterterrorism operations in Iraq. With a new commander Gates thought a new commander's review of the situation on the ground was reasonable, especially because Mullen and others continued to suggest that even more forces beyond the 21,000 just approved would be necessary. When Gates explained at a White House meeting with the president that he had asked McChrystal to conduct the review, as he put it, "the room exploded." "The president said testily there would be no political support for any further troop increase—the Democrats on the Hill didn't want one, and the Republicans would just play politics" (Gates 2014, 349).

Nevertheless, McChrystal discovered that Kabul and NATO were starting to lose in Afghanistan and told Mullen in July 2009 that he was planning to request 40,000 more troops. Gates knew the president and his advisors would hate such a proposal, and Gates himself wondered how he could "personally reconcile all my public statements expressing concern about our military footprint with supporting McChrystal" (Gates 2014, 353). Later, in a secret meeting with senior DoD leaders, Gates explained that of the "four pressure points associated with any force increase," two involved politics: "White House and congressional political opposition" and "the need for additional supplemental funding," another congressional hurdle (Gates 2014, 354). Gates then met with President Obama and some of his advisors to present McChrystal's findings about Afghanistan and manage their expectations without focusing on troop levels.

Tailoring his personal interactions with the president and other senior civilian leaders and adjusting his advised strategic approach in Afghanistan to domestic political concerns would be Gates's theme for the remainder of 2009. His efforts at civil-military diplomacy were most imperiled when McChrystal's review was leaked to the *Washington Post* amid discussions at the White House. White House staff believed it was yet another effort by the military to force the president to send more forces to Afghanistan. It took three months and extensive negotiating over force levels before President Obama accepted Gates's compromise proposal of 30,000 additional troops—splitting the difference between the National Security Staff's suggestion of 20,000 and McChrystal's request for 40,000. Gates wrote himself a note at the time that read, "I'm really disgusted with this process, I'm tired of politics overriding the national interest" (Gates 2014, 384).

By the time the 2011 deadline arrived, Gates had left and Leon Panetta had become secretary of defense. Panetta was moving to the Pentagon from the CIA, where he had participated in the "AFPAK reviews" and, most famously, led the agency through the raid that killed Osama bin Laden. His son, James (Jimmy), was a sailor who had deployed to Afghanistan. Between Jimmy and the CIA, Panetta knew Afghanistan policy well. He also understood politics from Washington's vantage, having already judged the domestic political importance to President Obama of keeping his military advisors on his side. He explained in his memoir that the 2009 Afghanistan policy review "largely boiled down to two questions: How many troops were needed to stabilize Afghanistan, and how long would they have to stay?" (Panetta 2014, 251) At the end of 2010 and start of 2011, Panetta participated in another series of meetings with the president on the administration's national security priorities, including Afghanistan. He found the president and his team were sober about the level of political support among the public and Congress for an open-ended commitment to Afghanistan. The administration was coalescing around a strategy of "sufficiency" in Afghanistan—sufficient military capability to repel al Qaeda and sufficient political stability that the government would not fall (Panetta 2014, 287). Panetta felt personally uncomfortable with the slogan for the new approach, "Afghanistan Good Enough" but he saw no political alternative. As President Obama had announced a year prior, troop levels would begin to come down in the middle of 2011, and by the time Panetta took the reins at DoD, the trajectory of reductions was set.

Although two more secretaries would serve in the Obama administration after Panetta, their roles in Afghanistan force levels were similar to Panetta's: they implemented the punctuated withdrawals and participated in reviews of political and security progress at the NSC. The security situation in Afghanistan never stabilized, but what mattered most were the domestic politics of the Afghanistan war, which mixed public disinterest in the war overall and disgust with its length. By 2014, when the Gallup organization once again asked Americans whether "the United States made a mistake in sending military forces to Afghanistan," 51 percent of Americans said the invasion was a mistake. Although there were moments when the president paused troop reductions, the eventual withdrawal from Afghanistan seemed politically inexorable to Barack Obama.

When the Trump administration took office in 2017, there were still approximately 9,000 troops still in Afghanistan, a reduction of some 90,000 from the peak of the surge in 2010 and 2011. Trump wanted the remainder withdrawn, but his secretary of defense disagreed. Retired General James "Jim" Mattis had the unusual background of being a career military officer. During his forty-one years in the Marine Corps, Mattis had led troops in Iraq and Afghanistan, been the commander of Central Command overseeing all forces in the Middle East and Central Asia, and had counted CJCS General Joseph Dunford as his deputy in combat. In short, he was a military expert, not an expert in politics. Yet his ability to navigate the tumultuous and hyperpartisan Trump administration signaled that he had developed some political intuition along the way. And true to the incentives of the institutional position of the secretary, the domestic and international political context affected Mattis's control choices.

Where Afghanistan was concerned, Mattis believed the mission to eliminate al Qaeda was essential and that staying the course with NATO allies and the Afghan government underwrote that mission. He was a creature of the last four decades of American foreign policy and agreed with its core precepts: that American leadership and global military presence helped stabilize world politics, and that international institutions, especially military alliances, were critical components of that stability (Mattis 2018). He gave very few media interviews, likely a coping mechanism for surviving in the Trump administration where media spectacle was a high wire act designed to get the president's attention (a resource Mattis didn't need more of) but that risked attracting the president's anger. Because he has betrayed so little of his thinking, analyzing Mattis's views is challenging. But reports by others of NSC meetings and his few later statements indicate Mattis opposed a complete withdrawal from Afghanistan, which he saw through the lens of alliance politics and counterterrorism. Unilateral withdrawal without concern for partners' security was antithetical to America's stabilizing purpose in the world, in Mattis's view (Schake et al. 2020), and he did what he could to constrain President Trump's efforts to do so. He ultimately resigned from office over the matter, after President Trump ordered him to begin planning withdrawals from Afghanistan and Syria in rapid succession in the fall of 2018.

As far as Trump's later Secretary of Defense Mark Esper was concerned, "getting out of Afghanistan . . . was a core Trump promise" (Esper 2022, 208). And, as Esper writes in his memoir, "By the time I became secretary of defense in July 2019, Trump wanted out immediately" (Esper 2022, 211). Esper had been the secretary of the army for the previous two years and had come to understand the politics of the Trump administration and the futility of open opposition to the president. Nevertheless, he did think he could find a way to get the president the withdrawal he wanted while preventing a full Taliban takeover of the country.

Luckily for Esper, he agreed with the president's view that the US was not going to be able to fight its way out of Afghanistan; only a political settlement with the Taliban would allow for a graceful American exit. Esper learned about the content of the secret State Department–led negotiations with the Taliban when he became the acting secretary of defense. Although Esper agreed with the idea of negotiating, he cautioned that the US should not withdraw until the Taliban made some concessions. "The two biggest levers we had over [the Taliban] were the US military presence and our ability to inflict violence upon them," Esper writes. He didn't think the US should give away those levers. (Esper 2022, 216) He also pointed out that the Afghan government valued the American military presence as well. The US could afford to wait a while longer to make a good deal.

Esper convinced everyone but President Trump, whose single contextual factor in his force management decisions was his own reelection. When he tweeted a month before the election that all US forces "should" be out of Afghanistan by Christmas, Esper worried about how American troops, NATO allies, and the Afghans themselves would react. And like his predecessors, Esper found himself in the middle between the White House and military officers at the Pentagon. CJCS Mark Milley and National Security Advisor Robert O'Brien traded barbs in the press over troop levels in Afghanistan (Cooper 2020; Crowley 2020). Esper wanted to back his military leadership but also convince the administration to slow down the pace of withdrawal to match conditions met by the Taliban. He counseled Milley that the best way to do so would be to "let it go." "The last thing we need," he told the chairman, "is for the president to intervene and give us a direct order to withdraw" (Esper 2022, 618). Esper showed, yet again, that in the case of Afghanistan, secretaries of defense chose to exercise constraining control over the president if possible.

Conclusion

The war in Afghanistan finally came to an end in August 2021, under the Joseph Biden administration.[14] Until then, every president, secretary of defense, and SASC chair read the domestic political context to mean that incentives to prevent future attacks on the US countervailed against incentives to end the war. It made presidents strike a middle course between hawks in the military and Congress and those who wanted a full withdrawal, and exercising constraining control over the former and the latter. The practical result was a low-level force presence over the entire course of the war. Bush launched the war in the wake of the 9/11 attacks with strong public support, then shifted both forces and policy attention to Iraq. Obama campaigned on the notion that Afghanistan was "the good war," feeling the pressure of that commitment in addition to the domestic and bureaucratic politics of military requests for more forces, backed by some members of Congress. Trump also read the mood of the country, also succumbed to Pentagon pressure to maintain a residual force presence, and belatedly and unsuccessfully attempted to override it. For all three men, public opinion and the perspectives of other politicians mattered most, with the advice of the military and other specialists a consideration of secondary importance.

The chairs of the SASC struggled with competing demands: bipartisan control over the military, partisan solidarity with colleagues and presidents, and exercising control over the executive branch regardless of partisan affiliations. In short, for SASC chairs party loyalty, control over other civilians, and control over the military were in steady competition.

Secretaries of defense, as in the post–Cold War period, balanced the advice of the military and senior civilians with the survival needs of politicians to calculate their own choices. Several of the secretaries examined here sided with the military's preferences to maintain or increase force presence. But those that didn't drew on their understanding of both domestic American politics and, in Rumsfeld's case, domestic Afghan politics to make the case that sending more troops would not be productive. What is most striking in the Afghanistan case were efforts by many of the secretaries to constrain the president's use of the military. Mattis and Esper, in particular, attempted to guide President Trump toward the DoD's preferred course of action. In Mattis's case, this was to extend the effort to defeat the Taliban; for Esper, it was to maintain force presence as pressure

140   Chapter Four

against the Taliban to implement negotiated concessions. Both were counter to what the president wanted.

All of the civilians examined here filtered the political context through their professional-institutional types to make decisions about whether and how to compel, constrain, or defer to each other and the military. Each man (and, again, they were all men) used force presence as a way to control military policy toward Afghanistan—and to control each other.

FIVE

Civilian Control and Capabilities

POLITICAL CONTEXT AND PROFESSIONAL-INSTITUTIONAL TYPE framed the control choices civilians made in the post–Cold War period and over the course of the war in Afghanistan. In both cases, civilian controllers made choices about shaping the whole military enterprise and aiming it at strategic-level goals under extraordinary circumstances and public scrutiny. Those choices were about the relationship between national goals and military action; whether the country would send its military to fight, and where and why. In this chapter, I turn to civilian control over *how* the military fights by examining the civilian role in the development and uses of a military capability.

Military capability refers to the knowledge, tools, and power to perform a complex task that helps achieve military objectives.[1] Put simply, it means the military is able to do something. A capability is more than a single tool; it typically involves coordinating the actions of people and military assets, including weapons. Not all capabilities are lethal, but all military capabilities contribute to achieving military missions, whether the mission is to seize territory or deliver assistance to victims of a hurricane. The power to choose which capabilities the military develops and uses gives civilian controllers the power to decide how the military will use force.

Because military personnel are the "end-users" of these tools and techniques, their expertise is essential to developing and integrating capabilities

142   Chapter Five

into military doctrine and operations. But military capabilities are neither exclusively nor ultimately the military's responsibility. Because civilians exercise control over the decision to use force and decisions to build forces in the first place, controlling which capabilities the military develops is a natural extension of civilian authority over the military. As with other aspects of military policymaking, civilians make choices about capabilities in the context of international, domestic, interagency, and even interpersonal politics. Prohibiting the use of chemical weapons, cancelling plans to buy certain types of fighter jets, and expanding the production of mine-resistant, ambush-protected vehicles are all examples of civilians exercising control over how the military uses force by controlling capabilities.[2]

This chapter examines how civilians controlled the development and the military's uses of one particular capability: uninhabited aerial vehicles (UAVs).[3] UAVs make it possible for the military to fly a platform over targets or terrain relevant to military operations and gather and transmit information about them or attack them, and then return to the launch site to be used again.[4] Compared to the previous two cases, the military played a more authoritative role in decisions about building and using UAVs given the technical expertise often required to understand what the platforms could do. The case therefore tests how overall political salience affects whether civilians choose to exercise control or simply defer to each other and, especially, the military. After all, an obscure capability still in development does not have the political resonance of major shifts in international power or of a war. The UAV case, in fact, shows that until UAVs became salient in a political context, senior civilian controllers generally deferred to their civilian subordinates and military experts. Consequently, this case examines the choices made by undersecretaries and staff directors in addition to secretaries of defense, presidents, and armed services committee chairs.

The case of UAVs reveals an important dynamic behind civilian control choices: during wartime, civilians tend to defer to warfighter demands for capabilities because doing so builds a politically valuable reputation for supporting the troops. At the same time, civilians' endorsements of UAVs also increased because using them meant fewer American forces were sent into combat. Meanwhile, foreign publics' anger at drone warfare barely registered with civilian controllers. When it came to how the US military

Civilian Control and Capabilities   143

used force—in this case, developing, buying, and using UAVs—politics at home mattered much more to civilians than politics abroad.

Political Context

By the 1980s, the United States military had been trying to find uses for uninhabited aircraft for more than sixty years.[5] But small communities of UAV developers in the services could never overcome institutional antipathies or technical problems. All four military services concluded that their experiments with UAVs proved the platforms were too costly and frail to ever replace the manned surveillance and fighter aircraft. Consequently, and despite sustained UAV development efforts from the DoD's Advanced Research Project Agency (DARPA), service leaders continued to budget for those legacy platforms and underfund or cancel UAV programs (Dombrowski and Gholz 2006).

But when a UAV was useful and reliable as a reconnaissance and target-identifying capability in the skies over Bosnia and Kosovo, senior leaders at DoD began to pay attention. A few years later, the Predator flew its first mission over Afghanistan just weeks after the 9/11 attacks. Once the War on Terrorism began, UAV development, acquisition, and deployment increased rapidly. Colloquially known as "drones," UAVs were symbols of the War on Terrorism. As counterterrorism missions wound down, however, concerns about the technological sophistication of the growing Chinese military drove new thinking about UAVs and other kinds of autonomous systems. The perceived threat from China convinced many civilians and some military leaders to develop UAV capabilities and integrate them into war-fighting concepts, but the costs created competition for budget share, spurring others in DoD and on the Hill to defend legacy platforms and ways of fighting. Administrators often took sides in military arguments, and members of Congress championed platforms built by companies in their districts in the face of service opposition.

The success of the Predator was largely possible because the intelligence community had seen the value of uninhabited aircraft since 1960 when the Soviet Union shot down an American U2 spy plane and took the pilot hostage. To prevent another such crisis, the intelligence community had begun to develop uninhabited spy planes, footing the bill but relying on the organizational capacity at DARPA and the Air Force for engineers and remote pilots. The collaboration also meant that UAVs were originally designed to collect intelligence, not to be weapons delivery platforms. Although the services opposed combat applications for UAVs, they were more tolerant of intelligence, surveillance, and reconnaissance (ISR) platforms sponsored by the intelligence agencies.

UAV producers were among congressional constituents, and some businesses survived the early decades of UAV development by appealing to their members of Congress for help with government contracts. UAV makers were small businesses, though, making them a minor feature of the political landscape compared to the large defense industry contractors (Dombrowski and Gholz 2006). Once the larger companies, especially Northrop Grumman, General Atomics, Boeing, and Lockheed-Martin, began investing in uninhabited systems after 9/11, UAV policy became important to a wide range of domestic economic actors and therefore many members of Congress.

The budgetary politics of UAVs therefore went through phases connected to their technological development and their use in wartime. During the long development phase of UAV capabilities, UAVs were generally experimental research efforts and rarely transitioned to become major budget programs with enough sustained funding for aircraft—or the businesses producing them—to survive.[6] A belief among politicians that UAVs ought to be cheaper than inhabited planes also often set development efforts up for failure when members of Congress saw large bills associated with UAV research and development. Downward pressure on UAV spending melted away during the War on Terrorism, however, as UAV's endurance and usefulness matured just in time for the invasion of Afghanistan and the counterinsurgency operations in Iraq.

Wartime also elevated the domestic political salience of warfighters. Statistics on UAV use in Iraq after 2003 demonstrates how much data military personnel gathered through UAVs and suggests that information encouraged operators to use UAVs more. For example, between 2003 and 2006 UAVs' flight hours went up sevenfold to 300,000 hours per year (AP 2008). But warfighter demand kept increasing, especially during the long stabilization phase of the war. "It was only after the military turned to new counterinsurgency techniques in 2007," the *New York Times* reported, "that demand for drones became almost insatiable" (Drew 2009). The public admired military personnel's sacrifices and professionalism; civilian controllers were aware of warfighters' political status and valued their combat expertise. Civilian controllers therefore wanted to accommodate warfighters' preferences for the acquisition and uses of UAVs.

Finally, civilian defense intellectuals were a small but relevant group of actors who pressed for spending on UAVs for Iraq and Afghanistan and who later advocated for broadening the capabilities offered by UAVs to incorporate them in future conflicts with peer competitors, especially China. Defense intellectuals are important civilian partners to military leaders and form a key constituency for DoD administrators—partly because they often become administrators themselves, and partly because they contribute to public debates about the wisdom of civilian controllers' guidance, budgeting, and force management choices.

The Civilians

Each aspect of the political contexts outlined above triggered some part of civilians' professional or institutional identity and motivations to shape their UAV control choices. The War on Terrorism activated presidents' re-election concerns and their desire to leave a legacy that, at a minimum, did not involve a failed conflict or additional terrorist attacks. Presidents encouraged more spending on UAVs and deploying more of them to conduct operations without the risk to pilots that manned systems presented, and because UAVs enabled the long loiter times necessary for counterterrorism surveillance and strikes while minimizing risk to the lives of special operators on the ground.[7] Presidents did not press administrators or the military services to develop UAVs to offer new capabilities, leaving that level of guidance to their administrators. Members of Congress, on the other hand, applied budgetary pressures along two lines: the first was to develop UAVs at a low cost, especially relative to manned capabilities; the second was to develop specific platforms that benefited companies headquartered in their districts or that employed significant numbers of people in their

146   Chapter Five

districts or states. Both types of politician compelled spending on UAVs and deployment of the platforms in wartime so long as supplying warfighters with UAVs—along with other popular equipment—contributed to their political survival.

The case also explores how administrators' authority to settle disputes between military stakeholders often means they merely take sides in a debate led by the military. If they took the side of less-powerful military actors, they were often unable to exercise meaningful control. Again, the conditions of conflict and peace changed the political context and affected civilian control choices. In peacetime, UAV proponents—even the few interested civilian controllers—struggled to overcome service opposition to investments in the capability. Most civilian controllers simply deferred to service judgments about UAVs. But in wartime, warfighter preferences became more politically salient and administrators allied with them, resulting in more UAV investment and deployments. But even in the context of the War on Terrorism, Secretaries Rumsfeld and Gates could allocate money to buy more existing UAVs but they couldn't compel the services to rebalance their manned and unmanned investments for the long term, nor to develop new UAVs that provided a conventional combat capability. As Iraq and Afghanistan became politically unpopular, however, the military services gained the political upper hand once again.

Politicians and administrators alike wrestled with the ethics of UAVs. The civilian ethic pointed unambiguously toward using uninhabited systems because they reduced risk to military personnel by reducing ground operations and putting remote pilots in trailers far removed from battlefields. UAVs also generally offered greater targeting precision, reducing civilian casualties relative to other aerial and ground attack options. At the same time, reliably identifying suspected terrorist targets was difficult, and mistakes meant that the US military killed innocent people. Even with accurate intelligence and minimized casualties, pilots' mental health was adversely affected by spending long hours observing enemy targets and then triggering and witnessing their deaths (Dao 2013), leaving many pilots with posttraumatic stress and moral injury (Wood 2016).

Finally, the ethics of hunting "high-value targets" (terrorists) in the midst of civilian settings was a matter of ongoing debate. Was it better to prevent another mass murderer from staging more terrorist attacks? Or was it impossible to accurately identify the person or people the military was hunting, and killing them did not justify the loss of any innocent civilian lives? Politicians—especially Democrats—had constituents who were antidrone activists and who therefore played a greater role in their political contexts than for administrators. But administrators also grappled with the reputational implications of drone strike controversies for their institutions and for themselves. But for civilians in control positions, the political benefits of minimizing American military casualties tended to outweigh the risks.

LEGISLATIVE POLITICIANS

For members of Congress, three elements of political context drove how they used UAV development to exercise control over the use of force: constituent interests in the defense budget, their electoral relationships with defense industry funders, and warfighter demands for access to more UAVs. The salience of each of these factors varied over time and across individual members, however, and sometimes Congress was able to coordinate its control activities because they felt common political pressures and sometimes individual members of Congress acted on their own political survival interests.

These pan-congressional dynamics shaped how chairs of the armed services committees approached authorizing UAV development and funding. For a time, the armed services (and appropriations) committees attempted to enlist administrators at DoD as their allies in forcing the services to develop more capable UAVs at lower costs. After 9/11, when UAVs had recently become more capable, warfighter demand for more UAVs combined with a defense industry response to that demand signal. Therefore, for the first half of the case period, Congress generally tried to compel the military to develop UAVs while constraining the military's spending on the capability. In the post-9/11 wartime budget context, Congress deferred to DoD administrators and the military alike.

From the 1980s and into the 1990s, Congress didn't champion a particular approach to the use of force that made UAVs more relevant. Instead,

148   Chapter Five

individual services approached the Hill with UAV programs to which Congress reacted. Even then, legislative politicians focused on the costs of the systems. They believed uninhabited aircraft should be cheaper than those that carried pilots and were irritated by the duplication of UAV projects across the services which in their view wasted money. One Congressional Research Service report explained that in general, "armed services and appropriations committees in both houses have sought to encourage the procurement of UAVs because of their comparatively low cost . . . and to do so in a way that would avoid unnecessary duplication among any UAV programs that might be initiated" (Best 1993, 13). Congress didn't choose to exercise control over how the military fought so much as how they developed the tools they would use to fight. But for many years, that control was constraining, expressed via reductions in UAV budgets rather than forcing the Pentagon to rationalize UAV development across the entire military, let alone to justify the operational uses of uninhabited aircraft and how they fit into the military's force structure.

It was the Army's Aquila system that prompted legislative civilians to shift from constraining to compelling control over UAV development. By 1987, after ten years of work, the Army had spent a billion dollars on the Aquila (Blom 2010).[8] But, as the General Accounting Office reported, the Aquila was still "not ready for production."[9] Believing that centralized civilian management of service UAV projects would reduce redundancy and keep costs down, the armed services and appropriations committees used the budget to consolidate all service UAV programs under a single office and funding account managed by OSD. In the FY 1988 defense authorization and appropriations acts, the armed services committees and the defense appropriators took UAV spending authorities away from the services and gave it to OSD in the form of a new Unmanned Aerial Vehicle Joint Program Office (JPO or "Jay-Poe"). This move simultaneously controlled the military and civilian administrators, because it withheld the cash for UAV development until OSD, working with the services, provided Congress with a UAV "master plan."[10] It was an unusual act of coordination between the two committees, and an instance of politicians in the legislative branch forcing administrators in the executive to take control over a military capability themselves—a trick of civilians in one branch compelling the civilians in another to do something, but deferring to them on exactly what that something would be.

And it didn't work. UAV development costs kept climbing and the platforms continued to struggle under the technical demands heaped on them. As one historian noted, "In the years that JPO oversaw DoD development of UAVs, not a single system moved from development to full production" (Blom 2010). Noting the failure of JPO to produce a working UAV program, the House Appropriations Committee wrote in 1991, "the Committee sees a UAV requirements process that is clearly broken."[11] The SAC-D expressed similar frustrations, and the armed services committees conference report added the authorizing committees' "serious reservations over the management of these [UAV] programs by the joint project office."[12]

It was inauspicious timing where the politics of national budgeting were concerned. By the mid-1990s the politics of the post–Cold War peace dividend only made politicians in the legislative branch more skeptical of nonessential military capabilities. Congress therefore exercised increasingly tight control over DoD, mixing constraining and compelling legislative language to force DoD to buy more capable, lower-cost UAVs. The FY 1994 appropriations act, for example, specified that no money for the Hunter UAV could be disbursed until DoD supplied proof of successful tests for flight readiness and logistical support and had certified that at least two manufactured Hunters met those testing requirements.[13] This was a pattern that would repeat itself into the future. After the financial crisis of 2008, the then HASC Seapower and Projection Forces Subcommittee chair, Representative Randy Forbes (R-VA), wrote to the Navy of its Unmanned Carrier-Launched Airborne Surveillance and Strike (UCLASS) UAV, "the UCLASS platform must ensure long-term utility to warrant full funding amidst severe defense budget constraints" (Eckstein 2014). Forbes, a UCLASS champion, was not writing to discourage Navy investment, but to urge them to navigate the budgetary politics more wisely.

Congress was not always of a single mind about UAV development, however. For reasons of political survival—procurement contracts for their constituents—a few members of Congress were the source of continued legislative commitment to developing UAVs. Representative Jerry Lewis (R-CA) of the HAC-D was one such UAV champion. General Atomics, the maker of the Predator UAV, had a development and test site in his district at El Mirage Field. Lewis put $20 million for an endurance UAV in the FY 1995 appropriations bill (Whittle 2014). Representative Buck McKeon (R-CA), the HASC chair from 2011 to 2015, championed UAVs while Northrop Grumman, Boeing, and Lockheed Martin had UAV facilities in his district (McKelvey 2013). The ranking member of the House Appropriations Committee, Representative Norm Dicks (D-WA), directed funding toward Boeing, headquartered in Washington state, which developed the Dark Star UAV in the 1990s (Ehrhard 2010). These parochial projects kept UAV development alive through the budget reductions of the post–Cold War era, enough to continue spending on the Predator and sustain spending on UAV designs and testing.

Such efforts were so narrow, however, that they moderated the strength of legislative politicians' potential control over administrators and the military. Internecine competition for UAV dollars kept members of Congress deferential to how military proponents explained UAV requirements and fixated on their pet programs rather than a broader vision for UAV capabilities. And the disjointed approach kept most UAV projects from moving to the procurement phase of acquisition. Although the House appropriators and the House intelligence committee supported Dark Star, for example, the Senate was skeptical, in part because of testimony it received about "serious difficulty" with the platform. It cut $95 million from UAV programming as a result for fiscal year 1998 (CQ Almanac 1997). These fratricidal tendencies within Congress prevented the institution from compelling DoD to make progress on UAV development or to rationalize spending in precisely the way the defense oversight committees had hoped the JPO would do.

Despite the internal funding traffic jams, committee chairs managed to exercise power over UAV policy processes. Before McKeon leveraged his HASC chairmanship to advance UAV development, Senator John Warner had his first tour as the SASC chair. His interest in UAVs was spurred by his staff director, Les Brownlee, and the ideas behind defense transformation. Warner appreciated that UAVs did not risk the lives of pilots, and Brownlee's advocacy on behalf of the potential capabilities UAVs could bring to combat operations turned Warner into a proponent of not just developing the technology but buying actual systems and getting them into the service inventories. Yet, to his dismay, he encountered service resistance. They were simply not interested in conventional applications of UAVs, nor in replacing manned fighters and bombers with unmanned aircraft. Years later, he explained:

> I told the services, give me your budget submissions for UAVs, and they didn't come to me and they didn't put it in [budget proposals] and they fought it, and this went on for over two years. "Fellows, I'm offering you money for what you want, tell me what you want!" Finally, one night I was in a bar with some of these guys from the services and we're joking, and this guy had a little bit too much to drink. He was in the Air Force and he said "What you don't understand, Senator, is they look upon these things as taking our pilot seats away and we're all about pilots. Since the beginning of the Air Force that's what we've been about, pilots and pilot seats." I say, jeez, you're kidding me. I said enough's enough, I'm going to require it by statute.[14]

Warner then, as he put it, took out his "shotgun and fired it into the heavens," putting language into the 2001 NDAA compelling DoD to ensure that as of 2010, one-third of all "deep strike" aircraft across the military services would be uninhabited (Wilson 2000). Section 220 of the law stipulated, "It shall be a goal of the Armed Forces to achieve the fielding of unmanned, remotely controlled technology."[15] To enforce compliance, the law required the secretary of defense to submit a report fourteen months later detailing each military service's progress toward demonstrating technical feasibility and showing an "acquisition strategy" for combat UAVs in the future-years defense program. The incident demonstrated the SASC chair's power over the annual defense authorization—as well as the power of his staff director, who would have worked out the detailed legislative language in conference with his HASC counterparts—and how that vehicle helps Congress exercise control over executive civilians and the military alike.

We'll never know how effective Warner's legislative control mechanism would have been at compelling DoD to acquire combat UAVs, because a major element of the political context shifted eleven months later. 9/11 ushered in the War on Terrorism, the war in Afghanistan, and later the war in Iraq. Budgetary politics swung from long-term planning to short-term exigency.

152   Chapter Five

The Predator symbolized the shift in congressional control, proving Warner and Brownlee prescient while bypassing their specific guidance. The Predator demonstrated that UAVs could be very useful, but it was not the kind of combat platform the transformation community had been imagining just a few months prior. It was a medium-altitude, long-endurance hunter-killer UAV that worked best against enemies who didn't have sophisticated air defenses—an unconventional weapon for an unconventional war. Thoughts of replacing manned "deep strike" platforms with UAVs lost relevance. What the American military personnel on the ground in Afghanistan and later Iraq loved was the capability to find and attack terrorists and insurgents. UAVs gave them that capability.

Parochial and collective interests merged. The political clout of warfighter requests dovetailed with congressional electoral interests not only as a general matter of public opinion but also pertaining to business interests in a member's district. Representative Brian Bilbray (R-CA) for example requested an earmark for two Predator UAVs in 2009 after General Atomics donated $50,000 to his reelection campaign. Bilbray explained the move as a request from the commanding general in Afghanistan. "I could care less who makes the product if it's the best possible equipment we can get to protect our troops," he said (Sifuentes and Walker 2009). Bilbray's explanation that his budgeting was responsive to a warfighter request demonstrated the political utility of supporting the troops. The war also helped unify legislative politicians. Representatives Buck McKeon (R-CA) and Henry Cuellar (D-TX) cofounded the Congressional UAV Caucus (later renamed the Unmanned Systems Caucus), a kind of issue interest group that kept its members apprised of the politics of UAVs, including industry activities in members' districts (McKelvey 2013). As warfighter demand for UAVs increased and industry scrambled to offer platforms to meet those demands, members of Congress continued to respond to the double incentive to support the war effort and potential campaign funders. The result was increased spending overall.

But even during wartime, the defense budget was not immune from a national financial crisis, a budgetary context that, as with the peace dividend after the Cold War, involved more civilians in DoD budget controls than normal. As the effects of the housing market crash of 2008 spread

Civilian Control and Capabilities   153

throughout the economy, the public expected federal spending to focus on "main street" needs. By 2011, controversy over federal spending evolved into a crisis between Congress and the White House over the typically per-functory annual raise to the federal debt ceiling. Split between the major parties, the two branches eventually agreed to a measure that required $1.5 trillion in federal cuts over the next ten years—the Budget Control Act or BCA.[16] Although the BCA resolved the debt crisis in the short term, in the medium term it created a crisis for DoD budgeting by enacting a "sequester," an automatic and indiscriminate cut to discretionary spending if Congress could not agree to more tailored reductions by the deadline.

Even with the cuts associated with the Budget Control Act, legislative administrators and politicians protected spending on UAVs (Ackerman 2011). Between fiscal year 2010 and fiscal year 2019, administration requests for UAV accounts doubled from roughly $4.5 billion to more than $9 billion.[17] Spending on UAVs also dodged scrutiny because some of it was through the Overseas Contingency Operations (OCO) fund in addition to the "base budget" or main DoD budget request. OCO was the emergency war budget, supplementing the funds authorized and appropriated through the normal budgeting process, and it was not subject to the BCA sequester mechanism.[18] Because it bypassed many other standard civilian oversight checks on defense spending, its persistence throughout the war demonstrated legislative civilians' deference to civilians and the military in the executive. In 2018 alone more than 13 percent of spending on unmanned systems was funded from the OCO budget (Gettinger 2017). The persistence of OCO in the midst of a federal budget crisis also demonstrated that to members of Congress, supporting the war effort was even more important to their political survival than economic instability. Legislative politicians calculated that deferring to warfighter demands was the politically wisest choice.

EXECUTIVE ADMINISTRATORS

Most Americans—and many politicians—may only have learned about UAVs once the Predator went into large-scale production in the early 2000s, but administrators at DoD and their uniformed counterparts began

154   Chapter Five

to embrace the technology in the 1980s. They echoed legislative politicians in praising UAVs' ability to reduce risk to American military personnel. In a 1985 article, the new Pentagon undersecretary for research, development, technology, and engineering (RDT&E), Donald Hicks, told the *Washington Post*, "the United States can no longer afford to risk so many lives and airplanes against increasingly lethal Soviet defenses and must put more emphasis on unmanned weapons." Former secretary of defense Harold Brown and future secretary of defense William Perry joined Hicks in praising the potential capabilities uninhabited systems offered. Bolstering these administrators' assertions, retired Air Force Lieutenant General Kelly H. Burke (who had been the service's RDT&E chief) said, "There may be such a thing as a cheap airplane, but there's no such thing as a cheap American pilot" (Wilson 1985).

But DoD administrators still largely deferred to the military services on UAV development. The vicious cycle of congressional pressures on costs and duplicative UAV projects across the military services therefore continued. Although civilian controllers in DoD recognized the ethical and political benefits of reducing military casualties using technology advancements, the internal politics of the Pentagon meant inertia in terms of many capabilities development programs, UAVs included. It would take some kind of force to change the speed and direction of service UAV programs.

Verne "Larry" Lynn took office as the deputy undersecretary for advanced systems and concepts at just such a turning point: the war in Bosnia. The operational problem for which warfighters hoped there was a technical solution was the weather. Cloud cover over Bosnia blocked views for satellites and high-altitude spy planes, preventing policymakers and uniformed war planners alike from understanding the disposition of Serbian forces around Sarajevo, the besieged capital of Bosnia. At the same time, the domestic politics of the Bosnia intervention were controversial, and neither the outgoing Bush administration nor the new Clinton administration at that time could see a political benefit to involving American military personnel in the conflict—especially when they couldn't even make independent assessments of what intervention might entail. The US needed something that could get below the clouds and see what was going on without running the risks that Americans could be killed or captured.

Lynn had arrived at DoD already sold on UAV capabilities. He had participated in an OSD-sponsored study on strategic reconnaissance that praised long-endurance UAVs, and he had been convinced of their battlefield benefits (Van Atta et al. 2003). As the author of a history about the Predator UAV wrote, "In [Lynn's] view, drones were a potentially lifesaving reconnaissance technology that would have been operational by now if the armed services weren't so myopic or the acquisition system such a mire" (Whittle 2014, 76–77). Lynn proposed to his boss, Undersecretary of Defense for Acquisition, Technology, and Logistics (AT&L) John Deutch, that OSD create a Defense Airborne Reconnaissance Office to encourage investments in UAVs. Lynn also pitched Deutch on a rapid acquisition mechanism he called Advanced Concept Technology Demonstration (ACTD). Echoing the JPO mechanisms, both proposals were bureaucratic tools designed to compel the military services to commit to developing, testing, and buying UAVs at a larger and sustained scale. Deutch and Lynn used the first ACTD to get Predators flying over Bosnia.

Although the ACTD process was designed to compel the military to build more UAVs, it was also a venue for civilian deference to military preferences. The way that Lynn got the services to participate somewhat willingly in the ACTD process was by seeking the "early participation of the user community." This approach allowed military actors to guide the earliest stages of development for UAVs and determine their uses (Van Atta et al. 2003, 47). As the 1997 DoD Annual Report to Congress explained, ACTDs provided "the users with a basis for evaluating and refining their operational requirements, for developing a corresponding concept of operations, and ultimately for developing a sound understanding of the military utility of the proposed solution, before a formal acquisition decision" was made.[19] Executive administrators suspected UAVs were broadly useful, but their top-of-mind application for the capability was in the Balkans. They left military operators to fill in the gap between the immediate uses of the aircraft and the abstract possibilities, partly as a device for securing military participation in development, and partly because the politics of

156   Chapter Five

imagined wartime uses were not nearly so compelling to civilians as the politics of the war right in front of them.

Meanwhile, the technology making uninhabited aircraft flight more reliable increased its sophistication, and defense intellectuals inside and outside the Pentagon proposed a series of concepts they grouped under the titles "revolution in military affairs" and "transformation." Both rubrics embraced technological advances to imagine fundamental changes in the ways the US military would fight wars (Gray 2006). Uninhabited systems, with UAVs as the most proven platforms, were centerpieces for these ideas. And the entire conceptual edifice turned on a new kind of combat that reduced casualties—effectively buying down the political costs of warfare.

Having demonstrated their utility in the wars in the Balkans in the 1990s, UAV capabilities piqued the interest of a growing number of civilian administrators at increasingly senior levels. When Donald Rumsfeld became President George W. Bush's secretary of defense, he was an advocate for the transformation concept of changing DoD force structure and the military's operational activities by embracing new technologies (Dombrowski and Gholz 2006). UAVs fit perfectly into the transformation theory of defense organization. And initially, he had a supportive SASC chair in the person of John Warner. But Rumsfeld struggled with the bureaucratic politics—including interagency politics—of fielding UAVs to the operational force. "When [UAVs] first had been ready for operations," he writes in his memoir, "Defense and CIA officials debated over who would control them and who would pay for their use" (Rumsfeld 2011, 389). In his 2002 Annual Report to Congress, he leveraged UAV's successes in Afghanistan and the appeal of their low risk profile to pole-vault over legacy service foot dragging. "Unmanned surveillance and attack aircraft like Global Hawk and Predator offered a glimpse of their potential in Afghanistan," he reported. "The 2003 budget increases the number of unmanned aircraft being procured and accelerates the development of new unmanned combat aerial vehicles capable of striking targets in denied areas without putting pilots at risk" (House of Representatives 2002, 200). To work around Air Force resistance to trading their preferred fighter jets for UAVs,

Rumsfeld simply added the remote systems to the normal budget items the service wanted, giving it "the largest budget of the services—$107 billion" along with "most of the UAV and UCAV increases" (Loeb 2002). In this way, Rumsfeld mixed compelling the service to adopt UAVs with deferring to their budgetary and force structure preferences.

Despite Rumsfeld's efforts, service opposition persisted, and civilian administrators at all levels encountered that resistance. This was especially the case when proposed UAVs might replace traditional inhabited fighter jets. The Joint Unmanned Combat Aerial System was one such victim (Axe 2011b). In 2004, the Defense Science Board, a kind of combination board of advisors and think tank for the undersecretary for acquisition, technology, and logistics, published a study on UAVs that observed organizational cultures made the military services "reluctant to incorporate unmanned systems into the regular force structure." But it also depicted the "pressure on the military by political authorities and the general public to minimize casualties and capture of aircrews by the enemy" along with and "perhaps most importantly, the generally high marks accorded Predator and Hunter during Operation Allied Force in the 1999 air war against Serbia, and . . . to Predator and Global Hawk during Afghanistan operations, and to UAVs overall in Operation Iraqi Freedom" (Defense Science Board 2004, 3–4). Civilians continued to choose compelling control over military headquarters to meet political demands to reduce risks to servicemembers—and to give warfighters what they wanted. The civil-military fights over UAVs showed civilian administrators' tendency to mix exercising control over the military with deferring to it, often by control of one element of the bureaucratic military and deferring to another. In wartime, the service headquarters lost political power relative to warfighters, and civilian administrators and politicians alike managed to compel the services in part by deferring to the warfighters.

Although the successful use of the Predator and Global Hawk systems in Afghanistan boosted interest in UAVs, it took the war in Iraq to institutionalize commitment to the capabilities they provided. The domestic politics of Iraq vaunted the warfighter into a political and social status that prioritized their preferences over other political pressures. By the time

158   Chapter Five

Robert Gates became secretary of defense, his embrace of UAVs at warfighters' behest was wholesale. As he writes in his memoir:

> I directed [CJCS Admiral Michael Mullen] to develop and implement a process by which I would be informed immediately of *any* request specifically addressed to me by our commanders in Iraq and Afghanistan. The immediate problem . . . was the difficulty we were having in meeting our field commanders' need for intelligence, surveillance, and reconnaissance (ISR) capabilities. (Gates 2014, 127)

This small move wasn't nearly enough for Gates to overcome persistent service resistance. So, Gates also directed the Air Force's top military officer and its civilian secretary to submit a plan to increase UAV procurement, a plan that disappointed him with its overlong timeline. Complaining that "the military too often stifled younger officers, and sometimes more senior ones, who challenged current practices," Gates next tried to compel reallocation of UAVs to Iraq and Afghanistan by setting up an ISR task force (Gates 2014, 133). Led by the civilian director of program assessment and evaluation, the ISR task force was not solely about UAVs, but its first order of business was to examine specific uninhabited aircraft, including the Predator (Muñoz 2008). Announcing the task force before an audience at Maxwell Air Force Base, Gates explained, "In my view, we can do—and we should do—more to meet the needs of men and women fighting in the current conflicts while their outcome may still be in doubt" (Gates 2008). Gates also selected General Norton (Norty) Schwartz to be chief of staff of the Air Force in part because Gates believed Schwartz would support UAV procurement. In his own memoir, Schwartz acknowledges "the traditional 'fighter/bomber' culture seemed to cloud the leaders' abilities to consider new paradigms" (Schwartz and Schwartz 2018, 255).

At the same time that Gates was trying to compel the military to build and use UAVs, he was trying to evade congressional control over his efforts. Gates relays in his memoir that "congressional appropriations committees . . . continued to press for dissolution of the task force and a return to regular procedures." To confuse congressional overseers, Gates confesses, "I changed the structure of the task force a couple of times—and renamed it in the Obama administration—which amounted to a bit of a shell game with the Hill." He justifies his evasion of congressional control by echoing other civilians' deference to warfighter demands. The task force, he explains, was "a mechanism at my disposal in Washington that could effectively serve the commanders in the field" (Gates 2014, 133). To win a war in service of two presidents, Gates deferred to warfighters, controlled service headquarters, and dodged Congress.

Gates's approach to controlling UAV policy during the Obama administration did not change from his approach during the Bush presidency, and neither did warfighter demand, except in the sense that it kept expanding to fill the space allotted—which itself appeared nearly infinite. One former senior OSD official under Obama confirmed that upon entering office, the Obama team learned first-hand that "the demand from CENTCOM for ISR in Afghanistan was insatiable."[20] One former Obama official also found in subsequent research on policymaker attitudes toward UAVs that "demand rather than effectiveness and appropriateness often set the pace for drone allocation under the Obama administration" (Schulman 2018, 1). As the undersecretary for AT&L's 2012 report to Congress on UAS training and sustainment explained it, "The emphasis on long-endurance, unmanned intelligence, surveillance and reconnaissance (ISR) assets—many with strike capabilities—is a direct reflection of recent operational experience and further Combatant Commander demands" (US Under Secretary of Defense 2012).

That is not to say that domestic politics applied consistent pressures on civilian administrators. Controversy over federal spending in 2011 threatened to overwhelm civilian efforts to control capabilities development for the wars in Iraq and Afghanistan. As a preemptive maneuver, Secretary Gates undertook an "efficiencies" process to seek savings in the DoD budget before Congress imposed them, and he used the final submission to protect UAVs from deep cuts (Axe 2011a).

Meanwhile, with the waning of the Iraq war came a commensurate decline in warfighter political salience—removing the element of the political context that helped civilians unify around UAVs—and a resurgence in competing service interests in other kinds of capabilities. The *Unmanned Systems Integrated Roadmap for FY2013–2038* by the undersecretary of defense AT&L illustrated the shifts in the political context. The report noted the "downward pressures" on the defense budget and the resulting

160   Chapter Five

need for cost savings—including an approximately 34 percent reduction in RDT&E for unmanned systems in the coming fiscal year. The report echoed the language of the 1980s with its emphasis on UAVs as cheaper than manned platforms: "Unmanned systems must provide capabilities with superior cost, schedule, and performance metrics to compete against other systems" (DoD 2013, 21). It also observed the ongoing priority of reducing risk to American personnel, something UAVs offered by design. As the authors explained, reducing dangers to personnel allowed UAVs to perform missions that would be too risky using manned platforms: "Unmanned systems will be critical to US operations in all domains across a range of conflicts, both because of their capability and performance advantages and because of their ability to take greater risk than manned systems" (DoD 2013, 14). And it struggled with "questions that extend quickly beyond mere engineering challenges into legal, policy, or ethical issues." These included "what overarching guiding principles should be used to help discern where more oversight and direct human control should be retained" (DoD 2013, 15).

DoD administrators believed they had adequate answers to these questions, especially that they balanced legal concerns with operational objectives. Secretary of defense from 2011 to 2013, Leon Panetta argues in his memoir that "the singular preoccupation with drones distracts from the larger context of the struggle we are waging." The technology itself was beside the point, in Panetta's view. Instead, decision makers focused on how drones were used and why—under the rule of law to protect American lives. According to Panetta, uses and purposes were the important considerations and should logically precede the selection of capabilities. Moreover, Panetta argues that UAVs minimize the carnage of war, because of their precision and the long-associated benefit of reducing risk to American military personnel. "All of which," Panetta concludes, "argues not only for the effectiveness of unmanned aerial vehicles but also for their morality" (Panetta 2014, 391).

The renewed budgetary pressures once again cut into UAV development, but spending during the Afghanistan and Iraq wars was high and sustained enough that a few systems found their way into long-term programs. The Predator in particular has left a legacy on the UAV fleet, as many UAVs in use by the US military today derive technology and even their airframe designs from the Predator (Hoehn and Kerr 2022). By the end of 2019, DoD was still receiving deliveries of MQ-9 Reaper UAVs, the Predator's offspring, and had orders for more through fiscal year 2023.[21]

EXECUTIVE POLITICIANS (PRESIDENTS)

Although the president submits a proposal for the federal budget to Congress each year, and the proposal includes funding for the DoD, presidents do not typically engage in decision making about developing military capabilities. Instead, they tend to delegate those decisions to their secretaries of defense and other civilian administrators to help control defense budgeting and force management decisions at that level of specificity. The reason for this has partly to do with the level of detail involved, but it also has to do with political context. Most Americans do not cast votes for president on the basis of UAV policy. Thus, other than Barack Obama (whose particular political context pressed him to address UAVs), presidents exercised control indirectly over whether and how the military fought using uninhabited aircraft.

Bill Clinton inspired the CIA and DoD to find the Predator (and in the CIA's case, its less capable variant, the Gnat) to supply him with more information about the military posture of Serbian forces around Sarajevo (Whittle 2014). But in that case, he deferred to his intelligence and defense administrators and military advisors. He triggered using the Predator again at the end of his second term when he authorized a hunt for Osama bin Laden in Afghanistan—but again, he didn't specifically compel use of the Predator, but relied on his subordinates to determine the most useful tools. Instead, he was responding to the political contexts of war and terrorism to give general guidance. Even in blessing some of the ideas behind the so-called revolution in military affairs, Clinton did not connect politics to UAVs.

George W. Bush embraced a similar set of ideas as the so-called revolution in military affairs on the campaign trail but approached UAVs more closely. As early as 1999 in a speech at the Citadel, candidate Bush declared, "Our forces in the next century must be agile, lethal, readily deployable."

162   Chapter Five

He went on to describe the kinds of capabilities that UAVs were on the cusp of being able to provide: "Our military must be able to identify targets by a variety of means. . . . Then be able to destroy those targets almost instantly" (Bush 1999). It is no wonder then that he reportedly said, after taking a briefing on Predator strikes in Afghanistan, "We ought to have 50 of these things" (Woodward 2002, 223). Within two months, he was back at the Citadel again as president telling the cadets, "The military does not have enough unmanned vehicles. We're entering an era in which unmanned vehicles of all kinds will take on greater importance" (Bush 2001e). The political pressure to win a war while reducing casualties was the major contextual factor for George W. Bush.

For Barack Obama, the politics of UAVs were a balance between suppressing the political costs of military casualties and the ethics of remote-control killing. Especially as American operations in Iraq wound down, Obama's administration found itself defending reported drone strikes in Pakistan, Somalia, and Yemen—countries outside areas publicly understood to be war zones. Although classification issues and the difficulty of attributing strikes to DoD or the CIA make the real number of strikes hard to track, President Obama began to build a reputation for embracing UAVs for counterterrorism operations. Public criticism mounted. In April 2013, the *New York Times* editorial board ran a piece entitled, "The Trouble with Drones." In it they argued, "popular discontent with the drone program has built slowly as drone missions grew from 50 strikes under President George W. Bush to more than 400 under President Obama, and it dawned on Americans that remote-controlled killing had become a permanent fixture of national policy" (Editorial Board 2013). The president had leaned into the use of drones for counterterrorism partly to minimize the domestic political risks from military casualties, and now he was facing a domestic political backlash for using drones too much.

A little over a month later, at the National Defense University in Washington, DC, the president revealed his new Presidential Policy Guidance, "Procedures for Approving Direct Action Against Terrorist Targets Located Outside the United States and Areas of Active Hostilities."[22] He succinctly asserted the effectiveness of drone strikes while spending the balance of the speech assuring the public that "the use of drones is heavily constrained" and conducted within legal parameters (Obama 2013). The announcement was designed to reduce domestic political pressure.

He did so partly by adjusting the way he controlled the military's use of UAVs. The Presidential Policy Guidance, which has since been declassified, was a way for the president and his White House advisors to constrain how the military conducted terrorist attacks, and UAVs were an element of that control. And they exercised that control because of the way executive politicians interpret domestic politics. In Obama's case, a legal justification for using UAVs derived from how he campaigned for office and presented his administration: His was a team defined by being scrupulous. To ensure values drove the use of force, policy judgments were required to approve drone strikes. The process then involved the preparation of operational plans, legal and policy reviews by the agencies with chairs on the NSC, and precautions to ensure the correct targets had been identified and civilian casualties can be avoided. It was methodical and bureaucratic, clearly designed to prevent rushed decisions even as it provided a continued pathway to using UAV strikes as a major part of ongoing counterterrorism policy.

Conclusion

The interactions of political context and civilian type do not just affect civilian control choices over whether to go to war, how much to spend on the overall defense budget, or how many troops to deploy overseas. Politics also shape why civilians make the force structure choices they do. Over forty years, UAV development and deployment showed that political pressures permeate the bureaucracy. It is not just presidents and armed services chairs who calculate their choices based on which issues are salient to voters and other powerful people; administrators at lower levels of the legislative and executive branches understood the art of the politically possible—whether those politics were national or bureaucratic.

The case also shows how both civilians and the military can evade efforts to control their actions. Politicians' efforts to constrain military spending on UAVs failed repeatedly, and administrators' efforts to press the services to develop combat UAVs met even more resistance. At numerous points, politicians and administrators alike chose to defer to military preferences regarding guidance for the development and uses of UAVs. At first, military preferences were to limit the uses of UAVs to intelligence platforms. But as the Predator, in particular, became useful to warfighters, their advocacy reshaped the political context for civilians, and thereby invigorated civilians' efforts at controlling how the military fought the War on Terrorism. For politicians, public support for the military in general suggested they would earn voter approval by answering (or at least not ignoring) warfighter demands. Administrators read this prevailing political context for politicians and also wanted to perform their own roles well—and when their political bosses and their bureaucracies were aligned, they went along.

Even over seemingly technocratic aspects of defense policy, politics and professional roles shape civilian control choices.

CONCLUSION

The Civilian Ethic

IT WAS THE FIRST DAY of June, and the president of the United States asked the CJCS to accompany him on a walk. The setting was unusual for a president and his chairman. Protestors associated with the Black Lives Matter movement had been gathering in DC for several days to demonstrate for racial justice as part of a nationwide wave of marches. The president had responded by calling up the National Guard to increase security around the White House. That day in June, the US Park Police forcibly removed protestors from the area in front of St. John's Episcopal Church at the far side of Lafayette Square across from the presidential residence. The incident was covered prominently in the media. Later in the day, as the president and the chairman walked across Lafayette Square, reporters filmed them and took pictures.

Although a later Department of Interior inspector general report found no connection between the Park Police's actions and the president's visit to the church, at the time a media firestorm ensued.[1] Ten days later, General Mark Milley apologized for accompanying the president on the walk across Lafayette Square in such a controversial political context. "I should not have been there," he said in a prerecorded commencement speech for National Defense University. "My presence in that moment, and in that environment, created the perception of the military involved in domestic politics" (Lamothe 2020). Milley was taking responsibility for his part in violating a principle of civil-military relations—that of the nonpartisan nature of the military.

But it was the president who asked Milley to be there. Trump, a politician running for reelection amid domestic unrest, violated the civilian ethic by using the CJCS to project control over domestic stability—in one sense, to suggest control over other civilians. For Trump, it was not an unusual reaction to the political context. He had been referring to the military as partisan loyalists throughout his presidency.[2]

But the event, while breaking new ground in one sense, had antecedents. "Many presidents," civil-military relations scholar Richard Kohn explained to one reporter at the beginning of Trump's term in office, "pander to the military and through it to voters who focus on national defense." Kohn allowed that Trump was unusual in that his speeches to military personnel often "mimicked a campaign rally" (Gordon 2017b). But he wasn't the first politician to use the military when campaigning. In recent decades, presidential candidates have built lists of retired military officers who endorsed their bids for president using their military ranks—a clear violation of the principle of treating the military as a nonpartisan actor.[3] Candidates for Congress have also increasingly referred to their approval among military officers, or to their own experience in the armed forces, some going so far as to use their rank upon retirement in official campaign materials. Politicians are tempted to invoke their bona fides with military personnel because the latter have long been popular with Americans. As one news article put it, party officials often "see candidates with a military pedigree as an appealing contrast to entrenched, career politicians" (Huetteman 2017).[4] The contrast is rooted in a shared belief that a military identity suggests more competence, more wisdom, and more honor than that possessed by the average civilian official (Krebs, Ralston, and Rappaport 2021).

Accompanying civilian controllers' waning legitimacy in comparison to military personnel is a reduction in civilian mastery of military matters. Although civilians' expertise is in politics, integrating military policy into politics requires sufficient knowledge of military affairs. Yet studies of defense and national security bureaucracies in democracies around the

The Civilian Ethic   167

world show a decline in civilian defense expertise and a steady delegation of civilian policy roles to senior military officers (Pion-Berlin, Acacio, and Ivey 2019; Kim 2014). This development allows the military more opportunities to influence defense policy, thus undermining civilian authority (Pion-Berlin and Trinkunas 2007).

What ought to counterbalance the civilian tendency to act in accordance with their own political survival is something I call the *civilian ethic*—that is, civilians' duty to protect the organizational health of the military, treat those who volunteer with dignity and respect, and guard the country against military influence in domestic politics. But if politicians and administrators keep losing sight of the civilian ethic and continue to defer to their copartisans and the military itself, they risk abdicating their control responsibilities and thereby politicizing the military.

Summary of the Argument

By design, civilian control of the military in the United States is hamstrung. Because the Founders were so anxious about a despotic civilian leader gaining control of the military, they ensured that civilian leaders could always check each other's power. But that dynamic almost universally precludes the unity among civilian policy and political commitments necessary to exercise strong control over the military instrument. Instead, as the cases in this book showed, the executive and legislative branches, themselves divided among politicians and administrators, are nearly doomed to make guidance, budgeting, and force management decisions that often contradict each other or at least diverge in ways that undercut effective defense and civilian control. This may be the subliminal reason that civil-military relations scholars in the United States have overemphasized military professional self-policing when it comes to nonpartisanship and subordination to civilian control: in reality, if the military does not separate itself from domestic partisan power struggles and make itself obey the chain of command, civilians are unlikely to unite effectively against a rogue military institution.[5]

And yet, this overemphasis has deferred too much to the military. This book has argued that civilians are worthy of study in their own right

168   Conclusion

because they still play the defining role in the civil-military relationship, a role carved out by their status, functions, and expertise. They have authoritative control over government to establish social order and allocate public resources. They are charged not only with controlling the military itself but also with controlling each other's uses of the military. To perform these functions in the democratic context, civilians become experts in politics. They understand the processes behind making collective decisions. They also become expert administrators of the branches of government in which they serve.

The professional and institutional features of American government mean that the most prominent civilians in positions of control over military policy divide into professional-institutional types. In the legislative and executive branches there are politicians and administrators. Politicians propose rules and survive in office by winning votes. Administrators implement rules and run government organizations, and they survive in office by winning the confidence of politicians and maintaining positive professional reputations among their peers and the bureaucracies they run.

Being a civilian is a role, but it is also an identity, and that identity allows for variation in beliefs across individuals. Civilians choose careers as politicians or administrators, in part because they are animated by certain core beliefs and traits. Politicians approach the world differently than administrators, not just by virtue of their formal-legal responsibilities, but also because they prefer the notoriety, the relationships with constituents, and the power to influence a broad range of issues. Administrators tend toward specialization in particular areas of foreign and security policy and toward executive leadership. Administrators do not choose to become politicians, but politicians must also choose them, much the way voters choose politicians. Administrators' dependence on politicians makes them sensitive to the political climate, and their desire to lead organizations effectively attunes them to bureaucratic politics.

This combination of institutional imperatives and professional convictions shapes civilian interactions in the exercise of control over military policy and can vary from person to person. From a democratic perspective, this is not a bad thing. For voting to be a meaningful choice, different candidates for public office must behave at least somewhat differently in the same institutional position. But the exigencies of office exercise strong, systematic influences on civilians' choices.

The cases show this systematic association between professional-institutional type, political context, and control choices. They illustrate how civilians interpret political contexts to exercise constraining and compelling control via the mechanisms of guidance, budgeting, and force management. They also show that civilians will defer to each other or to the military when they judge that doing so helps their chances of professional survival.

In the immediate post–Cold War period, the domestic political context exercised strong influence on politicians' and administrators' control choices. The economic recession of 1989–1992, which coincided with the collapse of the Soviet Union, drove domestic demand for a "defense dividend," a reinvestment of federal spending in domestic programs at the expense of military budgets. Although George H. W. Bush and Bill Clinton subscribed to very different political ideologies, they both acknowledged the domestic political context demanded cuts to defense spending. Both politicians therefore issued strategic guidance, and endorsed DoD budgets, designed to address regional threats with a smaller, cheaper force structure. They also both launched interventions in foreign conflicts in response to domestic and international political pressures. Meanwhile, the chairs of the SASC and HASC adjudicated partisan interests based on pressures from pro- and anti-defense-spending constituents. When their co-partisans occupied the White House, they were especially careful to walk the line between party solidarity and congressional control over executive policymaking, showing how civilian control of civilians is mediated significantly by party identity.

The secretaries of defense after the Cold War struggled to balance political incentives with military preferences with varying degrees of success. Dick Cheney, who had become secretary just as he was beginning to amass power as a member of the House of Representatives, was attuned well enough to domestic partisan politics to understand when he was unlikely to achieve his often more-conservative goals. He was also careful to strike a balance between deferring to military advice and reminding

170   Conclusion

senior officers to act consistently with administration policy. In contrast, Les Aspin read political context badly and did not develop strong trust relationships with either the military or the White House; as a consequence, he lost the president's confidence and then his job. William Perry benefited from taking office after the Clinton White House had already gone through a period of learning about the significant political clout of the military and its partners in Congress, and mainly focused on the administrative and technocratic aspects of his position without contradicting the president's political goals, including regarding the intervention in Bosnia.

The case studies of the war in Afghanistan and UAVs demonstrated how politically powerful the military can become in wartime, and how all types of civilians will often defer to the military and Congress will defer to the president on force management decisions. Regarding Afghanistan, both Obama and Trump read in the domestic political context a public losing interest in the war and wavering in its support for deploying more forces, yet they also both faced and folded to early military pressure to increase the American troop presence, and both pressed for reductions at the tail ends of their presidencies. For both presidents, their own secretaries of defense joined forces with the military. It is hard to perceive whether secretaries' agreement with their military advisors is sincere or bureaucratically expedient. But Gates, Panetta, and Esper all acknowledge in their memoirs that they attempted to manage the relationship between senior military officers and the White House, and to act as translators even as they fought to defend their own prerogatives. All three evince patterns of "on the one hand, on the other hand" thinking, and all three concede that when presidents felt strongly, they felt compelled to obey—or, in Mattis's case, resign. Across the Bush, Obama, and Trump administrations the politics of NATO participation in the war and Afghan domestic politics were important but secondary factors in president's force management decisions. Analysis of NATO politics were often more aspirational than realistic; the same was true of how presidents thought about Afghan and broader South Asian politics. In particular, presidents misread Pakistani politics as open to revising its perception of the threat from India and dismantling its mutually beneficial relationship with the Taliban. This miscalculation of the international political context perhaps generated false confidence

The Civilian Ethic   171

that increases in the number of troops could generate long-term changes in the balance of power between the Afghan government and the Taliban.

SASC chairs had little influence over force management during the Afghan war, in part because their committee tended to be of two minds: no politician wanted to advocate a policy that might lose the war, but most politicians also read public opinion to be ambivalent at best about escalating the war with more troops. Senator McCain cut an unusual figure with his strong support of committing more forces at multiple decision points, including against his own copartisan in the White House. Both he and Trump were unusual personalities, however, illustrating the difference that individuals can make even within the strictures of professional-institutional incentives.

The UAV case best demonstrates the tension between military and civilian expertise (discussed more below), and also provides a view of civilian control at lower levels of government hierarchy. The military feels proprietary about their capabilities, generally believing their expertise is more relevant to the development of military technology and tactics than civilian expertise. But under the Constitution, civilians "raise and support" the military and allocate resources for doing so. Choosing the types of military capabilities the country develops presents a series of political decisions about where to accept risk, where to direct finite resources, and which interests to protect.

Yet UAV development and use is an illustrative case of civilian deference to the military, especially in wartime. After 9/11, neither politicians nor administrators constrained warfighter demand for UAVs—on the contrary, they did what they could to supply as many UAVs as they could, sometimes over the objections of the military departments themselves. Prior to 9/11, civilians left guidance about the uses of UAVs largely up to the services. The control they exercised was over budgets for UAVs, which they generally tried to constrain unless their constituents had an interest in particular budget line items. Such parochialism meant UAV development was extended and halting. Once UAVs were beloved by warfighters, claiming to rush them to the front had political benefits. The UAV case thus shows the difference that wartime makes for the civilian control choices, even regarding narrow capabilities, but it does so in contradiction of some

172   Conclusion

of the classic literature that argues civilians exercise more control when threats are existential. This was also true in the case of the Afghanistan war. But in the UAV case, civilian deference was only to part of the military. Civilians were more likely to defer to the preferences of the operational military during war, but this often meant siding with warfighters over the military departments. Secretary Gates in particular pressed the Air Force to invest more in UAVs.

All three cases show the considerable overlap in civilian and military expertise and administrative capabilities, something that can make civilian control over the military contentious in times of disagreement. After all, military officers also run large government organizations, and despite their idealized apolitical status, those in the senior ranks regularly engage in political processes to pursue their budgetary and force management preferences. They are also adept at shaping the guidance civilians give them—something I have explored in depth previously (Friend 2020a). Despite clarity in their status, the firewall between civilian and military functions can look artificially drawn, simply a division of labor between otherwise interchangeable national leaders. But this is because what divides civilians from the military is not their innate capacities, but what structures their patterns of behavior and thought. Huntington's argument that there is no single civilian mind dismissed the task of conceptualizing civilians too hastily. Military officers follow and enforce the rules; civilians *make* the rules. The personalities drawn to a political or administrative career combined with the features of that career mold the individuals we call "civilian" in different ways than the individuals we call "military." The cases bear this out. Presidents and members of Congress look to public opinion to determine popular priorities; administrators tack between political pressures and technocratic rationales, enjoying governance while preferring force structure debates over polling numbers.

In each of the cases, politicians are consumed by politics, and rightly so: their role in government and in civil-military relations is to build and use political expertise. This is not to say that they are ignorant of or unaffected by purely military considerations, but their control choices are generally shaped by the political contexts they encounter. Politicians are pragmatists in that way, but political pragmatism can lead to military fantasizing.

The Civilian Ethic   173

Believing that regional wars can be mitigated, or new defense technologies developed at low costs, or that a few thousand more troops might turn the tide of a war imagines the future based on what is politically rather than materially feasible. Administrators, for their part, struggle more than politicians to navigate domestic politics, although they tend to do better with bureaucratic politics and almost always compel military action more effectively than presidents and members of Congress. Civilians who combine political and administrative expertise seem best positioned to control the military and other civilians.

Toward an Agenda for Further Research on Civilians

I wrote this book for three audiences. The first audience is civilians themselves. Civilian defense policy practitioners have few sources to which they can turn to understand their role in the civil-military relationship. Although most of them know instinctively that they occupy a status, fulfill specific functions, and have mastered political expertise, this book gives them a systematic framework for thinking about what it means to be a civilian, the responsibilities they have under the civilian ethic, and what their professional backgrounds and institutional positions mean for how they participate in democratic control of military policy. The concept and framework building chapters together with the case studies show civilian practitioners that their job is both vital and nearly impossible, because the need to control other civilians often conflicts with the exercise of civilian control of the military. Civilian unity facilitates control over the military but is hard to achieve unless some civilians defer to others. In many cases, a civilian or group of civilians enlists the military's assistance to compete with political opponents, a phenomenon that aids in controlling other civilians but violates the civilian ethic and degrades control of the military.

That civilian control is a contradictory phenomenon is already well understood by civil-military relations scholars. Democratic civil-military relations are filled with normative paradoxes—two or more ideals that need to be true for democracy to function but that counteract each other so fundamentally that there can never be a stable equilibrium in the civil-military relationship.[6] Countries need strong militaries to survive external

174 Conclusion

threats, but strong militaries make the state vulnerable to internal coercion (Feaver 1996). Military professionals are expected to give apolitical, technocratic advice. Yet military advice has enormous political utility and "politics pervades nearly all aspects [of] military affairs" (Travis 2019, 3). And because "civilians solicit and rely on military expertise to fulfill their control functions, military expertise informs the manner in which civilians exercise that control" (Friend and Younis 2020).

Naturally, attempts to put paradoxical values into practice result in constant violations of those values. The contradictory nature of civil-military norms is the basis for declarations from scholars like Richard Kohn and Eliot Cohen that civil-military relations should be thought of as a dialogue, and civilian control of the military as a process. The persistent and inevitable civilian and military intrusion into each other's spheres of influence also contributes to equally persistent claims that civil-military relations in the United States is in crisis.

As the legally and hierarchically superior actor in the civil-military relationship, civilians shoulder more of the responsibility for navigating these minefields of contradictory expectations. But more and more, American society places the burden of civil-military equilibrium on military officers. We expect them to subordinate themselves to civilian rule, maintain their nonpartisanship, and limit their influence on public policy to the defense sector. We do not hold civilians to commensurate standards. The penalties for deferring to military preferences or involving the military in politics are social and electoral, and the eroding norms of civilian control have meant that in recent years, voters and civilian controllers' peers have levied those penalties less and less frequently.

Another, and significant, shortfall in civilian performance has been how representative they are—or rather, are not. The overwhelming majority of civilian controllers throughout American history have been White and male. One Black man and no women have been president. Ditto the secretary of defense. SASC chairs have always been White and male. Among the roles mentioned in these pages, the national security advisor has most often departed from the gender and racial standard: Although White men still make up the majority of national security advisors, two Black women and one Black man (as well as two Jewish men and a [closeted] gay man)

The Civilian Ethic 175

have also held the post.[7] Civil-military relations scholars often claim that civilian control of the military is more democratic, but the narrow, unrepresentative demographics of those who actually wind up in the roles responsible for exercising that control weakens that claim.

If civilians can't win, and if we expect so little of them as a culture, should they even try? The answer is yes. Democracy is not designed for perfect victories, but for compromise. In occupying their authoritative status, performing their governing functions, using their political expertise, and acting according to the civilian ethic, civilian controllers get us closer to policies based on shared values than we might be otherwise. There is a meaningful difference between the secretary of defense who tells a combatant commander to use his own judgment and the secretary who constrains military action to guard against future abuses. A SASC chair who does not hold oversight hearings removes a brake on civilian military adventurism. These politicians and administrators—with their civilian staffs, who deserve a book of their own—also preserve the capabilities and capacity of American defense while helping the military remain nonpartisan in domestic politics, ensuring it can implement the policies of whatever Congress or president is temporarily in power. That these functions are practiced imperfectly does not mean the attempt should be abandoned. They are among the activities that keep our country a democracy.

Of course, civilians cannot do all of this without significant cooperation from the military. Although the book puts the military much more to the side than most studies of civil-military relations, its second audience is military personnel. Military personnel, especially midcareer officers, tend to learn more about civil-military relations in classroom settings than civilians do, but the field's bias toward military institutions and behavior and its aversion to the political aspects of the relationship teach future military leaders a simplistic model of civilian behavior. The preceding chapters laid out the broader context for military policy choices and provide insights into civilian incentives and constraints. Most of all, they showed that civilians incorporate political factors into their control decisions so they can incorporate military policy into politics. Officers often understand, in an abstract sense, that civilians consider a broader context than that at the tactical and operational levels. But without specific examples, it

176   Conclusion

can be frustrating when politicians do not give commanders exactly what they believe they need to win a war or succeed at their missions. And it is easy to dismiss such constraints as ignorant or self-serving. Officers who understand that their advice is just one factor among the many that weigh on policymakers and that domestic politics in a democracy will often, as former CJCS Martin Dempsey used to put it, "tie one arm behind our backs" will be better servants of the American people whose values and preferences the politicians are attempting to referee.

The third audience is academics, who I hope will take what I have started here and go further. There is much left to do. Pioneering the study of civilians in the civil-military context means resetting Americans' ideas about politics and scholars' ideas about how to study politics and the military together. Increasingly, "political" is a derogatory term, associated with corruption and controversy. Disappointment and disgust with the quality of political discourse in the US in recent memory have driven many Americans to discount the value of politics itself and of civilians who engage in them in government settings. Military officers' own stock rose commensurate with the plummeting public approval of most civilian institutions in government, not so much because of their own job performance but because they seemed like the most selfless and least self-dealing alternative to a political class gone apparently petty and destructive.

But politics and the way it is conducted are two separate phenomena. Politics is simply a process of making collective decisions and allocating public resources—including power. Political context as I have used it here simply describes who has the power to make and influence those decisions, and which issues those with power believe are important enough to receive attention and money. As I have shown, political context obtains at multiple levels of analysis, making it unavoidable, even for the military itself. To ensure that decisions reflect the most widely shared societal values and priorities, civilians must engage in politics, and therefore must evaluate political contexts to understand what society wants. But this process is so intricate and complex that we need much more study of the relationships between power, interests, and civilian control choices before we will have a comprehensive understanding of civilian behavior.

The military is a prominently powerful actor in the American system. It has money and prestige, and the greatest capacity for violent coercion. It is an inherently political institution. So, another area in need of further study is the military's role in civilians' political contexts. Civil-military scholars have long considered the political influence of military institutions, especially in the comparative literature. It is my hope that more will think squarely about how civilians interact with the military in the domestic political context and make decisions about how to control their military agents—and each other—based on input from their agents.

Relatedly, we must also acknowledge that as much as civilians are experts in politics, military officers are not all political amateurs. If the military is a component of the political context and itself engages in domestic and international politics, then we also need to examine how much of civilians' expertise is shared by the military. I have argued here that the question is not one of exclusive or unique knowledge but specialization. Civilians engage in politics at all levels as their core function and expertise, to translate social priorities into government actions. Much the way civilians acquire knowledge about military affairs to do their jobs, the military develops knowledge about politics to do theirs. But the point of being a military expert isn't to give political advice, and the point of being a civilian isn't military expertise. Still, and as Risa Brooks has shown elsewhere, the military is not apolitical, and it is misleading to believe it is. Confronting this fact, rather than assuming it away with inaccurate normative civil-military models, will help scholars and practitioners better define the difference between partisanship and politics. We need an entire library of studies to show practitioners what that difference really looks like.

This book focuses on the United States, but I do not think civil-military relations in the US is truly unique. The subtitle of this book is meant in an aspirational way, built on the hope that other scholars will take the proposition here that I am describing civilians in democratic civil-military relations and investigate other empirical cases. More comparative studies of civilian control that incorporate the United States would benefit our growing knowledge about civilians in democratic civil-military relations, and the many forms civilian functions take in governing systems around the world.[8] It would be especially illuminating to compare the US with cases where former military dictatorships have since democratized to see how the civilian ethic in those countries compares to its practice in cases where military rule was never a factor.

Scholars could also interrogate further how different types of civilians behave. I first observed the substantial differences between the ways politicians and administrators approach their civilian control duties in the halls of the Pentagon. I noticed that administrators worked within political contexts but also delved into—and sometimes preferred—the more technocratic aspects of defense administration. Executive administrators at the Pentagon also interacted with the military far more often than other types of civilians, making their volume of control (and deference) decisions much higher and their expertise in military policy far greater. They were therefore much more likely to base their choices on similar rationale to the military's, especially the further down and farther out they were in the organization from the secretary. Updates to the literature on organizational capture in the civil-military context would be fruitful in understanding the kinds of incentives motivating civilians at the DoD, especially those outside of OSD. Similarly, studies of civilians in Congress—especially staffers—would dramatically improve our understanding of how the legislative branch controls and defers to the executive beyond just the debates over authorizations for the use of force. Future studies should include national security advisors, committee staff directors, and civil servants in empirical analysis. Scholarly studies of civil servants and congressional staffers are glaring in their paucity and could provide innumerable insights into military policymaking.

Budgetary politics is a major source of civilian control choices, and I have taken a broad view of a topic with endless potential for empirical analysis. Arnold Kanter (1983) and Sharon Weiner (1996) have each provided models of how to study the civil-military politics of defense budgeting. More research on how defense budgets shape politics and especially civilian control choices, including how civilians control each other through the DoD budget, would build useful knowledge for civilian controllers and scholars alike.

Finally, so much more could be done to examine the detailed exercise of civilian control rather than just evidence of its presence or absence. In recent years, comparativists have done important work in this regard, largely regarding democratizing regimes (e.g., Croissant et al. 2010). Lindsay Cohn's excellent article about the challenges of defense contractors, which I have referenced, contains a discussion of control that guided me and should guide Americanists as well (Cohn 2011). The fragmentary nature of civilian control—derived from the fragmented structure of civilian governance—also generates trade-offs between control mechanisms that scholars could scrutinize more. The UAV case demonstrates these trade-offs well: Congress constrained spending on UAVs, but in doing so also suppressed further development, including of combat applications for UAVs, that some executive administrators wanted to encourage.

In any case, it is long past time to pull the civilian side of the civil-military relationship into everyone's focus. To do so will not only enrich civil-military relations scholarship, it will also contribute to a revitalization of democracy. The more citizens around the world, Americans included, expect civilian leaders to use their status, functions, and expertise to exercise control over the armed forces, the more democratic that control will be.

ACKNOWLEDGMENTS

WRITING THIS BOOK WAS A passion project, and if it succeeds in any way, it is only because of the support I received from a humbling array of people. Sharon Weiner is my steadfast friend and sponsor, having guided me through a master's thesis, a doctoral dissertation, and now my first book. I am so grateful for her patience, her fierce loyalty, and of course her superbly insightful comments on very messy drafts—the best of which was: "Tell a chatty story with teeth."

Once again, Sarah Snyder kept my little trolley on its rails. That she lived through my whole dissertation process and was still willing to read book proposals and chapter drafts, share her own writing strategies, and even lend me office space speaks to her enormous generosity as a scholar and friend. The academy could do with a lot more Sarahs.

Peter Roady is a dear friend, a like-minded colleague, and possibly the best developmental editor in the world. He read multiple drafts with great care, and he could see what I was trying to do sometimes even before I could see it myself. He also knew when I needed encouragement and confidence. Our writing club of two has been enormously rewarding to me, and I am so grateful.

Kathleen Hicks deserves special mention because she let me go, again. Kath has always believed in me, helped me whenever I needed help, and

182   Acknowledgments

given me permission to go do what I dearly want to do, even when it was very inconvenient to her. The team in the deputy secretary of defense's front office also deserves credit for listening to me talk about this project and then being gracious and supportive when I departed their pattern to go get it done.

Mara Karlin and Loren Schulman are the only two people I know who like to gossip about civil-military relations as much as I do. They are so fun, and so supportive, and so wise. I count my lucky stars for their companionship. Stephen Tankel coached me through book proposals and reminded me over and over and over that writing a book is hard and confusing and eventually you figure it out. He also read a first, truly terrible draft of the book and kept being supportive anyway. Risa Brooks mentored me through the moments of disorientation and discouragement, and helpfully wrote some of the most brilliant recent work on American civil-military relations to shape my own thinking.

A scholar couldn't get luckier than to work with the kind, professional folks at Stanford University Press. My editor, Daniel LoPreto, was savvy, efficient, and delightfully communicative. Also he has excellent taste in TV shows. Marie-Catherine "Cat" Pavel took good care of my manuscript and answered my silly questions. I also know it is customary to thank the anonymous reviewers, but I really mean it. Their comments were thoughtful, precise, kind, and doable. Best of all, they really did improve the book in your hands substantially. Every author should be so lucky.

I got by with the help of colleagues at American University, the Center for Strategic and International Studies, the US Army War College, Perry World House at the University of Pennsylvania, the Institute for Security and Technology, and Georgetown University. The great and good Heidi Urben deserves special mention for bringing me in to teach the Bulldogs, for telling me I was going through all the normal book-writing stages of grief, and for metaphorically meeting me at the end of numerous life races with a thermal blanket.

Meredith Killough is my Cheese, the best Cheese, and the best bestie of all.

Then there are the people I've never even met: the archivists who are, even today, digitizing the treasures in America's historical archives. I wrote this book during a pandemic while raising two small children, and simply could not embark on trips to distant locales—many of which were closed to researchers in any case. But thanks to how many records have been uploaded for the world to find, I was able to do substantial amounts of research remotely. The National Security Archives at the George Washington University in Washington, DC, deserves special mention for their dogged stick-to-itiveness with the Freedom of Information Act process. I referred extensively to interviews the scholars at the Miller Center at the University of Virginia conducted with members of the H. W. Bush, Clinton, and G. W. Bush administrations and am extremely grateful for all the hard work that went into collecting and preserving those first-person accounts of history. The American Presidency Project at the University of California, Santa Barbara, has been good enough to collect media interviews with presidents, making that phase of research infinitely more efficient.

But the person who did the most to make this dream not only possible but meaningful was my husband. I got to be a civilian at DoD for so long because he left his nice life in California to be in DC with me. Then when I quit to write a book about it, he was all in. He always knew when I needed a break or a cookie or encouragement or to just babble about the constitutional ratifying conventions. He knew I needed to do this, and he made sure it happened. So, this book is for Kaleb Friend. Thank you for always being on my side, my love.

ALICE HUNT FRIEND
Washington, DC
June 2023

NOTES

Introduction

1. Congress amended Title 10 in 2021 to require that general and flag officers be retired for ten years prior to serving as secretary of defense. For officers at the rank of colonel and below, the law left the waiting period as seven years.

2. The Austin nomination also gave senators the opportunity to confirm the first Black head of DoD in the wake of renewed civil rights and racial justice unrest over the summer of 2020. See Bishop Garrison, "Representation at the Top: The Importance of Race in the Austin Nomination Debate," *Just Security*, December 11, 2020, https://www.justsecurity.org/73833/representation-at-the-top-the-importance-of-race-in-the-austin-nomination-debate/; Meg K. Guliford, "What Lloyd Austin's Nomination Really Reveals, and What It Really Means for Me," *Inkstick Media*, December 23, 2020, https://inkstickmedia.com/what-lloyd-austins-nomination-really-reveals/.

3. For an exploration of the qualifications that career military officers bring to the secretary of defense role, see Alice Hunt Friend, "A Military Litmus Test? Evaluating the Argument that Civilian Defense Leaders Need Military Experience," *Just Security*, August 19, 2020, https://www.justsecurity.org/72084/a-military-litmus-test-evaluating-the-argument-that-civilian-defense-leaders-need-military-experience/.

4. The historian of American revolutionary thought Bernard Bailyn references John Trenchard as an influence on American colonists.

186   Notes to Introduction

5. *Extracts from the Votes and Proceedings of the American Continental Congress Held at Philadelphia on the 5ᵗʰ of September 1774* (Philadelphia: William and Thomas Bradford, 1774), 8.

6. *Federalist*, no. 51, 317. The Federalists were highly partisan, and I use the *Federalist Papers* here not because they reflect general sentiment at the time, but because they represent the strain of thought that came to dominate and justify the content of the Constitution.

7. Of course, the civilians included in government as reflected in the Constitution of the late eighteenth century was a category limited to free Americans eligible to vote, run for office, and wield economic power. Congress, the presidency, and the judiciary represented a generally free, White, male, and monied subset of the American population. Only those with enough social power were invited to participate in the balancing of interests in government. The idea that both the militia and the government controlling it represented "the people" elided these qualifiers placed on representation.

8. House of Representatives, *Hearing before the Select Committee on Post-War Military Policy*, "Proposal to Establish a Single Department of Armed Forces," 78th Congress, 2nd Session, April 26, 1944.

9. Department of Defense Reorganization Act of 1958, Section 202, (c)(7).

10. Representative Carl Vinson, chairman, House Armed Services Committee, *Report Accompanying the Department of Defense Reorganization Act of 1958*, May 22, 1958, 85th Congress, 2nd Session. Emphasis mine.

11. Cole et al. 1978, *Secretary Lovett's Letter—18 November 1952*, 119.

12. SASC. "Defense Organization: The Need for Change: Staff Report to the Committee on Armed Services." 99th Congress, First Session, October 16, 1985, page 40 and 45. Of course, any statistician will point out that the probability of an event is not determined by the frequency of previous occurrences of such an event.

13. *The Future of Defense Reform: Hearing before the Committee on Armed Services of the United States Senate*, October 21, 2015, 3.

14. Public Law 114-328: National Defense Authorization Act for Fiscal Year 2017, December 23, 2017. Hostility toward large staffs in OSD and the military departments persisted into the Trump administration. Secretaries Mattis and Esper both abhorred large headquarters, with the latter taking action to cut the size of leader support staffs. See Seamus P. Daniels, "Understanding DoD's Defense-Wide Zero-Based Review." Center for Strategic and International Studies, September 4, 2019, https://www.csis.org/analysis/understanding-dods-defense-wide-zero-based-review.

15. Public Law 114-328, Section 921.

Notes to Introduction and Chapter One   187

16. US Senate Armed Services Committee. *National Defense Authorization Act for Fiscal Year 2017*, 2. https://www.armed-services.senate.gov/imo/media/doc/FY17%20NDAA%20Bill%20Summary.pdf.

17. The concept of civilian and the framework for civilian control here sets aside the judiciary branch and the enforcement of both military and civilian law. I recognize the vital role played by the judiciary in civil-military relations and bracket it here for simplicity and because it is possible to analyze the major elements of military policymaking without reference to court proceedings. The book does examine the legislative process and the definitions of civilian and civilian authorities provided in law, particularly Title 10 of US Code. For a recent look at civilian efforts to reform military justice systems, see Kyle and Reiter 2021.

18. I am grateful to Sara Plana for observing this point to me about the book while it was in progress, before I had quite perceived it myself.

19. Peter Feaver calls this tension between a military powerful enough to win on the battlefield but controlled enough not to overthrow civilian government "the civil-military problematique" (Feaver 1996). Feaver approaches it as an agency problem. Here I also highlight the ethical responsibilities civilians have to manage the tension.

Chapter One

1. The conduct of modern war, particularly insurgencies, has blurred the distinctions between combatants and civilians. But the abstract concept of civilian in the wartime context still refers to those without a persistent role in combat or other types of violence, and authors often use the terms *civilian* and *noncombatant* interchangeably.

2. Although there are many professions considered "civilian," such as business, law, and medicine, and many professions in the broader national security community are dominated by civilians, such as intelligence, being a civilian in the context of military policy is not generally considered a professional status. It is even more confusing that the word *civilian* is often used to mean a person who is not a professional. The Oxford English Dictionary even gives one definition of civilian as "a person who is a not a member of a specified profession or group" (OED 3rd ed., modified version, published online March 2022).

3. The argument developed here began as a short exploratory essay (Friend 2020b).

4. Public consent as the basis of authority was captured in other contemporary documents, such as the Virginia Declaration of Rights.

5. This is the conclusion that Eliot Cohen comes to in the first chapter of his book *Supreme Command* (2002a). Cohen points out that civilians, by virtue of

188   Notes to Chapter One

their involvement in politics, have the right to involve themselves in every realm into which politics extend, including all corners of military affairs. Cohen adds that *whether* civilians should intervene is a "prudential" matter, but the fact remains that they *may* intervene due to their status.

6. Online Etymology Dictionary. https://www.etymonline.com/word/civil.

7. Former deputy secretary of defense Robert Work enumerated the range of business-like entities for which DoD administrators are responsible: "They include, among other things, a standalone recruiting force and processes; four different training and academic institutions; a uniquely complicated payroll system; a giant real estate operation; an enormous health care system; a global grocery and retail chain; the largest email system in the world; an information technology portfolio that exceeds $45 billion; a global distribution system that rivals FedEx; and a vast research and development and acquisition enterprise" (Galvin 2019, vi).

8. This section benefits from Shannon Culbertson's insights about civil-military working relationships at the policymaking level.

9. Another type of civilian contributes to civilian control functions but is not responsible for them. These civilians are technocrats. The civil service, junior political appointees, and congressional staffers facilitate civilian control by enabling politicians and administrators to perform their functions and by complementing political and administrative expertise with detailed procedural and substantive knowledge. In OSD, civilian technocrats craft the formal guidance that the secretary of defense issues to military organizations. Hill staff organize hearings about the defense budget, identifying witnesses and preparing talking points for committee members. Staffers develop the agendas for NSC meetings and prepare background materials on proposed or ongoing military operations for attendees. An office supplies the secretary of defense with information and policy proposals concerning the combatant command that covers the Asia-Pacific region. Technocrats educate politicians and administrators, provide them with policy options, and implement their decisions. The relationship is mutually beneficial, because technocrats need politicians' and administrators' power to be effective in their own roles.

10. As the political scientist Theodore Lowi once wrote: "Finding different manifestations or types of a given phenomenon is the beginning of orderly control and prediction" (Lowi 1972, 299).

11. This rare event was even more remarkable because Tower was a former senator and former SASC chair, proving that political connections and support are dynamic.

12. Of course, some administrators may stay in place at a politician's request, but then their tenure simply transfers its dependence on one politician to another.

Notes to Chapter One   189

13. I am grateful to Susanna Blume for highlighting that early, negative reactions to the typology from practitioners were rooted in frustrations over the tensions between formal hierarchy and policy relevance.

14. For a good primer on military planning see Joint Chiefs of Staff, *Joint Publication 5-01: Joint Planning*, 2020. https://www.jcs.mil/Portals/36/Documents/Doctrine/pubs/jp5_0.pdf.

15. There is also a reasonable argument that every member of Congress exercises some control over military affairs because they all vote on the annual NDAA and on the appropriations bills. This narrowing to just three roles is partly logical, as explained in the main text, and partly pragmatic. In a democracy, every civilian has some share in controlling the military, but the scope of this book is to concentrate on those who do so more than most.

16. Statistics compiled by the author. Members who served in the Coast Guard and reserve component are included. See US Office of Personnel Management 2021.

17. For an overview of the role of secretary of defense and the men who have occupied the position, see Stevenson 2006.

18. The party caucus is the main gatekeeper and mechanism of decision. Matt Williams, conversation with the author, February 18, 2022.

19. https://www.reed.senate.gov/news/releases/changing-of-the-guard -reed-ascends-to-top-of-senate-armed-services-committee.

20. In Senator Reed's case, he was made SASC chair in S. Res. 27: 117th Congress Organizing Resolution.

21. Even when Congress began to achieve some demographic representation of the country, progress was not steady, and falls short of a representative sample of the American population to this day. Black Americans broke into the Senate in 1870 in the person of Hiram Revels of Mississippi, with Blanche Bruce, also of Mississippi, following in 1875. But there wouldn't be another Black senator until 1967, when Edward Brooke of Massachusetts joined the club. See https://www .senate.gov/artandhistory/history/common/briefing/minority_senators.htm . Rebecca Felton of Georgia was the first woman to join the Senate in 1922. She was appointed rather than elected and in office briefly; it took almost another decade for the first woman to be elected to the Senate. Of the 1,314 Americans who have served as senators, just 58 have been women. Women have been just 355 of the 12,421 representatives. There have been 122 Latino members of Congress, 112 since 1950. Only 11 have been in the Senate. See https://www.senate .gov/senators/hispanic-american-senators.htm.

22. To get a sense of the share of the US population with direct livelihood ties to the military, consider that the DoD employs approximately 3 million people, military and civilian, as well as approximately 251,000 contractors.

190   Notes to Chapters One and Two

(More precisely, DoD reports the number of full-time equivalent or FTE personnel to Congress every year. See Heidi M. Peters, "Defense Primer: Department of Defense Contractors," Congressional Research Service, January 17, 2023). The families of those in uniform are considered "military dependents," and in 2017 they numbered some 2,667,909 people. See Le Menestrel and Kizer 2019. The military itself, particularly the officer corps, is increasingly drawn from family and regional groups already entwined with the military. See Council on Foreign Relations 2020; see also Schaefer 2017. Meanwhile, the defense industry accounted for around 2 million jobs in all fifty states, 1.4 percent of American employment in 2020, generating approximately 2 percent of national labor income (Aerospace Industries Association 2021, 7). But as of this writing, the CEOs of Boeing, Lockheed-Martin, and Airbus were all White men. Northrop Grumman's CEO was a White woman, as was Lockheed-Martin's board chair. But industry also has a long way to go to reflect America in its executive suites.

23. Scott Arceneaux, conversation with the author, February 17, 2022.

Chapter Two

1. A mentor of mine in the military policy community is very fond of saying about the DoD budget: "All problems are solved in the out-years."

2. "Global force management" is the term of art at DoD and is designed to ensure the military services "provide sufficient ready and available forces to execute the National Defense Strategy." See https://www.thelightningpress.com/global-force-management-gfm/.

3. Undue military influence was a major focus of civil-military relations scholarship in the US in the 1990s. See, e.g., Dunlap 1992/93 and Kohn 1994.

4. Lindsay Cohn (2011) has argued persuasively that analysts should think about control as a mechanism for positive action. Using a Weberian transactional model, Cohn lays out a two-step exchange where a principal issues a command or expresses a preference, and then an agent receives and acts on the principal's order. The process by which the principal arrives at the command naturally matters, and the way the agent receives the command also matters. Moreover, how the actors perceive each other will shape their conduct during, and in response to, the exchange.

5. Representative Mikie Sherrill from New Jersey's 11th District invited a prominent Ukrainian-American to be her guest at the State of the Union address during the conflict, and she met with members of the Ukrainian American Cultural Center. See https://sherrill.house.gov/media/press-releases/rep-sherrill-invites-local-ukrainian-american-leader-virtual-guest-state-union.

Notes to Chapters Two and Three   191

6. I am grateful to Mara Karlin for pushing me to consider this element of civilian motivation as I constructed the model. Conversation with the author, January 22, 2022.

7. In asserting the possibility that some civilians may privilege beliefs over survival, I am differing somewhat from Deborah Avant's assertion that "substantive goals . . . will be conditioned by what [civilians] believe is necessary to remain in power" (Avant 1994, 8). Although I agree that civilians privilege survival, I relax the assumption that survival is always at issue or that civilians are universally unwilling to risk everything for their beliefs.

8. The timeline presented here relies on Chivvis 2013. I also draw on the memoirs of Barack Obama, Robert Gates, Carl Levin, and John McCain, along with contemporary news items. See also Chollet and Fishman 2015.

9. Gates relays a story, contemporaneous with the Libya policy debate, about the HAC-D chair, Representative Bill Young, blocking more funding for intelligence, surveillance, and reconnaissance platforms for DoD. Gates criticized Young publicly for his stance in the appropriations committee hearing room on March 2, suggesting Young put his constituents' business interests ahead of service members' safety (the move was informed by the fact that one of Young's campaign contributors manufactured Humvees, the account from which the funding for the ISR assets would be taken). Although Gates regretted the tactic, it was effective; Young relented on the ISR funding.

10. Levin announced in 2013 that he did not intend to run for Senate again. Whether he was already considering retirement is unclear. He states in his memoir that he began to consider retirement in early 2013, two full years after the events in Libya.

11. *Reprogramming* refers to changes in how an agency uses its funds and may only be done with authority provided by statute. For more on how the DoD executes reprogramming, see https://comptroller.defense.gov/Budget-Execu tion/ReprogrammingFY2022/#:~:text=A%20reprogramming%20is%20a %20change,be%20performed%20without%20statutory%20authority.

Chapter Three

1. Sharon K. Weiner explores the political power of the chairman of the joint chiefs of staff extensively in her book *Managing the Military* (Weiner 2022).

2. Because Nunn was the SASC chair, a nontrivial amount of correspondence came from outside Georgia. His office tracked the origins of each letter, presumably to distinguish between constituents and others.

192   Notes to Chapters Three and Four

3. Moreover, as Bush explained to his diary on November 30, 1992, the political perceptions surrounding these humanitarian crises were critical: "There is a feeling that we won't help black nations, so that [intervening in Somalia] would be a peripheral benefit showing that the United States does care. There is a feeling in the Muslim world that we don't care about Muslims. A large US humanitarian effort backed by force would help in that category" (Meacham 2015, 529). In any case, Bush's national security advisor, Brent Scowcroft, assured members of Clinton's team that the forces would be withdrawn again before Clinton's inauguration (Chollet and Goldgeier 2008).

4. Les Aspin, Opening Statement as Delivered, Secretary of Defense Confirmation, January 7, 1993, https://www.c-span.org/video/?36865-1/secretary-defense-confirmation-part-1.

5. The "Two MRC" force sizing construct has been a staple of the Quadrennial Defense Review and its successor National Defense Strategy as well, to include the 2022 NDS.

6. "Defense Secretary Nomination," C-SPAN, January 24, 1994, https://www.c-span.org/video/?54008-1/defense-secretary-nomination, 16:38.

7. "Weapons' Modernization and Bosnian Rescue," C-SPAN, December 9, 1994, https://www.c-span.org/video/?62086-1/weapons-modernization-bosnian-rescue, 39:00.

8. "Weapons' Modernization and Bosnian Rescue," C-SPAN, December 9, 1994, https://www.c-span.org/video/?62086-1/weapons-modernization-bosnian-rescue, 39:00.

9. "Weapons' Modernization and Bosnian Rescue," C-SPAN, December 9, 1994, https://www.c-span.org/video/?62086-1/weapons-modernization-bosnian-rescue, 39:00.

Chapter Four

1. For a comprehensive overview, see: "A Timeline of US Troop Levels in Afghanistan Since 2001," Associated Press, September 8, 2019, https://apnews.com/article/fd2ec2085b0b4fd3ae0a3b03c6de9478. Special operations numbers estimated by the author using public US government documents. See especially "Appendix A: US Army Units in Operation ENDURING FREEDOM—Afghanistan, Order of Battle: October 2001–September 2005," in Wright et al. 2010.

2. See Megan Brenan, "Americans Split on Whether Afghanistan War Was a Mistake," *Gallup News Service*, July 26, 2021, https://news.gallup.com/poll/352793/americans-split-whether-afghanistan-war-mistake.aspx.

3. Several former government officials who were in office during the 9/11 attacks refer in their memoirs to the newspaper headlines on September 12 as a way to convey the emotional impact of the attacks on themselves and on the American public.

Notes to Chapter Four   193

4. Although the use of force against Iraq is not the focus of this chapter, several of Bush's advisors, including Secretary of Defense Rumsfeld, argued in the days after 9/11 that the president's desire to fight terrorists anywhere and to punish state sponsors of terrorism justified a campaign against Iraq. See Rumsfeld 2011, Feith 2008, and Woodward 2002.

5. For a detailed history of the ideas behind the racist, antisemitic, xenophobic "America First" slogan, see Churchwell 2018.

6. The University of California at Santa Barbara's American Presidency Project keeps daily presidential tweet records starting with June 15, 2015. The full text of @realDonaldTrump's tweets on October 7, 2020, is accessible at https://www .presidency.ucsb.edu/documents/tweets-october-7-2020.

7. Examples of bipartisan respect for Levin are available in the collection of tributes from his senatorial colleagues upon his retirement from the Senate in 2015. See: "Carl Levin, US Senator from Michigan: Tributes Delivered in Congress," Government Printing Office, 2015, https://www.govinfo.gov/content/pkg/CDOC-113sdoc34/pdf/CDOC-113sdoc34.pdf.

8. GovTrack rated Warner just right of center, and far left of most of his Republican colleagues in 2008, on their "Ideology-Leadership Chart." See https://www.govtrack.us/congress/members/john_warner/300099.

9. The content of the shared-topic hearings reflected the persistent imbalance of attention between Iraq and Afghanistan. As an example, at a hearing on both wars on September 9, 2003, senators and witnesses together said the word "Afghanistan" 62 times and "Iraq" 414.

10. Although outside the scope of this case study, McCain led what he called "a revolt of Republican hawks" against the Bush administration's use of torture to extract intelligence from detainees in Iraq and Afghanistan. McCain explained that he believed a Republican-sponsored bill "would have a greater restraining impact on the administration." His efforts culminated in the Detainee Treatment Act of 2005. See McCain and Salter 2018, 90.

11. Secretary of Defense Confirmation Hearing, June 9, 2011, https://www.c -span.org/video/?299943-1/secretary-defense-confirmation-hearing.

12. At the time he made these remarks in the 2017 hearing, McCain had just won reelection in the 2016 contest by approximately 10 percent. Data compiled by the Associated Press and presented on the *New York Times* website: https://www.nytimes.com/elections/2016/results/arizona-senate-mccain-kirkpatrick.

13. The Army's term of art for the ratio of time deployed to time at home was called "BOG/Dwell," with BOG standing for "boots on the ground."

14. At the time of this writing, insufficient memoirs and archival materials of Biden's policymaking process prevented me from including the final withdrawal decision in the case study. In full disclosure, I was working in the Pentagon as a Biden appointee in the secretary of defense's immediate office at the time.

194   Notes to Chapters Four and Five

Although I did not have duties directly pertaining to Afghanistan, that experience made it all the more important for me to be able to draw on a wide range of sources to develop a more empirical, objective picture of the decision-making process. I hope scholars will be able to use this framework to do so in the future.

Chapter Five

1. For a discussion of the range of definitions of the term *capability*, see "What Is a Capability, and What Are the Components of Capability?" in Taliaferro et al. 2019.

2. Scholars point out that control over chemical weapons is rooted in moral judgments as well as pragmatic reasons. For example, see Price 1997 and Brodie 1973. For an exploration of how the military expanded its procurement of MRAPs, see Weiner 2010.

3. Some portions of this chapter are adapted from earlier work on civilian preference formation. See Friend 2020a.

4. There is a great deal of debate over the appropriate terminology for aircraft that fly without a pilot or crew onboard. The term "unmanned aerial vehicles" was popular for many years, but it encountered two meaningful critiques. The first critique, that the term "unmanned" made it sound like there were no pilots or crew involved in UAV operations, came from the Air Force. The second critique was that the word was unnecessarily gendered. The Air Force long preferred the term "remotely piloted aircraft"; others offered the term "uninhabited" to replace "unmanned" while also limiting the term to meaning no person rode inside the aircraft. I adopt "uninhabited" here mostly for the legibility of keeping the widely understood acronym UAV, not because I have any objection to the Air Force's term. These days one is more apt to hear about autonomy in any case, but as this is a historical case study, I want to preserve some sense of the contemporary terminology. Thus throughout I also retain the terms "manned" and "unmanned."

5. Partly because the definition of UAVs is indistinct, there isn't agreement about the date that the first military UAV flew successfully. Some claim that the UAV era began when Europeans delivered bombs via balloons in the mid-nineteenth century. Most historians of American UAV development point to the Kettering Bug, a remote-controlled bomb delivery aircraft developed (but never used) during WWI. In any case, UAVs were in development long before the first Predator flew over Afghanistan.

6. The transparent defense budgeting process was separate from the classified intelligence budget, where funding for UAVs was likely much greater for several decades (Erhard 2000).

Notes to Chapter Five 195

7. Reporters and expert analysts have noted that even with full motion video ISR, counterterrorism operations relied on human intelligence to narrow down search areas, meaning the risk to American personnel is reduced by UAVs but never eliminated.

8. See also General Accounting Office, *The Army's Remotely Piloted Vehicle Shows Good Potential but Faces a Lengthy Development Program,* February 26, 1982; General Accounting Office, *Aquila Remotely Piloted Vehicle: Recent Developments and Alternatives,* GAO/NSIAD-86-41BR, January 4, 1986.

9. General Accounting Office, *Aquila Remotely Piloted Vehicle, Its Potential Battlefield Contribution Still in Doubt,* October 1987, GAO/NSIAD-88-19. NB: The GAO's name would later be changed to Government Accountability Office.

10. United States Senate, Department of Defense Appropriations Act 1988 Report, 250.

11. House of Representatives Committee on Appropriations, *Department of Defense Appropriations Bill, 1992, Report Number 102-95* (Washington, DC: Government Printing Office, 1991), 334.

12. US Congress, 102d Congress, 2d session, Committee of Conference, *National Defense Authorization Act for Fiscal Year 1993, House Rept. 102-966,* 635.

13. Department of Defense Appropriations Act 1995, Public Law 103-335, Sec. 8146 (a) and (b), Sept. 30, 1994.

14. John Warner, interview with the author, August 13, 2019.

15. Public Law 106-398, October 30, 2000, National Defense Authorization, Fiscal Year 2001.

16. For further background on the debt ceiling crisis and the Budget Control Act of 2011 see CRS 2015 and 2019.

17. Calculated by the author using multiple sources. See Ackerman 2011; Gettinger 2018.

18. For an analysis of OCO funding patterns, see Congressional Budget Office, *Funding for Overseas Contingency Operations and Its Impact on Defense Spending,* October 2018, https://www.cbo.gov/system/files/2018-10/54219-oco _spending.pdf.

19. Cohen 1997 (DoD Annual Report), 71–72.

20. Senior OSD Official, interview with the author, June 3, 2019.

21. Department of Defense, "MQ-9 Reaper Unmanned Aircraft System (MQ-9 Reaper)," Defense Acquisition Management Information Retrieval, December, 2019, https://www.esd.whs.mil/Portals/54/Documents/FOID/Reading %20Room/Selected_Acquisition_Reports/FY_2019_SARS/20-F-0568_DOC_61 _MQ-9_Reaper_SAR_Dec_2019.pdf.

196   Notes to Chapter Five and Conclusion

22. Original PPG Document available at https://www.justice.gov/oip/foia-library/procedures_for_approving_direct_action_against_terrorist_targets/download.

Conclusion

1. The original IG report appears to have been removed from the Department of Interior website, but a copy is available embedded in the text of a National Public Radio story. See Montanaro 2021.

2. For a review of civil-military relations during the Trump presidency, see Brooks 2021.

3. The dueling lists of retired general and flag officers who endorse presidential candidates has been an arms race for every campaign season since retired Marine Corps General P. X. Kelley appeared in a TV advertisement for George H. W. Bush's run for president in 1988 and reached its apogee (or nadir) during the 2016 campaign when each candidate amassed long lists of retirees' endorsements and featured fiery prime time speeches by prominent retired generals at the nominating conventions and gathered veterans out on stage. The 2020 campaign also featured such lists, although with fewer signatories than in the past.

4. Popular confidence is not invariant over time or across sections of the American population. There is a partisan effect in the statistics: Republicans tend to have higher and more durable confidence in the military, whereas Democrats' confidence is slightly lower on average. Partisans of all stripes increase their confidence when a copartisan is in the White House. See Burbach 2019.

5. Helpfully, the military's own internal divisions also prevent military regimes in democratic countries. For a convincing argument that military coups often fail elsewhere because of the collective action problem they pose for military organizations, see Singh 2014.

6. Risa Brooks refers to the paradoxes of military professionalism. Elsewhere scholars refer to the civil-military "problematiques" or "problematics," most notably Peter Feaver and Aurel Croissant.

7. Data gathered by the author. See Daalder and Destler 2009 and Burke 2017.

8. Lizamaria Arias and I contributed a case study on the United States to one such effort. See Kuehn and Levy 2021.

BIBLIOGRAPHY

Abrahamsson, Bengt. 1972. *Military Professionalization and Political Power*. Beverly Hills, CA: Sage.

Ackerman, Spencer. 2011. "Is the Pentagon's Drone Spending Spree Over?" *Wired*, February 14, 2011.

Aerospace Industries Association. 2021. 2021 Facts and Figures: U.S. Aerospace and Defense. https://www.aia-aerospace.org/report/2021-facts-figures-u-s -aerospace-defense/.

Ahlquist, John S., and Margaret Levi. 2011. "Leadership: What It Means, What It Does, and What We Want to Know about It." *Annual Review of Political Science* 14: 1–24.

Aspin, Les. 1992. *An Approach to Sizing American Conventional Forces for the Post- Soviet Era: Four Illustrative Options*. US House of Representatives: House Armed Services Committee, February 25, 1992.

Associated Press. 2008. "Military Relying More on Drones, Mostly in Iraq." *NBC News*, January 1, 2008. http://www.nbcnews.com/id/22463596/ns/world _news-mideast_n_africa/t/military-relying-more-drones-mostly-iraq/# .XTjTdC2ZOCQ.

Avant, Deborah. 1994. *Political Institutions and Military Change: Lessons from Peripheral Wars*. Ithaca, NY: Cornell University Press.

Avant, Deborah. 1998. "Conflicting Indicators of 'Crisis' in American Civil-Military Relations." *Armed Forces and Society* 24 (3): 375–88.

Axe, David. 2011a. "Killer Drones, Jamming Jets Win Big in New Pentagon Budget." *Wired*, January 6, 2011. https://www.wired.com/2011/01/killer-drones-jam ming-jets-win-big-in-new-pentagon-budget/.

Axe, David. 2011b. "The Secret History of Boeing's Killer Drone." *Wired*, June 6, 2011. https://www.wired.com/2011/06/killer-drone-secret-history/.

Bailyn, Bernard. 2017. *The Ideological Origins of the American Revolutions*, 50th anniversary ed. Cambridge, MA: Harvard University Press.

Baker, Peter, and Jeff Zeleny. 2009. "Obama Rules Out Large Reduction in Afghan Force." *New York Times*, October 7, 2009, A1.

Bawn, Kathleen. 1995. "Political Control Versus Expertise: Congressional Choices about Administrative Procedures." *American Political Science Review* 89 (1): 62–73.

Beerbohm, Eric. 2015. "Is Democratic Leadership Possible?" *American Political Science Review* 109 (4): 639–52.

Belasco, Amy. 2009. *Troop Levels in the Afghan and Iraq Wars, FY2001–FY2012: Cost and Other Potential Issues*. Washington, DC: Congressional Research Service.

Beliakova, Polina. 2021. "Erosion by Deference: Civilian Control and the Military in Policymaking." *Texas National Security Review* 4 (3): 55–75.

Bergen, Peter. 2022. *The Cost of Chaos: The Trump Administration and the World*. New York: Penguin Books.

Best, Richard A. 1993. *Intelligence Technology in the Post-Cold War Era: The Role of Unmanned Aerial Vehicles*. Washington, DC: Congressional Research Service.

Betts, Richard K. 1991. *Soldiers, Statesmen, and Cold War Crises*. New York: Columbia University Press.

Biden, Joseph R. 2020. "Why I Chose Lloyd Austin as Secretary of Defense." *The Atlantic Magazine,* December 8, 2020. https://www.theatlantic.com/ideas/archive/2020/12/secretary-defense/617330/#.

Blanton, Tom, Claire Harvey, Lauren Harper, and Malcom Byrne. 2021. "Afghanistan 20/20: The 20-Year War in 20 Documents." National Security Archive, August 19, 2021. https://nsarchive.gwu.edu/briefing-book/afghanistan/2021 -08-19/afghanistan-2020-20-year-war-20-documents.

Blom, John David. 2010. *Unmanned Aerial Systems: A Historical Perspective*. Fort Leavenworth, KS: Combat Studies Institute Press.

Blumenthal, Sidney. 1991. "The Mystique of Sam Nunn." *The New Republic*, March 4, 1991, 23–27.

Bresnahan, John. 2011. "Senate Dems Defend Obama on Libya." *Politico*, March 23, 2011.

Brooks, Risa A. 2008. *Shaping Strategy: The Civil-Military Politics of Strategic Assessment*. Princeton, NJ: Princeton University Press.

Brooks, Risa A. 2020. "Paradoxes of Professionalism: Rethinking Civil-Military Relations in the United States." *International Security* 44 (4): 7–44.

Brooks, Risa A. 2021. "Through the Looking-Glass: Trump-Era Civil-Military Relations in Comparative Perspective." *Strategic Studies Quarterly* 15 (2): 69–98.

Brooks, Risa A., and Sharan Grewal. 2022. "'Twice the Citizen': How Military Attitudes of Superiority Undermine Civilian Control in the United States." *Journal of Conflict Resolution* 66 (4–5): 623–50.

Bueno de Mesquita, Bruce, Alistair Smith, Randolph M. Siverson, and James D. Morrow. 2003. *The Logic of Political Survival*. Cambridge, MA: MIT Press.

Builder, Carl H. 1989. *The Masks of War: American Military Styles in Strategy and Analysis*. Arlington, VA: RAND Corporation.

Burbach, David. 2019. "Partisan Dimensions of Confidence in the U.S. Military, 1973–2016." *Armed Forces & Society* 45 (2): 211–33.

Burke, Frances Tilney, and MacKenzie Eaglen. 2020. "Is Veterans' Preference Bad for the National Security Workforce?" *War on the Rocks*, June 16, 2020. https://warontherocks.com/2020/06/is-veterans-preference-bad-for-the-national-security -workforce/.

Bush, George. 1989. *National Strategy Review 12: Review of National Defense Strategy*. Washington, DC: National Security Council, the White House.

Bush, George, and Brent Scowcroft. 2011. *A World Transformed*, 2nd ed. New York: Vintage Books.

Bush, George W. 2010. *Decision Points*. New York: Crown.

Cartwright, James E. 2015. "Best Military Advice." *Strategic Studies Quarterly*, Fall.

Caverley, Jonathan. 2014. *Democratic Militarism. Voting, Wealth, and War*. Cambridge: Cambridge University Press.

Cheney, Dick. 1991. *Annual Report to the President and the Congress*. Washington, DC: US Government Printing Office.

Cheney, Dick. 2011. *In My Time: A Personal and Political Memoir*. With Liz Cheney. New York: Threshold Editions.

Chivvis, Christopher S. 2013. *Toppling Qaddafi: Libya and the Limits of Liberal Intervention*. Cambridge, MA: Cambridge University Press.

Chollet, Derek, and Ben Fishman. 2015. "Who Lost Libya? Obama's Intervention in Retrospect." *Foreign Affairs* 94 (3): 154–59.

Chollet, Derek, and James Goldgeier. 2008. *American Between the Wars: From 11/9 to 9/11*. New York: PublicAffairs.

Clinton, Bill. 1993. "Address to the Nation on Somalia." Transcript of speech delivered at the White House, October 7, 1993. https://www.presidency.ucsb.edu/documents/address-the-nation-somalia.

Bibliography

Clinton, Bill. 2004. *My Life.* New York: Alfred Knopf.

Cohen, Eliot A. 2002a. *Supreme Command: Soldiers, Statesmen, and Leadership in Wartime.* New York: Free Press.

Cohen, William S. 1997. *Annual Report to the President and the Congress.* Washington, DC: Department of Defense.

Cohn, Lindsay. 2011. "It Wasn't in My Contract: Security Privatization and Civilian Control." *Armed Forces & Society* 37 (3): 381–98.

Cole, Alice C., Alfred Goldberg, Samuel A. Tucker, and Rudolph A. Winnacker. 1978. *The Department of Defense: Documents on Establishment and Organization, 1944–1978.* Washington, DC: Office of the Secretary of Defense Historical Office.

Coll, Steve. 2018. *Directorate S: The C.I.A. and America's Secret Wars in Afghanistan and Pakistan.* New York: Penguin Books.

Cooper, Helene. 2020. "General Tempers White House Chatter on Paring Troops in Afghanistan." *New York Times*, October 13, 2020, A9.

Correll, John T. 1992. "Washington Watch: The Base Force Meets Option C." *Air Force Magazine*, June 1, 1992. https://www.airforcemag.com/article/0692watch/.

Cottey, Andrew, Timothy Edmunds, and Anthony Forster. 2002. "The Second Generation Problematic: Rethinking Democracy and Civil-Military Relations." *Armed Forces & Society* 29 (1): 31–56.

Council on Foreign Relations. 2020. *Demographics of the U.S. Military.* Washington, DC: CFR.

CQ Almanac. 1993. "Hill Demands Early '94 Somalia Withdrawal." 49th ed., 486–93. Washington, DC: Congressional Quarterly. http://library.cqpress.com/cqalmanac/cqal93-1104663.

CQ Almanac. 1997. "Intelligence Bottom Line Disclosed." 53rd ed., 848–50. Washington, DC: Congressional Quarterly. http://library.cqpress.com/cqalmanac/cqal97-0000181121.

Croissant, Aurel, David Kuehn, Paul Chambers, and Siegfried O. Wolf. 2010. "Beyond the Fallacy of Coup-ism: Conceptualizing Civilian Control of the Military in Emerging Democracies." *Democratization* 17 (5): 950–75.

Crowley, Michael. 2020. "Trump Aide Insists US Will Reduce Forces in Afghanistan to 2,500 Troops." *New York Times*, October 17, 2020.

CRS (Congressional Research Service). 2017. *Additional Troops for Afghanistan? Considerations for Congress.* Washington, DC: Congressional Research Service.

CRS (Congressional Research Service). 2019. *The Budget Control Act: Frequently Asked Questions.* Washington, DC: Congressional Research Service.

CRS (Congressional Research Service). 2021. *Rules Governing Senate Committee and Subcommittee Assignment Procedures*. Washington, DC: Congressional Research Service.

Daalder, Ivo H., and I. M. Destler. 2009. *In the Shadow of the Oval Office: Profiles of the National Security Advisers and the Presidents they Served—From JFK to George W. Bush*. New York: Simon & Schuster.

Dao, James. 2013. "Drone Pilots Are Found to Get Stress Disorders Much as Those in Combat Do." *New York Times*, February 23, 2013, A9.

Defense Science Board. 2004. *Study on Unmanned Aerial Vehicles and Uninhabited Combat Aerial Vehicles*. February 2004. https://apps.dtic.mil/sti/pdfs/ADA423585.pdf.

Dempsey, Martin. 2012. *America's Military—A Profession of Arms*. Washington, DC: Joint Chiefs of Staff.

Desch, Michael. 1999. *Civilian Control of the Military: The Changing Security Environment*. Baltimore, MD: Johns Hopkins University Press.

Dewar, Helen. 1990. "Nunn Warns Pentagon to Fill Blanks in Budget." *Washington Post*, March 23, 1990. https://www.washingtonpost.com/archive/politics/1990/03/23/nunn-warns-pentagon-to-fill-blanks-in-budget/befff93f-c513-4c5c-aa1b-265e2e2a28be/.

Dickinson, John [attributed]. 1768. *Letters from a Farmer in Pennsylvania to the Inhabitants of the British Colonies*. Philadelphia: David Hall and William Sellers.

DoD (Department of Defense, Office of the Undersecretary of Defense, Acquisition, Technology, and Logistics). 2013. *Unmanned Systems Integrated Roadmap FY2013–2038*. Washington, DC: US Department of Defense. https://www.hsdl.org/?view&did=747559.

Dombrowski, Peter, and Eugene Gholz. 2006. *Buying Military Transformation: Technological Innovation and the Defense Industry*. New York: Columbia University Press.

Dreazen, Yochi J. 2009. "Call for an Afghan Surge." *Wall Street Journal*, September 17, 2009.

Dreazen, Yochi J., Neil King Jr., and Peter Spiegel. 2009. "Congress Presses on War Plan." *Wall Street Journal*, September 24, 2009.

Drew, Christopher. 2009. "For US, Drones Are Weapons of Choice in Fighting Qaeda." *New York Times*, March 17, 2009, A1.

Dubik, James M. 2016. "Taking a 'Pro' Position on Principled Resignation." *Armed Forces & Society* 43 (1): 17–28.

Dunlap, Charles Jr. 1992/93. "The Origins of the Military Coup of 2012." *Parameters* 22 (4): 2–22.

202 Bibliography

Eckstein, Megan. 2014. "Rep. Forbes Asks Navy to Ensure UCLASS Is a 'Warfighting' Platform Worth of Investment." *Defense Daily*, February 20, 2014. https://www.defensedaily.com/rep-forbes-asks-navy-to-ensure-uclass-is-a-warfighting-platform-worthy-of-investment/budget/.

Editorial Board. 2013. "The Trouble with Drones." *New York Times*, April 7, 2013, A20.

Ehrhard, Thomas P. 2000. "Unmanned Aerial Vehicles in the United States Armed Services: A Comparative Study of Weapon System Innovation." PhD diss, Johns Hopkins School of Advanced International Studies.

Ehrhard, Thomas P. 2010. *Air Force UAVs: The Secret History*. Arlington, VA: Mitchell Institute Press.

Esper, Mark. 2022. *A Sacred Oath: Memoirs of a Secretary of Defense During Extraordinary Times*. New York: HarperCollins.

Estabrook, Samuel. 1718. *A Sermon Showing that the Peace and Quietness of a People is a Main Part of the Work of Civil Rulers*. New London, CT: Timothy Green. Evans Early American Imprints series 1, no. 1955.

Feaver, Peter. 1996. "The Civil-Military Problematique: Huntington, Janowitz, and the Question of Civilian Control." *Armed Forces & Society* 23 (2): 149–78.

Feaver, Peter. 2003. *Armed Servants: Agency, Oversight, and Civil-Military Relations*. Cambridge, MA: Harvard University Press.

Feaver, Peter. 2011. "The Right to Be Right: Civil-Military Relations and the Iraq Surge Decision" *International Security* 35 (4): 87–125.

Feaver, Peter. 2016. "Make an Exception for an Exceptional Candidate as Defense Secretary." *New York Times*, December 6, 2016. https://www.nytimes.com/roomfordebate/2016/12/06/is-it-wrong-to-have-a-general-like-james-mattis-run-the-pentagon/make-an-exception-for-an-exceptional-candidate-as-defense-secretary.

Feaver, Peter, and Christopher Gelpi. 2004. *Choosing Your Battles: American Civil-Military Relations and the Use of Force*. Princeton, NJ: Princeton University Press.

Feith, Douglas J. 2009. *War and Decision: Inside the Pentagon at the Dawn of the War on Terrorism*. New York: HarperCollins.

Finer, Samuel. 1962. *The Man on Horseback: The Role of the Military in Politics*. New York: Praeger.

Fisher, Louis. 2013. *Presidential War Power*, 3rd ed. Lawrence: University Press of Kansas.

Fisk, Samuel. 1731. *The Character of the Candidates for Civil Government, Especially for Council*. Boston: Thomas Fleet. Evans Early American Imprints series 1, no. 3417.

Friend, Alice Hunt. 2020a. "Creating Requirements: Emerging Military Capabilities, Civilian Preferences, and Civil-Military Relations." PhD diss. American University, Washington, DC.

Friend, Alice Hunt. 2020b. "What Makes a Civilian?" *The War Room.* Carlisle: US Army War College, April 9, 2020. https://warroom.armywarcollege.edu/articles/what-makes-a-civilian/.

Friend, Alice Hunt, and Mara Karlin. 2020. "Towards a Concept of Good Civilian Guidance." *War on the Rocks,* May 29, 2020. https://warontherocks.com/2020/05/towards-a-concept-of-good-civilian-guidance/.

Friend, Alice Hunt, and Sharon K. Weiner. 2022. "Principals with Agency: Assessing Civilian Deference to the Military." *Texas National Security Review* 5 (4): 11–28.

Friend, Alice Hunt, and Reja Younis. 2020. *Nuclear Command and Civilian Control.* Washington, DC: Center for Strategic and International Studies: http://defense360.csis.org/wp-content/uploads/2020/11/Friend-Younis-Civ Mil.pdf.

Galvin, Tom, ed. 2019. *Defense Management: Primer for Senior Leaders.* Carlisle, PA: US Army War College.

Gates, Robert. 2014. *Duty: Memoirs of a Secretary at War.* New York: Alfred A. Knopf.

Gellman, Barton. 1993. "Witness Aspin Encounters Flak Back at 'Home.'" *Washington Post,* March 31, 1993. https://www.washingtonpost.com/archive/politics/1993/03/31/witness-aspin-encounters-flak-back-at-home/1c7ef298 -b361-44b2-845f-1c6e4f8324cb/.

Gelpi, Christopher, Peter D. Feaver, and Jason Reifler. 2009. *Paying the Human Costs of War: American Public Opinion & Casualties in Military Conflicts.* Princeton, NJ: Princeton University Press.

Gettinger, Dan. 2017. *Drones in the Defense Budget: Navigating the Fiscal Year 2018 Budget Request.* Center for the Study of the Drone at Bard College, October 24, 2017. https://dronecenter.bard.edu/files/2018/01/Drones-Defense -Budget-2018-Web.pdf.

Gettinger, Dan. 2018. *Summary of Drone Spending in the FY 2019 Defense Budget Request.* Center for Study of the Drone at Bard College, April 2018. https://dronecenter.bard.edu/files/2018/04/CSD-Drone-Spending-FY19 -Web-1.pdf.

Golby, James, and Mara Karlin. 2018. "Why 'Best Military Advice' Is Bad for the Military—and Worse for Civilians." *Orbis* 62 (1): 137–53.

Gordon, Michael R. 1994. "Secretary of Defense Wins Few Points for His Candor." *New York Times.* April 8, 1994, A10.

Gordon, Michael R. 2017a. "General Seeks More Troops in Afghan Stalemate." *New York Times*, February 9, 2017, A3.

Gordon, Michael R. 2017b. "Trump's Mix of Politics and Military Is Faulted." *New York Times*, February 8, 2017, A17.

Gordon, Michael R., Eric Schmitt, and Maggie Haberman. 2017. "Trump Chooses a 'Path Forward' for Afghanistan." *New York Times*, August 21, 2017, A1.

Graham, Lindsey, Joseph I. Lierberman, and John McCain. 2009. "Only Decisive Force Can Prevail in Afghanistan." *Wall Street Journal*, September 13, 2009.

Gray, Colin S. 2006. *Recognizing and Understanding Revolutionary Change in Warfare: The Sovereignty of Context*. Carlisle, PA: Strategic Studies Institute, US Army War College.

Gross, Jane. 1993. "Critic as Chairman Gets Praise as Both." *New York Times*, February 8, 1993, A12.

Gunzinger, Mark. 1996. *Beyond the Bottom Up Review*. Washington, DC: National Defense University.

Halberstam, David. 2001. *War in a Time of Peace: Bush, Clinton, and the Generals*. New York: Touchstone.

Hastings, Michael. 2011. "Inside Obama's War Room: How He Decided to Intervene in Libya—And What It Says about His Evolution as Commander in Chief." *Rolling Stone*, October 17, 2011.

Hendrickson, Ryan C. 2002. *The Clinton Wars: The Constitutions, Congress, and War Powers*. Nashville, TN: Vanderbilt University Press.

Herring, Pendleton. 1941. *The Impact of War: Our American Democracy Under Arms*. New York: Farrar and Rinehart.

Hoehn, Andrew R., Albert A. Robbert, and Margaret C. Harrell. 2011. *Succession Management for Senior Military Positions: The Rumsfeld Model for Secretary of Defense Involvement*. Arlington, VA: RAND Corporation.

Hogan, Michael J. 1998. *A Cross of Iron. Harry S. Truman and the Origins of the National Security State, 1945–1954*. Cambridge: Cambridge University Press.

Huetteman, Emmarie. 2017. "Democrats Court Military Veterans to Run for Congress." *New York Times*, July 6, 2017, A12.

Hulse, Carl. 2021. "John Warner, 94, Dies; Genteel Senator Led Virginia for 3 Decades." *New York Times*, May 26, 2021, B11.

Huntington, Samuel P. 1957. *The Soldier and the State: The Theory and Politics of Civil-Military Relations*. Cambridge, MA: Harvard University Press.

Huntington, Samuel P. 1961. *The Common Defense: Strategic Programs in National Politics*. New York: Columbia University Press.

Hoehn, John R. and Paul K. Kerr. 2022. *Unmanned Aircraft Systems: Current and Potential Programs*. Washington, DC: Congressional Research Service, April 13.

Hohmann, James. 2022. "Ukrainian Americans Overpower the Isolationist Impulses of Trump-Era GOP." *Washington Post*, March 2, 2022. https://www.washingtonpost.com/opinions/2022/03/02/what-ukrainian-american-voters-are-doing-to-gop-politics/.

Janowitz, Morris. 1960. *The Professional Soldier*. New York: Free Press.

John, Peter. 2012. *Analyzing Public Policy*. 2nd ed. New York: Routledge.

Johnson, Robert David. 2006. *Congress and the Cold War*. New York: Cambridge University Press.

Johnston, David Cay. 2014. "The Legacy of Carl Levin." *The American Prospect*. Fall 2014. https://prospect.org/power/legacy-carl-levin/.

Jones, Frank Leith. 2020. *Sam Nunn: Statesman of the Nuclear Age*. Lawrence: University Press of Kansas.

Kane, Paul. 2003. "Warner Soldiers On." *Roll Call*, January 24, 2003. https://rollcall.com/2003/01/24/warner-soldiers-on/.

Kanter, Arnold. 1983. *Defense Politics: A Budgetary Perspective*. Chicago: University of Chicago Press.

Karlin, Mara. 2022. *The Inheritance: America's Military After Two Decades of War*. Washington, DC: Brookings Institution Press.

Keller, Bill. 1986. "Pentagon's New Yes-and-No Man on Weapons." *New York Times*, February 18, 1986, B8.

Kier, Elizabeth. 1997. *Imagining War: French and British Military Doctrine between the Wars*. Princeton, NJ: Princeton University Press.

Kim, Ki-Joo. 2014. "The Soldier and the State in South Korea: Crafting Democratic Civilian Control of the Military." *Journal of International and Area Studies* 21 (2): 119–31.

Kingdon, John W. 1995. *Agendas, Alternatives, and Public Policies*. 2nd ed. Berlin: Longman.

Kohn, Richard, ed. 1991. *The United States Military Under the Constitution of the United States, 1789–1989*. New York: New York University Press.

Kohn, Richard. 1994. "Out of Control: The Crisis in Civil-Military Relations." *National Interest* 35 (Spring): 3–17.

Krauss, Clifford. 1993. "House Vote Urges Clinton to Limit American Role in Somali Conflict." *New York Times*, September 29, 1993, A1.

Krebs, Ronald R., Robert Ralston, and Aaron Rapport. 2021. "No Right to Be Wrong: What Americans Think About Civil-Military Relations." *Perspectives on Politics*, March 11, 2021. https://doi.org/10.1017/S1537592721000013.

Kuehn, David, Aurel Croissant, Jil Kamerling, Hans Leuders, and André Strecker. 2017. "Conditions of Civilian Control in New Democracies: An Empirical

Analysis of 28 'Third Wave' Democracies." *European Political Science Review* 9 (3): 425–47.

Kuehn, David, and Yagil Levy, eds. 2021. Mobilizing Force: Linking Security Threats, Militarization & Civilian Control. Boulder, CO: Lynne Rienner.

Kyle, Brett J., and Andrew G. Reiter. 2021. The Politics of Military Justice: Military Courts, Civil-Military Relations, and the Legal Battle for Democracy. New York: Routledge.

Lakshmanan, Indira A. R. 2009. "Democrats Aren't Yielding to Obama." *New York Times*, July 9, 2009.

Lamothe, Dan. 2020. "Pentagon's Top General Apologizes for Appearing alongside Trump in Lafayette Square." *Washington Post*, June 11, 2020. https://www.washingtonpost.com/national-security/2020/06/11/pentagons-top-general-apologizes-appearing-alongside-trump-lafayette-square/.

Larson, Eric V., David T. Orletsky, and Kristin Leuschner. 2001. *Defense Planning in a Decade of Change: Lessons from the Base Force, Bottom-Up Review, and Quadrennial Defense Review.* Arlington, VA: RAND.

Lee, Carol E., and Colleen McCain Nelson. 2015. "U.S. Slows Pace of Afghan Troop Withdrawal." *Wall Street Journal*, March 24, 2015.

Le Menestrel, Suzanne, and Kenneth W. Kizer. 2019. *Strengthening the Military Family Readiness System for a Changing American Society.* Washington, DC: National Academies Press. https://www.ncbi.nlm.nih.gov/books/NBK547615/#sec_ch3_1.

Levin, Carl. 2021. *Getting to the Heart of the Matter: My 36 Years in the Senate.* Detroit: Wayne State University Press.

Lewis, Michael. 2012. "Obama's Way." *Vanity Fair*, October 2012, 210–17, 259–64.

Lieb, David A. 2010. "Hartzler Defeats Longtime Missouri Rep. Skelton." *News Tribune*, November 3, 2010. https://www.newstribune.com/news/2010/nov/03/hartzler-defeats-longtime-missouri-rep-skelton/.

Lieberman, Joe. 2022. "The Case for a No-Fly Zone in Ukraine." *Wall Street Journal*, March 9, 2022. https://www.wsj.com/articles/case-for-no-fly-zone-ukraine-russia-offensive-defensive-bombing-civiliians-airpower-nato-human-rights-violation-war-invasion-11646837093.

Lipset, Seymour Martin. 1959. "Some Social Requisites of Democracy: Economic Development and Political Legitimacy." *American Political Science Review* 53 (1): 69–105.

Locher, James. 2002. *Victory on the Potomac: The Goldwater-Nichols Act Unifies the Pentagon.* College Station: Texas A&M University Press.

Loeb, Vernon. 2002. "New Weapons Systems Are Budget Winners." *Washington Post*, February 8, 2002, A29.

Lopez, Anthony C. 2020. "Making 'My' Problem 'Our' Problem: Warfare as Collective Action and the Role of Leader Manipulation." *Leadership Quarterly* 31 (2): 101294.

Lowi, Theodore. 1972. "Four Systems of Policy, Politics, and Choice." *Public Administration Review* 32 (4): 298–310.

Luce, Edward. 2006. "Robert Gates Iraq 'Realist' at the Gates." *Financial Times*, December 1, 2006.

Lupton, Danielle L. 2017. "Out of the Service, Into the House: Military Experience and Congressional War Oversight." *Political Research Quarterly* 70 (2): 327–39.

Malkasian, Carter. 2021. *The American War in Afghanistan: A History*. New York: Oxford University Press.

Mattis, Jim. 2018. "Resignation Letter from Defense Secretary James Mattis." December 21, 2018. https://www.documentcloud.org/documents/5656065 -Resignation-Letter-From-Defense-Secretary-James.html.

Mayhew, David. 1974. *Congress: The Electoral Connection*. New Haven, CT: Yale University Press.

McCain, John, and Mark Salter. 2018. *The Restless Wave: Good Times, Just Causes, Great Fights, and Other Appreciations*. New York: Simon and Schuster.

McCubbins, Matthew, Roger Noll, and Barry Weingast. 1987. "Administrative Procedures as Instruments of Political Control." *Journal of Law, Economics, & Organization* 3 (2): 243–77.

McFadden, Robert D. 2021. "Carl Levin, 87, Michigan Senator Who Was Feared by Corporate Titans, Dies." *New York Times*, July 31, 2021, B7.

McInnis, Kathleen. 2021. *The Position of Secretary of Defense: Statutory Restrictions and Civilian-Military Relations*. Washington, DC: Congressional Research Service.

McKelvey, Tara. 2013. "How Buck McKeon Created a Global Drone Enterprise." *BBC News Magazine*, August 2, 2013. https://www.bbc.com/news/ magazine-23024462.

McPherson, James M. 2008. *Tried by War: Abraham Lincoln as Commander in Chief*. New York: Penguin Press.

Meacham, Jon. 2015. *Destiny and Power: The American Odyssey of George Herbert Walker Bush*. New York: Random House.

Medvic, Stephen K. 2018. *In Defense of Politicians: The Expectations Trap and Its Threat to Democracy*. New York: Taylor and Francis.

Montanaro, Domenico. 2021. "Watchdog Report Says Police Did Not Clear Protestors to Make Way for Trump Photo Op." *National Public Radio*, June 9, 2021. https://www.npr.org/2021/06/09/1004832399/watchdog-report-says -police-did-not-clear-protesters-to-make-way-for-trump-last-.

Bibliography

Moten, Matthew. 2014. *Presidents and Their Generals: An American History of Command in War*. Cambridge, MA: Harvard University Press.

Moynihan, Daniel Patrick. 1998. *Secrecy: The American Experience*. New Haven, CT: Yale University Press.

Muñoz, Carlos. 2008. "Seven Pentagon Teams to Spearhead Reviews for ISR Task Force." *Inside the Pentagon* 24 (8): 12–13.

Murray, Shoon. 2014. *The Terror Authorization: The History and Politics of the 2001 AUMF*. New York: Palgrave MacMillan.

Obama, Barack. 2020. *A Promised Land*. New York: Crown.

Olson, Mancur. 1971. *The Logic of Collective Action*. Cambridge, MA: Harvard University Press.

O'Reilly, Robert. 2022. "Sam Nunn Constituent Issue Mail." UNC Dataverse. https://doi.org/10.15139/S3/3TI7VF. Version 1.0.

Panetta, Leon. 2014. *Worthy Fights: A Memoir of Leadership in War and Peace*. With Jim Newton. New York: Penguin Books.

Perry, William J. 2015. *My Journey at the Nuclear Brink*. Stanford, CA: Stanford University Press.

Peter, Fabienne. 2017. "Political Legitimacy." In *The Stanford Encyclopedia of Philosophy*, edited by Edward N. Zalta. https://plato.stanford.edu/archives/sum2017/entries/legitimacy/.

Phillips, Soren. 2009. "The Birth of the European Union: Challenging the Myth of the Civilian Power Narrative." *Historical Social Research* 34 (2): 203–14.

Pietrucha, Mike, and Mike Benitez. 2022. "The Dangerous Allure of the No-Fly Zone." *War on the Rocks*, March 4, 2022. https://warontherocks.com/2022/03/the-dangerous-allure-of-the-no-fly-zone/.

Pion-Berlin, David, Igor Acacio, and Andrew Ivey. 2019. "Democratically Consolidated, Externally Threatened, and NATO Aligned: Finding Unexpected Deficiencies in Civilian Control." *Democratization* 26 (6): 1070–87.

Pion-Berlin, David, and Harold Trinkunas. 2007. "Attention Deficits: Why Politicians Ignore Defense Policy in Latin America." *Journal of Latin American Research Review* 42 (3): 76–100.

Powell, Colin. 1992. "Why Generals Get Nervous." *New York Times*, October 8, 1992, A35. https://www.nytimes.com/1992/10/08/opinion/why-generals-get-nervous.html.

Powell, Colin. 1995. *My American Journey*. With Joseph E. Perisco. New York: Random House.

Price, Richard M. 1997. The Chemical Weapons Taboo. Ithaca, NY: Cornell University Press.

Priest, Dana, and William M. Arkin. 2010. "A Hidden World, Growing Beyond Control." *Washington Post,* July 19, 2010.

Putnam, Robert. 1988. "Diplomacy and Domestic Politics: The Logic of Two-Level Games." *International Organization* 42 (3): 427–60.

Rasky, Susan F. 1990. "Washington at Work: Two Unlikely Voices that Find Harmony on the Military Budget." *New York Times,* May 2, 1990, A18.

Riker, William H. 1986. *The Art of Political Manipulation.* New Haven, CT: Yale University Press.

Rosen, Stephen Peter. 1991. *Winning the Next War: Innovation and the Modern Military.* Ithaca, NY: Cornell University Press.

Rumsfeld, Donald H. 2002a. "Afghanistan." Memo to President George W. Bush, August 20, 2002. https://nsarchive.gwu.edu/document/24551-office-secre tary-defense-donald-rumsfeld-memo-president-george-w-bush-subject.

Rumsfeld, Donald H. 2002b. "Transforming the Military." *Foreign Affairs,* May/ June.

Rumsfeld, Donald H. 2011. *Known and Unknown: A Memoir.* New York: Sentinel.

Sanger, David E. 2009. *The Inheritance: The World Obama Confronts and the Challenges to American Power.* New York: Harmony Books.

Sanger, David E., and William J. Broad. 2022. "Putin Revives Global Shivers of Atomic Age." *New York Times,* June 1, 2022, A1.

Schaefer, Amy. 2017. *Generations of War: The Rise of the Warrior Caste and the All-Volunteer Force.* Washington, DC: Center for a New American Security.

Schake, Kori, Jim Mattis, Jim Ellis, and Joe Felter. 2020. "Defense in Depth: Why US Security Depends on Alliances—Now More Than Ever." *Foreign Affairs,* November 23, 2020.

Schelling, Thomas C. 1960. *Strategy of Conflict.* Cambridge, MA: Harvard University Press.

Schlesinger, J. A. 1966. *Ambition and Politics: Political Careers in the United States.* Chicago: Rand McNally.

Schmitt, Eric. 1993a. "Charting a Course at the Pentagon, Aspin Uses His Congressional Map." *New York Times,* February 17, 1993, A15.

Schmitt, Eric. 1993b. "Lawmakers Are Impatient to Start Pentagon Cuts." *New York Times,* March 31, 1993, A20.

Schmitt, Eric. 1994. "The Reporter's Notebook: In Perry's First 100 Hours, What Could Possibly Go Wrong?" *New York Times,* February 8, 1994, A20.

Schmitt, Eric. 1995. "Republicans Finding Dissension in Ranks on Military Issues." *New York Times,* January 29, 1995, A20.

210 Bibliography

Schmitt, Eric. 1999. "Senate's New Hand on the Military." *New York Times,* March 10, 1999, A17.

Schmitt, Eric, and David E. Sanger. 2009. "Obama Is Facing Doubts in Party on Afghanistan." *New York Times,* September 10, 2009, A1.

Schulman, Loren DeJonge. 2018. *Behind the Magical Thinking: Lessons from Policymaker Relationships with Drones.* Washington, DC: Center for a New American Security.

Schwartz, Norton, and Suzie Schwartz. 2018. *Journey: Memoirs of an Air Force Chief of Staff.* With Ronald Levinson. New York: Skyhorse Publishing.

Sciolino, Elaine. 1994. "Republicans Say Congress Could Balk on Bosnia Force." *New York Times,* February 24, 1994, A10.

Sciolino, Elaine. 1995. "Conflict in the Balkans: In Washington, Clinton's Policy on Bosnia Draws Criticism in Congress." *New York Times,* June 8, 1995, A10.

Shanker, Thom. 2010. "Senators Challenge Deadline for Afghan Troop Withdrawal." *New York Times,* June 16, 2012, A12.

Shelton, Hugh. 2010. *Without Hesitation: The Odyssey of an American Warrior.* With Ronald Levinson and Malcolm McConnell. New York: St. Martin's Press.

Shepsle, Kenneth. 2010. *Analyzing Politics: Rationality, Behavior, and Institutions.* 2nd ed. New York: W. W. Norton.

Sifuentes, Edward, and Mark Walker. 2009. "Bilbray Submits $26 Million Earmark for Predator Drones." *San Diego Union-Tribune,* March 21, 2009. https://www.sandiegouniontribune.com/sdut-exclusive-bilbray-submits-26-million-earmark-for-2009mar21-story.html.

Singh, Naunihaul. 2014. Seizing Power: The Strategic Logic of Military Coups. Baltimore, MD: Johns Hopkins University Press.

Snider, Don M. 1993. *Strategy, Forces and Budgets: Dominant Influences in Executive Decision Making, Post-Cold War, 1989–91.* Carlisle, PA: Strategic Studies Institute, US Army War College.

Stanton, Zack. 2021. "Carl Levin: The Senator Who Mastered Oversight." *Politico,* December 27, 2021. https://www.politico.com/news/magazine/2021/12/27/2021-obituary-carl-levin-525938.

Steinhauer, Jennifer, Eric Schmitt, and Luke Broadwater. 2020. "Congress Frets Over General in Civilian Job." *New York Times,* December 9, 2020, A1.

Stephen Peter Rosen. 1991. Winning the Next War: Innovation and the Modern Military. Ithaca, NY: Cornell University Press.

Stevenson, Charles. 2006. *SECDEF: The Nearly Impossible Job of Secretary of Defense.* Sterling, VA: Potomac Books.

Stuart, Douglas T. 2008. *Creating the National Security State: A History of the Law that Transformed America*. Princeton, NJ: Princeton University Press.

Taliaferro, Aaron C., Lina M. Gonzalez, Mark Tillman, Pritha Ghosh, Paul Clarke, and Wade Hinkle. 2019. *Defense Governance and Management: Improving the Defense Management Capabilities of Foreign Defense Institutions. A Guide to Capability-Based Planning (CBP)*. Alexandria, VA: Institute for Defense Analyses. http://www.jstor.org/stable/resrep22853.

Tau, Byron. 2011. "Levin Backs Obama on Libya." *Politico*, March 27, 2011. https://www.politico.com/blogs/politico-now/2011/03/levin-backs-obama-on-libya-034504.

Taylor, Andrew J. 2019. "Legislative Seniority in the Partisan Congress." *Social Studies Quarterly* 100 (4): 1297–307.

Travis, Donald S. 2019. "Pursuing Civilian Control Over the Military." *Armed Forces & Society* 45 (3): 546–60.

Trenchard, John. 1697. *An Argument Shewing that a Standing Army is Inconsistent with a Free Government, and Absolutely Destructive to the Constitution of the English Monarchy*. London. https://quod.lib.umich.edu/e/eebo/A63115.0001.001?view=toc.

Tucker, Robert C. 1985. *Politics as Leadership*. Columbia: University of Missouri Press.

US Office of Personnel Management. 2021. FedScope—Federal Workforce Data. https://www.fedscope.opm.gov.

US Under Secretary of Defense (Acquisition, Technology and Logistics). 2012, April. *Department of Defense Report to Congress on Future Unmanned Aircraft Systems Training, Operations, and Sustainability*. https://irp.fas.org/program/collect/uas-future.pdf.

Van Atta, Richard H., Michael J. Lippitz, Jasper C. Lupo, Rob Mahoney, and Jack H. Nunn. 2003. *Transformation and Transition: DARPA's Role in Fostering an Emerging Revolution in Military Affairs, Volume 1—Overall Assessment*. Alexandria, VA: Institute for Defense Analyses.

Walsh, Carl E. 1993. "What Caused the 1990–1991 Recession?" *Federal Reserve Bank of San Francisco* Economic Review, no. 2, 33–48.

Washington Post. 1993. "Sam Nunn on the Defense Budget." March 25, 1993. https://www.washingtonpost.com/archive/opinions/1993/03/25/sam-nunn-on-the-defense-budget/be97b60f-9c53-449f-bf10-c166f494fbdf/.

Weber, Max. 1964. *The Theory of Social and Economic Organization*. New York: Free Press.

Weiner, Sharon K. 1996. "The Politics of Resource Allocation in the Post-Cold War Pentagon." *Security Studies* 5 (4): 125–42.

Bibliography

Weiner, Sharon. 2010. "Organizational Interests versus Battlefield Needs: The US Military and Mine-Resistant, Ambush Protected Vehicles in Iraq." *Polity* 42 (4): 461–82.

Weiner, Sharon K. 2022. *Managing the Military: The Joint Chiefs of Staff and Civil-Military Relations*. New York: Columbia University Press.

Western, Jon. 2002. "Sources of Humanitarian Intervention: Beliefs, Information, and Advocacy in the US Decisions on Somalia and Bosnia." *International Security* 26 (4): 112–42.

Whittle, Richard. 2014. *Predator: The Secret Origins of the Drone Revolution*. New York: Henry Holt.

Wilson, George C. 1985. "Unmanned Weapons Gain Backing." *Washington Post*, September 5, 1985, A1.

Wilson, George C. 2000. "Senate Chairman Pushes Unmanned Warfare." *Government Executive*, March 6, 2000. https://www.govexec.com/federal -news/2000/03/senate-chairman-pushes-unmanned-warfare/1977/.

Wood, David. 2016. *What Have We Done: The Moral Injury of Our Longest Wars*. New York: Little, Brown, and Company.

Woodward, Bob. 1993. "The Secretary of Analysis." *Washington Post*, February 21, 1993. https://www.washingtonpost.com/archive/lifestyle/maga zine/1993/02/21/the-secretary-of-analysis/e9c838cb-9a4a-40ea-881e-c4a4 f7499339/.

Woodward, Bob. 2002. *Bush at War*. New York: Simon and Schuster.

Wright, Donald P., James R. Bird, Steven E. Clay, Peter W. Connors, Lieutenant Colonel Scott C. Farquhar, Lynne Chandler Garcia, and Dennis F. Van Wey. 2010. *A Different Kind of War: The United States Army in Operation Enduring Freedom (OEF) October 2001–September 2005*. Fort Leavenworth, KS: US Army Combined Arms Center, Combat Studies Institute Press.

Zelditch, Morris Jr.. 2001. "Theories of Legitimacy." In *The Psychology of Legitimacy. Emerging Perspectives on Ideology, Justice, and Intergroup Relations*, edited by John T. Jost and Brenda Major. Cambridge: Cambridge University Press.

Interview Transcripts and Videos

Bush, George. 1990. "Remarks at the Aspen Institute Symposium in Aspen, Colorado." Transcript of speech delivered at the Music Tent, August 2, 1990. https://www.presidency.ucsb.edu/documents/remarks-the-aspen-institute -symposium-aspen-colorado.

Cheney, Richard. 2000. Interview, "The Future of War." *Frontline*, PBS. https:// www.pbs.org/wgbh/pages/frontline/shows/future/interviews/cheney.html

.Miller Center. 2000–2013. *Presidential Oral Histories.* https://millercenter.org/the-presidency/presidential-oral-histories.

Nunn, Sam A. Jr. 2013. Interview by Myron A. Farber, June 3, 2013, Carnegie Corporation of New York Oral History Project, Columbia Center for Oral History, Columbia University, New York. https://dlc.library.columbia.edu/carnegie/cul:nvxok6dm3s.

Perry, William J. 1998a. "Interview with William J. Perry." October 6, 1998, Transcript by Historical Office, Office of the Secretary of Defense. https://history.defense.gov/Portals/70/Documents/oral_history/OH_Trans_PERRYWilliam%20J10-06-1998.pdf?ver=2017-10-04-102345-740.

Perry, William J. 1998b. "Interview with William J. Perry." October 22, 1998, Transcript by Historical Office, Office of the Secretary of Defense. https://history.defense.gov/Portals/70/Documents/oral_history/OH_Trans_PERRYWilliam%2010-22-98.pdf?ver=2018-04-10-070022-050.

Perry, William J. 2004. "Interview with William J. Perry." October 18, 2004, Transcript by Historical Office, Office of the Secretary of Defense. https://history.defense.gov/Portals/70/Documents/oral_history/OH_Trans_PerryWilliam10-18-04.pdf?ver=2017-11-17-134335-103.

Public Broadcasting Service. 2009. "Afghan Election Further Complicates Efforts to Shape Military Strategy." *PBS NewsHour*, September 29, 2009. https://www.pbs.org/newshour/show/afghan-election-further-complicates-efforts-to-shape-military-strategy.

Speeches

Brown, Harold. 1981. "Managing the Defense Department: Why It Can't Be Done." William K. McInally Memorial Lecture, University of Michigan, March 25, 1981.

Bush, George W. 1999. "A Period of Consequences," The Citadel, South Carolina, September 23, 1999.

Bush, George W. 2001a. "National Day of Prayer and Remembrance Service." September 14, 2001.

Bush, George W. 2001b. "Remarks to New York Rescue Workers." September 14, 2001.

Bush, George W. 2001c. "Address to the Joint Session of Congress." September 20, 2001.

Bush, George W. 2001d. "Address to the Nation on Operations in Afghanistan." October 7, 2001.

Bush, George W. 2001e. "Address at the Citadel." December 11, 2001. Charleston, South Carolina.

Bibliography

Gates, Robert M. 2008. "Remarks to the Air War College and the Air Command and Staff College," Maxwell Air Force Base, Alabama, April 21, 2008.

Obama, Barack. 2009. "Remarks by the President in Address to the Nation on the Way Forward in Afghanistan and Pakistan." Transcript of speech delivered at the U.S. Military Academy, December 1, 2009. https://obamawhitehouse .archives.gov/the-press-office/remarks-president-address-nation-way-for ward-afghanistan-and-pakistan.

Obama, Barack. 2013. "Remarks by the President at National Defense University." Fort McNair, Washington, DC, May 23, 2013. https://obamawhitehouse .archives.gov/the-press-office/2013/05/23/remarks-president-national-de fense-university.

Obama, Barack. 2016. "Statement by the President on Afghanistan." Transcript of speech delivered at the White House, July 6, 2016. https://obamawhitehouse .archives.gov/the-press-office/2016/07/06/statement-president-afghanistan.

Trump, Donald. 2017a. "Address on Afghanistan." Fort Meyer, Virginia, August 21, 2017.

Trump, Donald. 2017b. Inaugural Address. January 20, 2017.

Congressional Hearings

House of Representatives Committee on Appropriations. 2002. *Department of Defense Appropriations for 2003: Hearings before a Subcommittee of the Committee on Appropriations, House of Representatives.* 107th Congress, 2nd. Sess.

SASC (US Senate Armed Services Committee). 2002. "Operation Enduring Freedom." 107th Congress, 2nd Sess. February 7, 2002.

SASC (US Senate Armed Services Committee). 2005. "US Military Operations and Stabilization Activities in Iraq and Afghanistan." 109th Congress, 1st Sess. February 3, 2005.

SASC (US Senate Armed Services Committee). 2006. "Hearing to Consider the Nomination of Robert Gates to be Secretary of Defense." 109th Cong., 2nd sess., December 5, 2006.

SASC (US Senate Armed Services Committee). 2011. "Department of Defense Authorization for Appropriations for Fiscal Year 2012 and the Future Years Defense Program." 112th Congress, 1st Sess. February 17, 2011.

SASC (US Senate Armed Services Committee). 2017. "The Situation in Afghanistan." 115th Congress, 1st Sess., February 9, 2017 [Stenographic Transcript].

US Senate Select Committee on Intelligence. 1991. "Hearing to Consider the Nomination of Robert M. Gates, to be Director of Central Intelligence." 102nd Cong., 1st sess., October 3, October 4, and October 18, 1991.

INDEX

accountability, process of, 23–24
administrators/administration:
  authority in disputes by, 146;
  control by, 61–62, 63, 68; division of
  labor in, 29; in executive branch,
  38; expertise in, 25–27, 31–34;
  function of, 33; in legislative
  branch, 38; nomination of,
  33–34; political context and,
  70–71; political context of, 60–61;
  politicians as compared to, 168;
  power of, 36; requirements of, 26;
  unmanned aerial vehicles (UAVs)
  and, 153–61
Advanced Concept Technology
  Demonstration (ACTD), 155
Advanced Research Project Agency
  (DARPA) (DoD), 143, 144
Afghanistan: domestic politics
  of, 128–29; government in, 104,
  106, 114, 122; military training
  in, 114, 122–23; nation-building
  goal in, 111; political context of,

56, 129; Soviet Union role in, 131;
  topography of, 104. *See also* War in
  Afghanistan
Aideed, Mohammed, 73
al Qaeda, 103. *See also* War in
  Afghanistan
Aquila system, 148
Armed Servants (Feaver), 46
Army, competition of, 5. *See also*
  military and defense
Article I (US Constitution), 4
Article II (US Constitution), 4
Aspin, Les: Bill Perry and, 95; BUR
  and, 72, 93–94; Colin Powell and,
  93; leadership of, 170; "Option
  C" of, 92; overview of, 76–78;
  post-Cold War leadership of, 73,
  92–94; two major regional conflict
  (2MRC) and, 94; use of force and,
  94; win-hold-win scenario and, 94;
  work of, 85
assessments, bias and failure of, 61
Austin, Lloyd, III, 2–3

215

216 Index

authority, 6, 19, 22, 35
Authorization for Use of Military Force (AUMF), 103, 107

Bader Ginsberg, Ruth, 15
Baker, Jim, 89
Balkans, war in, 84
Bannon, Steve, 117
Base Force structure of military, 72, 82–83, 91–92
Battista, Anthony, 47
Bergen, Peter, 116
Biden, Joseph, 2–3, 65, 134, 138–39
Bilbray, Brian, 152
bin Laden, Osama, 104. *See also* War in Afghanistan
blood and treasure, 61
Blue Ribbon Commission on Defense Management, 8–9
Boeing, 150
Bosnia: Bill Clinton's leadership regarding, 86, 88, 97–98; Bill Perry's leadership regarding, 96–99, 100–101; crisis in, 73, 74; Dick Cheney's leadership regarding, 92; force management in, 98; George H. W. Bush's leadership regarding, 73, 84; lack of unity regarding, 80; multilateralism in, 100; policies regarding, 97–98; skepticism regarding, 79; Srebrenica massacre and, 99, 100; unmanned aerial vehicles (UAVs) and, 154–55
Boxer, Barbara, 124
Brooke, Edward, 189n21
Brooks, Risa, 12, 176
Brown, Harold, 34, 154
Brownlee, Les, 150, 152

Bruce, Blanche, 189n21
Budget Control Act (BCA), 153
budgeting/budgetary politics: for Base Force, 92; guidance and, 48; overview of, 47–48, 177; reconciliation process of, 53; of unmanned aerial vehicles (UAVs), 144, 152–53, 160–61, 171
bureaucracies, administration of, 26–27
bureaucratic politics, civilian interaction with, 14
Burke, Kelly H., 154
Bush, George H. W.: assassination attempt on, 15; Base Force structure and, 82–83; Bosnia crisis and, 73, 84; defense spending viewpoint of, 169; nominations by, 34, 75, 82; overview of, 80–84; quote of, 82, 191–92n3; Somalia crisis and, 73, 84, 86–87; war effect on, 107
Bush, George W.: criticism of, 128; Donald Rumsfeld and, 128; Iraq War and, 192–93n4; praise for, 30; quote of, 107, 109, 110, 161–62; terrorism viewpoint of, 111; unmanned aerial vehicles (UAVs) and, 161–62; War in Afghanistan and, 104, 106, 107–12, 131, 132, 133–34, 139, 170
Bottom-Up Review (BUR), 48, 72, 93–94, 96
Byrd, Robert C., 78

Central Intelligence Agency (CIA), 108
chairs, role of, 38–42, 62, 68, 69, 139. *See also specific persons*
Cheney, Richard B. (Dick), 59, 83, 88–92, 129, 169–70

Index   217

Christopher, Warren, 73, 79, 100

Churchill, Winston, 52

civilian control/controllers. *See* control/controllers, civilian

civilian ethic, 15–16, 167

civilians: authority of, 13, 19, 22; behavioral characteristics of, 178; choice source for, 14; in civil-military relations, historical trends for, 3–10; concept of, 21–29; defined, 23; dimensions of, 12–13; expertise of, 13, 25–27, 28; functions of, 23–25; further research agenda regarding, 173–79; identity of, 37, 41–42, 168; job requirement of, 37; knowledge and, 177; limitations of, 28, 34; as making the rules, 172; in the military, distinctions and overlaps in, 10–11, 27–29; motivations of, 42–43; obligations of, 24–25; overview of, 20–21, 167–73; political interactions of, 14–15; power of, 22–23; preferences of, 52; professional backgrounds of, 38–39; professional-institutional types of, 14, 17; requirements of, 186n7; in scholarly and contemporary context, 10–12; senior, 39; status of, 13, 21–23; as sustaining order, 23–24; as technocrats, 188n9; type overview of, 30–31, 42–43; typology of, 21–29, 31; variations of, 20

civil-military model: administration in, 26; burden in, 174; civilian ethic in, 15–16; civilian side of, 18–19; control in, 45; debates in, 27; Dick Cheney's viewpoint regarding, 90–91; overview of, 10; politics in, 19

Civil War, 5

Clinton, Bill: Bosnia crisis and, 86, 88, 97–98; campaign of, 72, 92; constraints of, 86, 87; defense spending viewpoint of, 169; memoir of, 15; military spending increase by, 97; nominations by, 34, 40, 75, 92, 94, 95; overview of, 85–88; quote of, 86, 87–88; Somalia crisis and, 73, 86–87, 88; support for, 78; unmanned aerial vehicles (UAVs) and, 161

Clinton, Hillary, 65

coalitions, effectiveness of, 70

Cohen, Eliot, 1, 2, 12, 61, 174, 187n5

Cohn, Lindsay, 46, 190n4

Collins, Susan, 2

Combatant Commands, 49

compelling, in civilian control, 51

Congress: administrators in, 38; allowances of, 53; authorization of the use of military force (AUMF) and, 103, 107; civilians in, 35–39; committee structure in, 7, 40; control exercising by, 69; demographic representation in, 189n21; Department of Defense (DoD) control by, 149; military affairs roles of, 189n15; military control of, 4; organizational elements of, 36; polarization of, 78–79; politicians in, 38; unmanned aerial vehicles (UAVs) and, 145, 147–53; Unmanned Systems Caucus of, 152

consensus building, in civilian control, 51–52

Constitution, division of labor in, 35

Index

constraint: ambiguity regarding, 86;
of Bill Clinton, 86, 87; in civilian
control, 51; of Dick Cheney,
91; example of, 78, 79; by the
president, 70
Continental Congress, 3
control/controllers, civilian:
budgeting and, 47–48;
calculating, 60–63; choosing,
49–50, 57–63, 68; compelling,
51; competitors for, 49;
consensus building and, 51–52;
constraining, 51, 78, 79; deference
and, 50, 70; degrees and
methods of, 62; demographics
of, 41, 174–75; effectiveness
factors of, 53; ethics regarding,
100–101; expertise in, 53; force
management and, 48, 72–73; force
structures and, 77; governance
methods and, 46; guidance and,
72–73; Joint Chiefs of Staff (CJCS)
and, 70; Libya intervention
example regarding, 63–67;
measurement of, 50; mechanisms
for, 48–49; military cooperation
and, 175–76; of military policy,
50; motivations and, 57–58;
overview of, 44–53, 67–68, 173–74;
policymaking and, 51–52; as
political activity, 52, 53; political
competition and, 51; political
context and, 54–57; progressive
types of, 51; resources and,
58–60; risk and, 61; of secretary of
defense, 6; selection process of,
40–41; strategies of, 51; unity and,
53; variation in, 101
Crowe, Jonathan, 81–82

Cuban missile crisis, 51
Cuellar, Henry, 152

Daley, Bill, 65
Dark Star UAV, 150
Declaration of Independence, 3, 22
defense. *See* military and defense
Defense Airborne Reconnaissance
Office, 155
Defense Planning Guidance, 47, 91
Defense Reorganization Act of 1986, 9
Defense Science Board, 157
deference, 50, 70, 142, 171–72
Dellums, Ron, 78–79, 80, 86
Democratic Party, 76, 86, 87
Department of Defense (DoD):
budgeting and, 47–48; civilian
control over, 6; civilian reduction
in, 9; Congressional control of,
149; Dick Cheney's viewpoint
regarding, 90; employment in,
189n22; management of, 26;
military control of, 8; organization
of, 8; Program Objective
Memoranda cycle, 53; reform of, 7;
responsibilities of, 188n7
Detainee Treatment Act of 2005, 193n10
Deutch, John, 155
Dicks, Norm, 150
director of defense research and
engineering (DDR&E), 7
DoD's Advanced Research Project
Agency (DARPA), 143, 144
Dole, Bob, 79
domestic politics, 76, 117, 128–29.
See also politics
Donilon, Tom, 65
Don't Ask, Don't Tell policy, 93
Douglas, Paul, 7

drones. *See* unmanned aerial vehicles (UAVs)

Dunford, Joseph, 137

economy, 72, 104, 153, 169

Eisenhower, Dwight, 6, 7, 39

Esper, Mark, 118, 137-38, 140

executive branch. *See* president

expertise: in administrators/administration, 25-27, 34; in civilian control/controllers, 53; of civilians, 13, 25-27, 28; debates regarding, 28; in government, 26; of military, 141-42

Feaver, Peter, 2, 46

Federalist 51, 4

Feingold, Russ, 124

Feinstein, Diane, 124

Feith, Doug, 128

Felton, Rebecca, 189n21

Finer, Sam, 51

Forbes, Randy, 149

force management, 48, 72-73

foreign policy, constituent views regarding, 75

Forrestal, James, 88-89

Franks, Tommy, 127

functions, of civilians, 23-25

Future Years Defense Plan (FYDP), 48

Gates, Robert: Bill Young and, 191n9; experiences of, 30-31; Libya intervention and, 64, 65-66, 67; military policy approach of, 30; quote of, 34, 66, 131, 134, 135, 158; unmanned aerial vehicles (UAVs) and, 158-59; War in Afghanistan and, 124, 130-35

gay and lesbian community, Don't Ask, Don't Tell policy regarding, 93

General Atomics, 149-50, 152

George III (King), 3

Germany, general staff model of, 8

Ghani, Ashraf, 114

Global Hawk UAV, 157

global integrator, debate regarding, 29

Goldwater Nichols Department, 9

Gorbachev, Mikhail, 71, 82

Gore, Al, 34, 95, 99

Gramm-Rudman law, 76

Grumman, Northrop, 150

guidance, 46-47, 48, 72-73, 94

Halberstam, David, 83-84

Hicks, Donald, 47, 154

hierarchy, 35

Holbrooke, Richard, 96

House Armed Services Committee (HASC) chair, 40, 69. *See also specific persons*

House of Representatives, 53. *See also* Congress

Hunter UAV, 149

Huntington, Samuel P., 11-12

Hussein, Saddam, 83

informational resources, 59

Inman, Bobby Ray, 94

institutional capacity resources, 59

interest group politics, 14

international politics, 14, 81, 89, 105, 115

Iran, 8

Iraq War. *See* War in Iraq

Islamabad, 108

Joint Chiefs of Staff (CJCS), 7, 8-10, 29, 70, 91

220 Index

Joint Program Office (JPO or Jay-Poe), 148–49
Joint Staff, military planning process and, 49
Joint Unmanned Combat Aerial System, 157

Kanter, Arnold, 177
Karzai, Hamid, 104, 106, 125, 129
Kelley, P. X., 196n3
Kennedy, John F., 51
Kettering Bug, 194n5
Kohn, Richard, 166, 174
Kuwait, 83

Lee, Barbara, 107
legislative branch. See Congress
legitimacy, 22
Levin, Carl, 40, 64, 66, 67, 118, 119–21, 122–24, 131, 191n10
Lewis, Jerry, 149–50
Libya, 63–67
Lieberman, Joe, 64
Lincoln, Abraham, 5
Lockheed Martin, 150
Los Angeles Uprising, 72
Lovett, Robert, 6, 8
Luce, Edward, 130
Lugar, Dick, 95
Lynn, Verne "Larry," 154–55

Madison, James, 4
Malkasian, Carter, 113
Mansfield, Mike, 7
Mattis, James, 1, 2, 116–17, 136–37, 139–40
McCain, John, 9, 40, 64, 104, 118, 124–26, 171, 193n10
McChrystal, Stanley, 113, 124, 134–35
McDonough, Denis, 65

McKeon, Buck, 150, 152
McKiernan, David, 133–34
McMaster, H. R., 116–17
McNeill, Dan, 131
McPeak, Merrill A., 93
meaning, in political context, 54
military and defense: Base Force structure of, 72, 82–83, 91–92; centralized control over, 4; civilian control of, 8; civilian roles in, 4; constituent views regarding, 75; context of, 11; disagreements regarding spending for, 76; distinctions and overlaps in, 27–29; Don't Ask, Don't Tell policy of, 93; expertise of, 141–42; failures of, 8; feasibility of, 29; new era purpose of, 85; nonpartisan professional ethic of, 24–25; oppression and, 3–4; peacetime control of, 4–5; planning process of, 49; policy control in, 50; political influence of, 176; professionalism, 11, 12; reduction of, 77; as resource, 24; size considerations of, 72; spending reduction of, 72, 81–82; spending restoration to, 97; use of force of, 28; wartime control of, 4–5
military capability, 141–42. See also unmanned aerial vehicles (UAVs)
Milley, Mark, 138, 165–66
moral evaluations, 24
motivations, 57–58, 61–63
MQ-9 Reaper UAV, 161
Mullen, Michael, 65, 67, 133
Musharraf, Pervez, 108, 111
Myers, Richard, 127

Index   221

National Defense Authorization Act (NDAA), 9, 48
National Defense Strategy, 47
national politics, civilian interaction with, 14. *See also* politics
national security, 95-96
National Security Act of 1947, 6-7
National Security Review 12 (NSR 12), 81
National Security Strategy, 96
Navy, competition of, 5. *See also* military and defense
network politics, civilian interaction with, 14
Nicholson, John, 116
Niger, 56
9/11 attacks. *See* September 11, 2001, attacks on
North Atlantic Council, 64
North Atlantic Treaty Organization (NATO): Bosnia crisis and, 73, 86, 98-99, 100; Libya intervention and, 63-64, 66-67; Russo-Ukrainian war and, 55; War in Afghanistan and, 103, 105, 116, 120, 122, 132-33, 135, 170
Nunn, Sam, 25, 34, 74-80, 86, 95

Obama, Barack: campaign of, 104; experiences of, 30-31; Iraq War and, 56; Libya intervention and, 64-65, 66-67; nominations by, 40; political position of, 113-14; quote of, 30, 65, 112, 114; unmanned aerial vehicles (UAVs) and, 159, 161, 162-63; viewpoint of, 30; War in Afghanistan and, 104-5, 106-7, 112-15, 123, 126, 135-36, 139, 170
O'Brien, Robert, 138

Office of the Secretary of Defense (OSD): authority of, 6; bureaucratic capacity of, 6; civilian technocrats in, 188n9; control of, 6, 68; direction of, 6; expansion of, 7; experience of, 39-40; military planning process and, 49; nomination process for, 1; overview of, 38-42, 139; power of, 36; president negotiations with, 70; requirements for, 3, 185n1; Unmanned Aerial Vehicle Joint Program Office (JPO or Jay-Poe), 148-49. *See also specific persons*
Operation Enduring Freedom. *See* War in Afghanistan
Operation Iraqi Freedom. *See* War in Iraq
oppression, 3-4
orders, policy guidance as compared to, 47
Overseas Contingency Operations (OCO), 153

Pakistan, 108, 111, 128, 131, 133
Panetta, Leon, 113-14, 135-36, 160
people, in political context, 54-55
Perry, William, 33-34, 94-101, 154, 170
Persian Gulf War, 71
personal politics, civilian interaction with, 14
policymaking, 46, 51-52, 60
political context: of Afghanistan, 56, 129; calculating control and, 60-63; civilian control and, 54-57; civilian interpretation of, 82; civilian perception of, 70; differences of perspective regarding, 60-61; at domestic

222   Index

political context (*continued*)
levels, 55; as dynamic, 56;
at international level, 55,
56; interpretation of, 57–63;
issues and, 54; meaning in, 54;
motivations and, 57–58; overview
of, 44, 68, 71–74; people in, 54–55;
of post-Cold War period, 71–74,
90, 169; resources and, 58–60;
risk and, 61; salience in, 54; Sam
Nunn's use of, 75; strategic, 56; of
unmanned aerial vehicles (UAVs),
143–45; usage differences of,
70–71; of the War in Afghanistan,
103–5, 108
political parties, 32, 36–37. *See also*
specific parties
politicians: administrators as
compared to, 168; civilians as,
31–34; control by, 61–62, 63, 68;
electoral imperatives of, 32; in
executive branch, 38; influences
on, 32–33; in legislative branch, 38;
persuasion by, 33; political context
and, 60–61, 70–71; power of, 36;
pragmatism of, 172–73; unmanned
aerial vehicles (UAVs) and, 147–53.
See also specific persons
politics: actors in, 22; allies in, 25–26;
approaches to, 22–23; budgetary,
144, 152–53, 160–61, 171, 177; civilian
expertise in, 25–27; in civil-
military model, 19; context of, 14;
defined, 14, 22, 54; division of labor
in, 29; domestic, 72; function of,
25; levels of, 55–56; military policy
into, 166–67; national, 14; personal,
civilian interaction with, 14; power

in, 22–23; purpose of, 24; survival
in, 57–58
Pompeo, Mike, 116–17, 118
post-Cold War period: Base Force
structure and, 72, 82–83,
91–92; Bill Clinton's leadership
regarding, 72, 73, 75, 78, 85–88;
Bill Perry's leadership regarding,
94–101; civilian control and, 72–73;
Congressional control during,
69; Congressional polarization
during, 78–79; constraint during,
70; defense spending reduction
in, 72, 81–82; Dick Cheney's
leadership regarding, 88–92;
domestic politics and, 72, 76;
economy downturn of, 72; George
H. W. Bush's leadership regarding,
75, 80–84; HASC chair guidance
during, 69; John Shalikashvili's
leadership regarding, 99–100;
Joint Chiefs of Staff (CJCS) and, 70;
Les Aspin's leadership regarding,
76–78, 92–94; Los Angeles Uprising
and, 72; military spending and,
76; national security and, 95–96;
political context of, 71–74, 90, 169;
presidential decisions during,
70; Ron Dellums' leadership
regarding, 78–79; Sam Nunn's
leadership regarding, 74–80;
SASC chair guidance during, 69;
secretary of defense negotiations
during, 70. *See also* Bosnia;
Somalia
Powell, Colin, 82, 83, 84, 87, 91–92, 93,
99–100, 131
power, 22–23, 41, 58

Power, Samantha, 65
Predator UAV, 143, 152, 157, 160–61, 164
president: administrators in, 38; authority of, 35; campaign strategies of, 166; cares of, 54–55; civilians as, 35–38; as commander-in-chief, 4; constraint by, 70; control exercising by, 70; executive prerogatives of, 89; hierarchy of, 35; military responsibility of, 50; military service of, 39; overview of, 38–42; politicians in, 38; secretary of defense negotiations with, 70. *See also specific persons*
Presidential Policy Guidance, 163
principal-agent theory, 50, 53
Program Objective Memoranda cycle (DoD), 53
Putin, Vladimir, 110

Qaddafi, Muammar, 64

Reagan, Ronald, 8–9
Reed, Jack, 40
reelection, political importance of, 32
remotely piloted aircraft, 194n4. *See* unmanned aerial vehicles (UAVs)
representative government, 22
reprogramming, 191n11
Republican Party, 80, 87
Revels, Hiram, 189n21
Rice, Susan, 65
risk, 61
Rumsfeld, Donald, 15, 52, 126–29, 156–57

Russia, 54, 88. *See also* Russo-Ukrainian war
Russo-Ukrainian war, 55, 57

salience, in political context, 54
Scowcroft, Brent, 81, 89, 192n3
secretary of defense. *See* Office of the Secretary of Defense (OSD)
Senate Armed Services Committee (SASC) chair, 38–42, 62, 68, 69. *See also specific persons*
September 11, 2001, attacks on, 103, 107–8, 109, 147, 192–93n4. *See also* War in Afghanistan; War in Iraq
Shalikashvili, John (Shali), 99–100
Shelton, Hugh, 108, 127
Sherrill, Mikie, 190n5
Skelton, Ike, 37
Slotkin, Elissa, 37
social life, ordering of, 23
Somalia: Bill Clinton's leadership regarding, 86–87, 88; crisis in, 73, 84; George H. W. Bush's leadership regarding, 84, 86–87; military mission to, 56; skepticism regarding, 78, 79
Soviet Union, 131, 143
Spence, Floyd, 78, 79, 80
Srebrenica, 74, 86, 99
status, of civilians, 21–23
strategic environment, 56
strategy, in political context, 56
survival, political, 57–58

Taliban, 104, 108, 116, 118, 133. *See also* War in Afghanistan
Taylor, Gene, 77
technocrats, 188n9

terrorism, 111

Thurmond, Strom, 79, 80

Tillerson, Rex, 116–17

Title 10, 1, 35, 37

Tower, Jim, 89

Tower, John, 34

Townsend, Frances, 25–26

Trenchard, John, 3, 185n4

Truman, Harry, 6, 39

Trump, Donald: experience of, 39; foreign policy viewpoint of, 116; international politics viewpoint of, 115; Lafayette Square controversy and, 165–66; nominations by, 1; quote of, 115, 116, 117; War in Afghanistan and, 105, 106, 107, 115–18, 136–38, 139–40, 170

two major regional conflict (2MRC), 94

Ukraine, 54. *See also* Russo-Ukrainian war

United Kingdom, War in Afghanistan and, 110

unity, in civilian control, 53

Unmanned Aerial Vehicle Joint Program Office (JPO or Jay-Poe), 148–49

unmanned aerial vehicles (UAVs): acquisition strategy for, 151; Advanced Concept Technology Demonstration (ACTD) for, 155; Barack Obama's leadership regarding, 159, 161, 162–63; Bill Clinton's leadership regarding, 161; budgetary politics of, 144, 152–53, 160–61, 171; civilian overview regarding, 145–47; companies of, 144; Congressional

decisions regarding, 145; constraint regarding, 178; Dark Star, 150; debate regarding, 146–47, 154, 156–57; Defense Airborne Reconnaissance Office for, 155; deference and, 171–72; defined, 194n4; developments of, 143–44; Donald Rumsfeld's leadership regarding, 156–57; era of, 194n5; ethics of, 146–47; executive administrators and, 153–61; George W. Bush's leadership regarding, 161–62; Global Hawk, 157; Hunter, 149; John Warner's leadership regarding, 150–52; Joint Unmanned Combat Aerial System for, 157; legal justification for, 163; legislative politicians and, 147–53; MQ-9 Reaper, 161; overview of, 142, 163–64, 171; political context of, 143–45; Predator, 143, 152, 160–61, 164; presidential decisions regarding, 145, 161–63; Presidential Policy Guidance for, 163; purpose of, 144; Robert Gates' leadership regarding, 158–59; *Unmanned Systems Integrated Roadmap for FY2013-2038*, 159–60; usage statistics regarding, 144; Verne "Larry" Lynn's leadership regarding, 154–55

Unmanned Carrier-Launched Airborne Surveillance and Strike (UCLASS), 149

Unmanned Systems Caucus (Congress), 152

Unmanned Systems Integrated Roadmap for FY2013-2038, 159–60

use of force, 28, 77, 94

veterans' preference, 37
Vietnam War, 8, 29
Vinson, Carl, 6–8, 74
von Clausewitz, Carl, 12

War in Afghanistan: air campaign of, 110; American troop population in, 102, 112, 113, 114, 117, 126, 129, 132, 133–34, 135, 136; Barack Obama's leadership regarding, 104–5, 106–7, 112–15, 123, 126, 135–36, 139, 170; Carl Levin's leadership regarding, 118, 119–21, 122–24; Central Intelligence Agency (CIA) role in, 108; chairs overview regarding, 118–19, 139; as civil challenge, 128–29; criticism of, 112; domestic politics of, 128–29; Donald Rumsfeld's leadership regarding, 126–29; Donald Trump's leadership regarding, 105, 106, 107, 115–18, 136–38, 139–40, 170; end of, 138–39; George W. Bush's leadership regarding, 104, 106, 107–12, 131, 132, 133–34, 139, 170; international politics of, 105, 120; James Mattis' leadership regarding, 136–37, 139–40; John McCain's leadership regarding, 118, 124–26; John Warner's leadership regarding, 121–22; Leon Panetta's leadership regarding, 135–36; Mark Esper's leadership regarding, 137–38, 140;

negotiations for, 118; overview of, 102–3; Pakistani role in, 108, 111, 131, 133; political context of, 103–5, 108; presidential overview regarding, 105–7; public hearings regarding, 121–22; public opinion regarding, 105, 136; Robert Gates' leadership regarding, 130–35; secretary of defense overview regarding, 139–40; Stanley McChrystal's leadership regarding, 134–35; unmanned aerial vehicles (UAVs) in, 143, 144–45, 157–61; war fatigue regarding, 114

War in Iraq, 56, 104, 117, 145, 157–61, 192–93n4

Warner, John, 37, 118, 121–22, 130, 150–52

War on Terrorism. *See* War in Afghanistan; War in Iraq

wealth, political mobilization of, 61

Weiner, Sharon, 177

Western, Jon, 84

win-hold-win scenario, 94

Wolfowitz, Paul, 91–92

Woodward, Bob, 93

Work, Robert, 188n7

World War II, 5

Yeltsin, Boris, 88

Young, Bill, 191n9

Yugoslavia, 73, 83

Zelditch, Morris, Jr., 22

Printed and bound by CPI Group (UK) Ltd, Croydon, CR0 4YY
21/11/2024

14596796-0003